Thomas E. Randell

History of the Chippewa Valley

A Faithful Record of All Important Events

Thomas E. Randell

History of the Chippewa Valley
A Faithful Record of All Important Events

ISBN/EAN: 9783337762919

Printed in Europe, USA, Canada, Australia, Japan

Cover: Foto ©ninafisch / pixelio.de

More available books at **www.hansebooks.com**

HISTORY

OF THE

CHIPPEWA VALLEY,

A

FAITHFUL RECORD OF ALL IMPORTANT EVENTS, INCIDENTS AND CIRCUMSTANCES THAT HAVE TRANSPIRED IN THE VALLEY OF THE CHIPPEWA FROM ITS EARLIEST SETTLEMENT BY WHITE PEOPLE, INDIAN TREATIES, ORGANIZATION OF THE TERRITORY AND STATE; ALSO OF THE COUNTIES EMBRACING THE VALLEY, SENATORIAL, ASSEMBLY AND CONGRESSIONAL DISTRICTS, &c.

ALSO A BRIEF

BIOGRAPHICAL SKETCH OF THE MOST PROMINENT PERSONS IN THE SETTLEMENT OF THE VALLEY,

—BY—

THOMAS E. RANDALL.

1875:
FREE PRESS PRINT,
EAU CLAIRE, WIS.

PREFACE.

When this work was commenced as a contribution to the columns of the Free Press, it was not with the expectation of making a book, nor were the difficulties, and labor, of gathering the materials and connecting the facts—of determining what should be included in, and what excluded from such a work—fully realized.

The first settlers in a new country find little time or inclination to record even the most stirring events in journals and diaries, and hence many are very reluctant when called upon to make statements in regard to circumstances with which they are known to have been perfectly familiar. Others too, when applied to for information can remember nothing, except what pertained exclusively to themselves, and seem to consider all else as unworthy of record; and others still so modest that it has been difficult to prevail upon them to relate such things in their experiences as have been deemed essential to this work.

Of the many parties appealed to, to furnish the data on which many of the facts herein set forth, are founded, I cannot withhold the names of Hiram S. Allen, of Chippewa Falls, and Rev. Dr. Alfred Brunson, of Prairie du Chien, as gentlemen, whose interest in, and efforts to promote the objects I had in view, have afforded me much satisfaction and encouragement, and whose kindness and assistance will ever be remembered with heart felt gratitude.

The favorable notices of the Newspaper Press in this part of the State, and the flattering reception which the work found at the hands of the State Historical Society, and several of its learned members, together with numerous and repeated demands of the public, having responded liberally in subscribing for the work have induced me to republish it in a form better adapted to its preservation and the wants of the student of history. Trusting that some little service has been rendered to the cause of science, and that some events have been redeemed from oblivion which would otherwise have been lost to history for which posterity will feel grateful and conscious that in this my labor is not in vain. I submit this work to a generous public.

THE AUTHOR.

HISTORY OF THE CHIPPEWA VALLEY.

From the Daily Free Press.

We commence to-day the publication of a series of letters concerning the Chippewa Valley, which, when finished, will be a minute and full sketch of all incidents worthy of note, from the advent of the first white settler until the present date. It is true that some of the most important facts connected therewith have already become a part of the written history of the country, but still there remains much that is traditionary, only treasured in the minds of the oldest settlers, to be recalled at their semi-occasional gatherings. It is this class of matter that the author will weave into narrative.

We are glad, too, that it is to be done, for this valley is bound to bear an important part in the history of the State; hence it is fit that all those matters incident to the early trials and hardships of the settlers, and the development of the country become matters of record.

We need not say what is so well known hereabouts, that the gentleman who has undertaken it, Mr. T. E. RANDALL, better known as "Uncle Tom Randall," is just the man to accomplish the work. Coming here as he did in 1845, possessed of large observation and a retentive memory, it will readily be preceived that his own knowledge will grasp a large portion of this time. H. S. Allen, Alfred Brunson, and others, furnish the matter with which he is not conversant; hence, the narrative may be relied upon as correct in all essential details. And, too, in a literary point of view, Mr. Randall is not altogether unfitted for the task. Although he is a self-made man, and has been a hard working one all his life, he is an extensive reader, a clear thinker, possesses eminent good-sense, and his frequent contributions to the public press denotes him not devoid of literary excellence. This, however, we will not discuss, but let the reader judge for himself. Of this, all may be assured, that his contributions will possess the rare merit of accuracy and nice delineation of occurrence, so much desired in productions of this character.

The one which appears to-day is merely introductory. They will all be published first in the Daily, and then reproduced in the Weekly.

INTRODUCTION.

The close of the Black Hawk War, so called, and the extinction of the Indian title to the rich prairie lands in Northern Illinois, Southern Wisconsin, and West of the Mississippi in what is now Iowa, gave a new impulse to eastern emigration, and from Pennsylvania, Maryland, Virginia, the Carolinas, Tennessee, Kentucky, Ohio, and Indiana, could be seen long lines of "prairie schooners," their white canvass tops shining in the summer sun, filled with tired mothers and towhead children, and followed by droves of cattle, sheep and hogs, and on horseback boys and girls bringing up the rear, bound to "Black Hawk's purchase," while over the Lakes come pouring out from New York and New England a new installment of the restless but enterprising sons and daughters of the Pilgrims, as if bound to take possession of all the territory promised and guaranteed to their fathers by the British King, in a certain charter granting within certain parallels all the lands to the great "Southern (Pacific) Ocean."

The banks of the "Father of Waters" soon swarmed with these hardy adventurers, and towns and villages sprang up as if by magic, while the virgin prairies in their rear gave evidence of their boundless fertility in the most exuberant crops of golden grain, the lead and coal mines gave up their long-hidden wealth and commerce, manufactures, science and the arts began to flourish. But no single locality or section of country posessses all the advantages. Nature reserves something for all, and as no man is so vile but that we can discover some good traits in him, so no region is so destitute but we can find some bounty lavished upon it from Nature's ample store house; and as the best men have some faults, so the richest countries lack some element essential to human wants.

And thus it was with the rich and fertile West. With all its vast agricultural and mineral wealth, it lacked lumber to fence its fields, store its grain, or build its farm-houses and barns.

The scarcity and high price of this commodity was for many years a serious drawback to the progress of the farmers of Illinois, Missouri and Iowa, and a large share of that used in the erection of the first houses built in Burlington, Muscatine, Davenport, Rock Island, Galena, and Dubuque, came from the Alleghany river, by raft to Cincinnati, thence by steamboat to its destination, and sold at $75 to $100 per 1,000 feet. And in the summer season, long lines of wagons, each drawn by six yoke of oxen, and laden with whitewood lumber from the Wabash country, could be seen winding over the prairies, and across the sloughs and rivers of Illinois, their drivers mounted ten feet high on the clear, white lumber, and cracking their long "sucker whips" over the lolling oxen, as they floundered on over quagmire, marsh and bottomless flag-pits to the far-off embryo villages of Iowa; and these were the only available supplies of lumber for all that timberless region.

But, as through nature's handiworks, there is no want of anybody or anything without an adequate supply, so the allwise Creator has so arranged that these treeless but luxuriant and smiling prairies of the West shall have a bounteous supply of pine, away up in the frozen regions of the North, with the current of a hundred streams to bear it on to that wonderful river on whose bosom for two thousand miles floated the commerce of the West.

No wonder then that the moment, or even before, the Government had extinguished the Indian title, swarms of adventurous Yankees, brought up to the lumbering business, rushed up these rivers, out upon these hitherto unscathed forests, and, with axe, saw and cable, commenced the business that in a few years assumed gigantic dimensions, and now employs a very large share of the capital and industry of our growing State.

The struggles and hardships encountered by the pioneers in the settlement of any new country bring them into very close—almost fraternal—relations with each other; and a common interest and common dependence is felt, even though separated by long distances, which, in their eagerness to secure the best natural positions, is seldom taken into account. Especially was it so with the settlers in this valley; the great expense and difficulty in getting here; their utter isolation— shut out for several months in the year from all intercourse or correspondence with the outside world—their nearest post-office at Prairie du Chien, three hundred miles away; the winter's supplies frequently running so low that every pound was distributed—those who had much lending to those who had none—without any possibility of replenishing until a boat came up in the spring; the immediate presence of powerful and sometimes turbulent and hostile bands of Indians on the north and west; the reckless and abandoned character of some of the immigrants; the total absence of legal and social restraint; all conspired to make every event of this early period full of interest to those who, coming at a later day, know nothing of those vicissitudes and experiences.

Having migrated to the valley at a comparatively early day, and becoming intimately acquainted with all the first settlers, and with most of the noteworthy events, scenes, circumstances and incidents attending our incipient settlement and civilization, and being importuned by several ladies of this city, whose request I could not be so ungallant as to refuse, I have concluded to furnish for the columns of the FREE PRESS a reliable and as readable a sketch of our Valley's history as my time and ability will enable me to accomplish, although, to tell the truth, I feel it to be a very difficult task, from the fact that many abler pens than mine have at different times given detached portions of these narrations to the public, in writing up the business of our flourishing villages through the respective journals in whose interests they wrote. But I hope, notwithstanding, by grouping together all the facts and incidents into one continuous story, to make it both instructive and amusing.

CHIPPEWA VALLEY HISTORY.

CHAPTER I.

In the spring of the year 1828, James H. Lockwood, afterward better known as Judge Lockwood, an Indian fur trader, and General Street, of the United States army, Indian Agent at Fort Crawford, obtained a permit from the great chief Wabashaw, of Wabashaw's band of Sioux Indians, and also from the chiefs of the Chippewa band that claimed the lands on the Chippewa and Red Cedar (now Menomonie) rivers to cut pine timber, to occupy a certain tract of land, and to build a saw-mill thereon, in consideration of certain articles of merchandise, blankets, beads, whisky, etc., to be paid annually in July to the former at Wabashaw's Prairie, now Winona, and to the latter at the mill to be built on the lands leased. The sanction of Goverment was also obtained and under this arrangement the aforesaid parties fitted out an expedition, and erected a saw-mill on Wilson's creek, a short distance from its confluence with the Red Cedar. This was the fiirst mill built in the Chippewa Valley, and its site is now the west-side center of of Menomonie Village.

At this time, and for several years subsequently, the above-named band of Sioux claimed the delta of the Chippewa and the territory lying between the Mississippi and Red Cedar rivers, but it was really the neutral or dark and bloody ground between the two great hostile tribes of Sioux and Chippewas. At this time, too, all the territory comprised in the States of Iowa, Minnesota, northern half of Illinois, Wisconsin, nearly all of Michigan, and parts of Ohio and Indiana, was held by various tribes of Indians.

Military posts were established at Fort Madison, in what is now Lee county, Iowa, at Fort Armstrong, on Rock Islands at Fort Crawford, at Prairie du Chien, and at Green Bay and Chicago. Goverment agencies and Indian trading-posts existed at all these and many other places in the Northwest.

The writer was personally acquainted with several of the agents and fur traders of that early period, including Col. George Davenport, of Rock Island, who was the victim of a murderous conspiracy in 1843, H. L. Dousman, of Prairie du Chien, and one of the Beaubeins, of Chicago.

And here I am tempted to digress a moment, to relate an episode in the life of those two brothers whose names are well known as the founders of that famous city, as related by one of them in my presence in 1837, while he, in company with one of the Railroad Commissioners for the State of Illinois, was on a visit to the camp of a surveying party to which I was then attached, and engaged in locating the old Illinois Central Railroad, H. P. Woodworth, formerly a professor in the Norwich University, Vermont, being in charge. Many anecdotes concerning these brothers have been told in the early Chicago journals, but I do not think this was ever made public. Beaubein's English was very imperfect, but I will give it as near as I can remember in his own words:

"Out in the direction of widow Barry's Point my brother and I had raised a field of oats to feed our ponies; we had a cabin near it to sleep in. In the fall before war broke out, we went to trash dem with flails, had cleaned off a bit of prairie for a floor, and began to pound out de oats. By-and-by we zee three Injuns coming on dere ponies; we not know den dey tink to make for war. Dey were Sacs, and came from big war-dance and council of braves. By-and-by dey want whiskey; we say, 'Have none,'—in Indian—'all gone.' Den dey speak very bold and saucee, and say, 'We burn you' wigwam, an' take you' ponies, and kill you.' Den, quick as flash, my brother look at me an' I at him, an' (rising to his feet, and motioning his cane in the attitude of threshing) me trash an' he trash, an' one Injun he get on his pony an' march on, but two of dem would never go for ride any more. Den we were scare, 'fraid, an' get on our ponies for ride to de fort. Den we were 'fraid an' no go for oats ver' soon; den some soldiers go, but find all burnt; no oats, no cabin, no Injuns, but den we knew war would come."

Prairie du Chien—with the exception of Green Bay—the oldest settlement in the Northwest, was, in 1820, selected by the American Fur Company as its headquarters on the Upper Mississippi, and the Government had established a military post there, occupying at first the same fort occupied by the British troops in 1813, '14 and '15, who, having established a sort of military government at Green Bay, took formal possession of the country; one Rolette, a French Canadian voyageur, of Prairie du Chien, being employed to pilot them up the Fox and down the

Wisconsin Rivers, receiving therefor $20,000 in British gold—so says report. One account says the British held this post until 1816, when it was formally surrendered to the United States.

The commerce of the Upper Mississippi at this time (1828), though considerable in furs, skins and goods for the Indian trade, was unequal to the support of regular steamboat navigation, and only when Government forwarded military stores on boats chartered for the purpose, could passage or freight be secured to those upper regions. The steamboat Warrior, so famous for the part she took in the battle of the Badaxe in 1832, was thus employed in carrying troops and military stores, and by the vigilance of her commander, Captain Throckmorton, was at the precise point required when the fugitive bands of Sacs and Foxes came to the river—hotly pursued by our brave Suckers and Regulars—first reaching the bank where the village of Victory now stands.

The British and American fur companies have always used two kinds of river crafts for the transportation of freight; on all the upper branches the inevitable canoe adapted to rapids and shallow waters. But on the Mississippi and lower branches of all its tributaries, the "Keel Boat" had been in use until the increased volume of business warranted its [supercedure by steam boats. These boats were constructed much like an ordinary barge, but shallower and provided with running boards on each side; their carrying capacity varied from seven to twenty tons, the large class usually manned by fourteen men, six on each side, with poles which constituted the propelling power, a helmsman and a cook, with sometimes a sub-agent of the company as supercargo.

A large number of these boats were put in requisition by the American Fur Company, some of the largest of which descended to St. Louis and made regular trips between that place and Prairie du Chien, occupying 40 to 50 days for each trip, cordeling over the Upper and Lower Rapids on their return against the current. The cargo consisted of goods for the Indian trade and supplies for the various trading posts above, to which the goods were re-distributed from the latter place, the headquarters for the upper Mississippi. These boats were usually manned by Canadian French and half-breads, [called "voygeurs," under the supervision of some active, intelligent sub-agent or interested trader, and at the time of which we are speaking, 1828, one of the most trusted and energetic of the company's agents was Jean Brunett, (John Brunie) a native of France, emigrated and came to St. Louis in 1818, was some time in the service of Chuteau Brothers, and transferred in 1820 to

Prairie du Chien, where he subsequently married a sister of the Rolette before named. He and several of his employes will find a prominent place in these pages as the first settlers at Chippewa Falls.

It was this class of men, together with discharged soldiers, who were employed to boat the supplies, assist in building the mills and make the first lumber manufactured in the valley, at the mill before spoken of. An ex-Lieutenant of the regular army, named George Wales, was placed in charge, and continued to conduct the business for the Company, Street & Lockwood, until 1835, and in the mean time had erected, for the same parties, another mill on what is now known as "Gilbert's Creek," a mile or so from its mouth and two miles below the first named. Who the millwrights were that planned and executed the millwright-work in the mill I have not been able to learn. It was to these mills that young Lieutenant Jefferson Davis is said to have been dispatched for lumber to rebuild Fort Crawford. An amusing incident is related by several of the old soldiers who were with Davis and some officers on one of these trips for lumber. The order had been filled at the mill, the lumber rafted down the Red Cedar in strings to the Chippewa, all safely coupled up, and an old voyageur shipped as pilot, the officer and all hands leaped on board, and all went well until they neared the head of Beef Slough. "To de right, hard," said the old Frenchman. "What's that, you villain?" said the West Pointer, "you're going to run this raft right to hell? I tell you to pull to the left where the main river is." It was done, and the lumber lost in Beef Slough, as the channel was effectually blocked with drift wood. The crew returned for more lumber, but the officers returned to Fort Crawford, in a canoe, and reported the raft as broken.

In 1835, Messrs. Street & Lockwood sold both these mills to H. S. Allen, with the permit from the Indians, together with all the teams, tools and all the appurtenances, who, on his part, agreed to fulfill all obligations they were under to the Indians. The consideration was made payable in lumber, at thirty dollars a thousand, in annual installments. This gentleman was of New England stock; came from Vermont, first to Galena, thence to Menomonie in 1834, and commenced the business of getting out logs and square timber, but soon discovered that without booms in which to secure logs near the Mississippi they must be sawed into lumber here, in order to a successful prosecution of the business, and therefore accepted the Company's offer to sell, with alacrity, although his means were very limited. But to good business qualifications he added untiring energy, economy and unflinching perseverance, and nothing short of unparalleled misfortunes has prevented his acquiring all his ambition aspired to.

Lieutenant, or Captain Wales, as he was called, on retiring from the management of these mills, passed over to Eau Galle and built a mill on the site where the present mill, now owned by Messrs. Carson & Rand, stands. He was educated at West Point, possessed every business capacity, but had contracted dissolute and extravagant habits, had picked up a woman in Baton Rouge, while quartered in that city, whom he brought to the pineries with him, but whether they were married is not known. Four children, however, were the result of their connection, and she was probably the first white woman that ever came into this valley, and will be the subject of further comment.

CHAPTER II.

The settler on any of our western prairies, and the axemen who enter upon the primeval forests, where no mark or sign of man's destructive force or redeeming power is seen or felt, is frequently the subject of strange reflections as he follows his plow, turning up the virgin soil that through all the ages has remained undisturbed, or hews down the stately pine, that for a thousand years has flourished and grown, unnoticed and uncared for by the hand of man, he wonders how it occurs that he, of all the people that have lived and still live on the face of the earth, swarming, as it does, with so many millions, should be the first to appropriate to his comfort and convenience the blessings so long held in reserve in Nature's vast store-house.

He wonders, too, why his race should require all the resources of earth, the productions of forests, mines, rivers, lakes, oceans—of the soil plowed, planted, cultured, and garnered; the flocks and herds, feeding and gamboling on a thousand hills—for his subsistence, while other races have remained from generation to generation in all the untamed wildness of the wild deer and elk on which they subsist. What of the race that but yesterday was here! Have these rivers, fields, and forest, now so peaceful, always been so calm and still? or have they, like the old world, been the scene of some savage and sanguinary conflict? We speculate in vain on the long-ago dwellers upon the banks of these pleasant streams; their war-dance and savage yells may have been the only sound that ever waked the stillness of these hills, or a race long since extinct may have plowed and sowed, and builded, and loved, and worshiped, and cultivated all the graces and amenities of civilized life, but the records of whose deeds and virtues have been obliterated by the convulsions of Time's relentless changes. Of the race whose steps are now fast receding and giving place to ours, we know comparatively little, as traditions, and their history written for the past two hundred years by foreigners, is very imperfect. A brief account of the Indians who once claimed this valley, will be the subject of this chapter.

The Chippewas, whose name our river bears, were considered by the French missionaries as the bravest, most war-like, and, at the same time, the noblest and most manly of all the tribes on the American continent. They were derived from the Algonquin race, or type, and were first met with by the French on the Chippewa river near Montreal, Canada, in 1642, and were immediately taken into alliance with them (political), but matrimonial alliances soon followed, and their relations became very intimate. The Jesuit missionaries speak of the language of the Chippewas as the most refined and complete of any Indian tongue. Their territory seems to have been confined at that time to what is now the New Dominion, and the lower peninsula of Michigan.

Of the Sioux or Dakotas, still less is known of their history, at the time of which we are speaking, 1642, they seem to have been in possession of all the territory south of Lake Superior, west of Lakes Huron and Michigan, south as far as Milwaukee, and west to, or even beyond the Missouri river, for at this period they took a Jesuit priest prisoner at Sault (Sue) St. Mary's, and killed him as an intruder on their territory. And in 1660, the Jesuits having established a mission at La Point, on Magdalen Island, Lake Superior, were driven off by the Sioux, (Wis. Hist. Col., vol. 4, p. 226). Soon after this, probably in 1670, the Chippewas commenced their inroads upon the territory of the Sioux on the north and east, and fought their way south and west to the lines hereinafter described.

In the mean time the Winnebagoes, a migatory tribe from Mexico, to escape the Spaniards came among the Sioux, who gave them lands near Green Bay, probably to shield themselves from the Chippewas. But the Sacks and Foxes came up from the South and took forcible possession of their territory and compelled them to "go West," and they in turn were crowded out by the Menomonies.

In consequence of these immigrations and predatory wars the claims of the several Indian nations to their respective territories became very complicated and the cause of almost incessant wars amongst them. To prevent this as much as possible the United States government, in 1825, authorized a general treaty to be held at Prairie du Chien between all the Indian tribes within a district of five hundred miles each way. This joint treaty, was signed on the part of the Government by Generals William Clark and Lewis Cass, and by Wabashaw and Red Wing, Little Crow and twenty-three other Chiefs and braves of the Sioux, and by Hole-in-the-day and forty other Chiefs and braves on the part of the Chippewas. The names of the other chiefs are ommitted as unnecessary and not specially interesting to my readers. To fix the boundaries between the various nations definitely was the first and principal object of this treaty. The eastern boundary of the Sioux commenced opposite the mouth of the Iowa river on the Mississippi, runs back two or three miles to the bluffs, following the bluffs to, and crossing Bad-axe to Black river, from which point the line described is the boundary between the Sioux and Winnebagoes, and extends in a direction nearly north to a point on the Chippewa river, half a days march from Chippewa Falls, (U. S. Statutes at large, vol. 7, Indian Treaties, art. 5, page 273.) From this point on the Chippewa which was fixed at or near the mouth of Mud Creek (near Rumsey's Landing,) the line becomes the boundary between the Sioux and Chippewas, and runs to the Red Cedar river, just below the Falls, from thence to the St. Croix river at a place called the Standing Cedar, about a day's paddle in a canoe above the Lake on that river, thence passing between two lakes called by the Chippewas "Green Lakes," and by the Sioux " The lake they bury the eagles in," from thence to the "Standing Cedar" that the Sioux split, and thence to the mouth of Rum river, on the Mississippi. (ibid.) The boundary line between the Chippewas and Winnebagoes was also defined at this treaty, as commencing at this same point on the Chippewa river, half a day's march below the Falls, and thence to the source of the Clear Water, (Eau Claire,) a branch of the Chippewa, thence south to Black river, thence to a point where the woods project into the meadows, and thence to the Plover Portage of the Wisconsin, (Ibid. art. 7. p. 274.)

Thus we see the boundaries of the Sioux, Chippewas and Winnebagoes, were brought to a point at the famous half a day's march below the Falls; we see also that the permit granted Street & Lockwood, and mentioned in the preceding chapter, was entirely within the limits of Sioux territory, unless they had occasion to go above the Falls, on the Red Cedar, which was not the case as an abundance of pine was found near by on the creeks that drove those mills.

The boundaries above described were pretty carefully observed by the respective parties to the treaty aforesaid, except when war parties were fitted out by the Sioux or Chippewas, (the Winnebagoes remained perfectly neutral,) when the intervening territory between the Mississippi and the first described boundary became the theatre of many a hard fought battle, and hunting here was regarded as very unsafe by all three of those tribes.

On the 29th day of July, 1837, at Ft. Snelling, Gov. Dodge on the part of the United States, and Hole-in-the-day with forty-seven other Chiefs and braves, on the part of the Chippewas, signed a treaty ceding to the United States, land as follows: Beginning at the confluence of the Crow Wing and Mississippi rivers, and running to the north point of Lake St. Croix, one of the sources of the river of that name, thence along the dividing ridge between the waters of Lake Superior, and those of the Mississippi to the source of the Ocha-sua-sepe, (Court Ourilles,) a tributary of the Chippewa river, thence to a point on the river twenty miles below the outlet of Lake de Flambeau, thence to the confluence of the Wisconsin and Pelican rivers, and thence by various points named, to Plover Portage, thence back along the boundary between the Winnebagoes and Chippewas, to a point on that river half a day's march below the Falls, thence to the mouth of Rum river and up the Mississippi to the place of beginning. (ibid, p. 536.)

On the 29th of September, the same year, (1837,) at Washington City, D. C., Joel R. Poinsett, Secretary of War, on the part of the United States, and Big Thunder with twenty other Chiefs, and braves on the part of the Sioux, made a treaty, when the latter ceded to the United States all their lands east of the Mississippi, and all their islands in said river. (ibid, p. 538.)

On the 4th day of October, 1842, at La Point in Lake Superior, Robert Stewart on the part of the United States, and Po-go-ne-ge-shik with forty other Chiefs and braves of the Chippewas held a treaty, at which all the Chippewa lands in Wisconsin were ceded to the United States. (ibid, p. 591.)

It is proper to state, however, that immediately subsequent to the cession of the last named lands, several bands of the Chippewas became very much dissatisfied with the treaty, and with the reservation set apart for them above Sand Lake, in Minnesota, and begged so hard to come back, that the Government, in 1854, gave them back several townships, and half-townships of the land on the Court Ourilles, and some other branches of the Chippewa river, and established an agency there for the distribution of part of the annuities promised them by the terms of the treaty, as consideration for the value of their lands.

One thing will strike the reader as remarkable in regard to the treaty of 1825, namely: the geographical accuracy with which the boundaries between the tribes are defined, especially when we consider that eleven years later when Congress annexed the northern peninsula to Michigan, the maps of these territories were so imperfect that great difficulty arose in defining the boundary between that State and this.

CHAPTER III.

Until the year 1836, the territory now composing the State of Wisconsin composed a part of the Territory of Michigan, but in that year Congress and the people erected that Territory into a soverign State, and the organic law was passed creating the Territory of Wisconsin, which also included Iowa, and in October of that year, (1836,) the first Territorial Legislature convened at Belmont, Iowa county, which with three others, (Brown, Milwaukee, and Crawford,) had been organized under the former territorial Government, and comprised what is now the whole State of Wisconsin. The latter (Crawford) included about one-half the Territory, (Wisconsin), and of course this valley, and was entitled to two Representatives, but no member of Council. At the first session, James H. Lockwood and James B. Dallam, were chosen to represent this (Crawford) county, and the next year, 1837, to the Legislature convened at Burlington, Iowa, Jean Brunett and Ira B. Brunson, were elected. There was a special session of this Legislature called, and Mr. Brunett attended both. He was also engaged quite extensively in trading with the Indians, and in lumbering.

At the treaty spoken of in the preceding chapter, held in Prairie du Chien, in 1825, it was stipulated that the Government should maintain an agency at La Point for the distribution of annuities, and to establish a farm and blacksmith shop with a competent workman therein at some point on the Chippewa river not far from the Falls.

Mr. Lyman Warren, of La Point, formerly of Newburg, New York, was appointed to the position of farmer, blacksmith, and sub-agent, and subsequently, by Governor Dodge, as justice of the peace, and established himself at Chippewa City, five miles above the Falls.

The Gothy family now located at the Court de Oreilles (Couterey) agency, and several other half breeds of note located there, and it soon became quite an important place for the sale of goods, and the collection of furs, the whole being under the direction and control of the American Fur Company and its agents. But in 1837, immediately after the treaty at Fort Snelling and the cession of these lands by the Indians, a number of those agents, including H. L. Dousman, Gen. Sibley, Col. Aiken and Lyman Warren, fitted out an expedition under the supervision of Mr. Brunett to erect a saw-mill at the Falls of the Chippewa. Why this point should have been chosen in preference to the Dells, either upper or lower, seems unaccountable; it is probable, however, that the difficulty of booming the river and securing the logs was never taken into account. Had men of larger experience in lumbering on large rivers, in damming, booming, and storing large quantities of logs been employed by this company, the probability is that the mill would have been located at some point where, by setting the water back over some lagoon or marsh flat, a safe reservoir for logs could be formed entirely outside of the rapid current. There were such points on the river, above and below, but no more expensive and difficult place could have been found on the whole river than the one selected, in which to stop and retain a season's supply of logs, as the result has shown by repeated disasters. Experience has also proved that it is far less difficult to obtain a head of water to drive a saw mill than to secure a stock of logs, on a rapid river like the Chippewa, hemmed in as it is between steep banks, and if there should ever come such a freshet as occured in 1838, and again in 1847, I am afraid there would be few logs left in any boom on the river.

It was necessary to engage all operatives, boatmen, axemen, mechanics, loggers, etc., and to bring all necessary supplies from Prairie du Chien, or points below, and those employed by Mr. Brunett in the construction and management of the mill at the Falls, were mostly the old voyagers, and Canadian French and half breeds, previously employed in the fur trade, and amongst the first who came to settle permanently, was Louis Demarie, notably conspicious as the father of five blooming daughters he was of pure Canadian French blood, from Montreal, and his wife French and Chippewa half-breed, born in Detroit. She was a woman of uncommon natural abilities, and with education and culture would have graced a high social position in any community. She was a born physician, and for many years the only one in the valley; and in making a diagnosis of disease, and her knowledge of the healing properties and proper application of many of the remedies used in the Materia Medica, exhibited extraordinary insight and skill in her practice. She was frequently called to attend upon myself and family, and her prescriptions were simple, natural, and always efficacious. Several of her daughters had attained the age of maidenhood before leaving Prairie du Chien, and were much admired belles in that old pioneer town, whose young swains sang their praises on many a night's camp ground.

The work of building the mill progressed slowly the first year; a great many unexpected obstacles impeded the undertaking; the rock encountered in excavating the race was of such intense hardness that the contractors threw up the job, and in re-letting the work a price almost fabulous had to be paid, running into many thousands. During the ensuing winter the supply of provisions failing, recourse was had to the stores of H. S. Allen, at Menomonie. On such occasions every one looked out for himself, and amongst those who suffered was Mr. Demaric, whose family being large, soon found it necessary to obtain a supply from that quarter. As spring advanced and the ground became bare, so that trains, (a short one-horse vehicle on runners much used in Canada) could not run, it was sometimes necessary to pack provisions over on their backs, and on one occasion, the two older girls, Mary and Rosalie were dispatched thither for flour, and other necessaries which led the way to more intimate relation. At this time, the Green Mountain adventurer and successful lumberman on the Red Cedar, had rebuilt the oldest of the Street & Lockwood mills, and looked forward to a prosperous career in the the business he had chosen. One thing he yet lacked, God's last, best gift to man, a wife, in the multiplicity of business cares he had neglected to take "unto himself"; perhaps too, away down amongst his native hills some school-girl's face still haunted his dreams, and he might have longed for the time to come, when he could get away from these wild scenes, and claim it as his own; but then, would she be willing to share with him the hardships and social privation to which she must be subjected in his exile home? Such reflections had made him hesitate, and when the fair but bashful Mary Demaric presented herself at his counter, it is not to be wondered at that she made an impression upon him that set at defiance all those preconceived notions of propriety, family pride and youthful fancy, and to ally himself with this unsophisticated girl of the pine woods. After several months wooing, they were married by Esq. Warren, and she being a devoted Catholic, their union was subsequently solemnized at Prairie du Chien, according to the rites of that

Church. In the spring and summer of this year, 1838, there came the most terrible flood ever known on this river, in the month of June; from Eau Claire to the Mississippi, the bottom-lands, from bluff to bluff, were covered with water from ten to fifteen feet deep. Mr. Brunett's keel boats were at Menomonie for lumber, when the water was highest, and entered through the woods and over the prairie bottoms, keeping close to the bluff's in order to enable them to reach bottom with their poles.

CHAPTER IV.

We left Captain George Wales in 1838-9, building a mill on the Eau Galle; he was in partnership in the undertaking with Thomas Savage, and a mill-wright called Captain Dix, most likely the same that had been employed in the erection of the two mills before named, on the Monomonie (Red Cedar,) by Street & Lockwood. Soon after this mill commenced operations in 1839, there came on to that stream two young men, named William Carson, and Henry Eaton, the former from Canada, the latter a Yankee, and as the mill company had no prescriptive or exclusive right to the pine, commenced getting out square timber and shingles, a business which their enterprise and economy made quite lucrative, but was very annoying to the company, not only because it took away the most convenient and valuable timber, but obstructed the navigation of the little river for their cribs of lumber. These operations continued for several years, and in the mean time, several others found their way on to that stream and the Red Cedar; amongst them a man named Lamb, who stuck his stakes and built the first house in Dunnville, which very soon became a noted "stopping place" for all the lumbermen and hunters that came to the country. It was then considered one of the best locations of the kind in the valley, and its owner soon found it necessary to procure "an help mate," which he found in the person of Margaret Demarie, adopted daughter of Louis Demarie, at the Falls, (Frenchtown). Lamb was an old soldier, very dissipated, with no business habits or industry, and being unable to keep up the place to the wants of the public, in 1841 sold out to his more energetic brother-in-law, Arthur McCann, who had just married Rosalie Demarie, sister of Mrs. Allen.

Three of these brothers, Stephen, Arthur, and Dan McCann, had come on to the river a year previous; they were originally from Marietta.

Ohio, had followed the river round, and like many other river men of that day, belonged to the more reckless strata of society.

The Eau Galle Company finding all efforts to induce the energetic young operators, Carson and Eaton, to leave the stream, unavailable, concluded to sell them an interest in the mill, which soon after resulted in the withdrawal of Savage & Dix from the concern, leaving Carson, Eaton & Wales as the firm, the latter being considered the financial partner, who necessarily spent much of his time at St. Louis, and other points on the Mississippi, selling lumber, leaving his family at the mill.

When young Tom Sheridan was requested by his father to take a wife, he replied, "that he had no objections if he only knew whose wife to take." There is wit and humor in such a remark, where plenty of other material to make wives of are at hand, ready and waiting for a fellow to propose. But it becomes a serious matter, and "no joke into it," when on looking "the landscape o'er," a young man in want finds that if he takes a wife at all it must be somebody else's wife. A bashful young man, whose heart comes right up into his throat the moment he finds himself in the presence of, and attempts to speak to a young lady who has taken his fancy, is frequently astonished at the ease and fluency with which he can address himself to a married one, and encouraged by the freedom and familiarity experienced in revealing his inmost thoughts to, and eliciting the sympathy of a married female acquaintance, many a virtuous young man has found himself contravening the tenth commandment in coveting his neighbor's wife. Which of these causes influenced or took possession of one of these junior partners, (Eaton) there is no record extant by which to determine, but one thing is certain: during the long protracted absence of the senior down the river, the junior's visits to the residence of his partner's mistress became alarmingly frequent. Free love as taught and exemplified by Mrs. Woodhull, of our time, may or may not have been a favorite theory with this exemplary lady at this time, but that she encouraged these visits, and did her best to render them agreeable is freely admitted. Perhaps she derived some secret satisfaction from so doing, in the fact that her lord, like John Quin, "carried his wife in his pocket," and when absent from her, squandered large sums for his gratification, but expected his wife to be a paragon of virtue. Such was the course of events until the fall of 1844, when matters culminated in open rupture between this historic couple, and finally separation; and as his extravagance had involved the firm in financial embarrassment, the other members compelled him to abdicate, when he left the valley forever, the oldest settler, and, as some say, the most wronged of any that ever came into it.

Some two miles below Gilbert's Creek on the West side of the Red Cedar, a small spring creek makes into the river, on which in 1839 H. S. Allen built a saw mill, making three mills owned and run by him at the same time, which gave to the one on Gilbert's Creek, the name of the "middle mill," by which it was known for many years. It was re-built in 1841. The same year Allen sold the lower or Spring Creek mill to Stephen S. McCann; it was to this mill that Simon and George Randall first came and took employment with McCann. It was burned in 1843, the loss falling on the orignal owner, Allen. In the fall of the year 1841, the mill on Wilson's creek was sold to one Green, and by him soon transferred to a Mr. Pearson, by whom the first dam across the Menomonee was erected, with a view to the establishment of a big mill, but for want of means was unable to go on, and finally sold out to an old gentleman by the name of Black, who in 1844 transferred a half interest to Knapp & Wilson, two of the present wealthy owners, and in the fall of the same year went down on a raft to Keokuk, Iowa, sickened and died, leaving the property to the other members of the firm, who, the following year, associated themselves with Mr Stout, under the firm name of Knapp, Stout & Co. While Mr. Black was in possession at this point in 1844, a most unprovoked murder was committed by a man whose name my informant cannot recall, the victim had retired for the night to the garret of an old log house, where he was stealthily shot. A warrant was issued by Esq. Branham, the offender arrested, taken to Prairie du Chien tried before Judge Dunn and acquitted. This is supposed to be the first murder of any white man in the valley, but was very soon followed by another, under the following circumstances: Arthur McCann and J. C. Thomas, in partnership had in 1843 commenced and nearly completed the Blue Mills, now so called, the former still residing at Dunville; they had employed on the work for some time, a man by the name of Sawyer, who when his time was up, went down to McCann's for a settlement, after which McCann proposed cards, at the same time treating freely.

The game went on until evening, when some dispute arose the latter threw a scale-weight at the former, whereupon he repaired to the cabin of Philo Stone, near by, carefully loaded his rifle, went back to the door of McCann's house and called him; on his appearance at the door Sawyer took deliberate aim, and McCann fell dead on his own door-step, the victim of a drunken brawl. Sawyer made his way up the river to Eau Claire, and thence to the Falls of Chippewa, where his pursuers lost track of him, since when he has never been heard of, although a large reward was offered for his apprehension by McCann's friends. His wife returned to her parents, and Philo Stone took possession of the tavern.

This man and his brother Rosewell Stone, came on to the river in 1838, from Vermont, and engaged in hunting on the neutral territory between the Sioux and Chippewas, which being seldom visited by either party of Indians, was most excellent hunting grounds for the whites who came early. Philo was a turbulent fellow, never avoided a quarrel, was brave, wiry, small in stature but quick as lightning, never was whipped, was frequently arrested and placed under bonds to keep the peace, and like many others had taken a full-blooded squaw, whom he trained to be a good housekeeper; the fact is, this class of women are all tractable, and easy to acquire all the arts and many of the graces of civilized life, and if the males were as readily molded into the ways of industry and progress as the females, they would be easily civilized.

CHAPTER V.

The settlement at the Falls will now claim our attention, and as indicating the social condition, and the difficulties under which the early settlers labored, I will quote from a letter just received from Rev. Dr. Alfred Brunson, of Prairie du Chien, he says: "In 1842, I was appointed Indian agent at La Point, Lake Superior, and in going there went up the Chippewa river in a keel boat to the mouth of the Red Cedar, It was in the month of November, and so cold that the floating ice cut a hole in the bow of our boat, and we were compelled to land. The next morning the river was closed with ice, and the snow was a foot deep. Mr. Jean Brunett was in charge of the boat, which was laden with provisions, clothing, etc., for the company's mill at the Falls, to which place Mr. Brunett sent messengers for teams to draw up the freight. But the cattle being out on the Rush bottoms, (Lowe's creek bottoms,) a week passed before the team arrived, and we were two days reaching the Falls. My position as Indian agent made Mr. Warren, (the sub-agent and blacksmith before named) one of my employees, and I went to his house and stayed several weeks waiting for the ice to bridge the rivers, lakes and swamps so that we could make a winter's passage through to La Point, which detained me until nearly Christmas.

Finding an excellent library at Mr. Warren's, I improved my time in reading; and Mrs. Warren, though seven-eights Indian and spoke only the Chippewa language, was an excellent cook and neat house-keeper. Their house was of hewn logs, two stories high, furnished with good beds, and I fared like a prince. The Indians for 40 or 50 miles around hearing that their "Father," the agent, was there came in to see me, and both they and the lumbermen who had troublesome teeth came in to have them extracted, the tools for which I carried with me, as every traveler among them should. In the meantime Mr. Warren fitted out the trains, one for dogs the other a one horse rig. These vehicles are very peculiar, being a thin rock-elm board 10 feet long, and from 12 to 15 inches wide, bent up at the forward end like a runner, and strips of cedar fastened to the edge having holes through them to facilitate binding on their loads. We reached La point in ten days, five men going ahead on snow-shoes, but I rode on the train."

The following summer Mr. Brunson made another trip, and writes as follows: "On the 24th day of May, 1842, I left Prairie du Chien with a company of miners, bound for the newly purchased copper mines of Lake Superior. We had three wagons, nine yoke of oxen, three horses and fourteen men. After the first ten miles we had to look out our own road, bridge some of the deep narrow streams and ford others. I had learned from Cadot, brother of Mrs. Warren, the previous winter, what the face of the country was between Black river and Chippewa Falls. At the former place we found the Mormons in possession getting out timber for their Nauvoo Temple; to them, and our company, I preached the first Gospel sermon ever delivered in that valley. We ferried over Black river on their keel boats, except the cattle who swam. The Trempeleau was crossed high up the valley, and thence over the ridge into the valley of the Eau Claire which we crossed on a raft, the water being too deep to ford, as we judged ten miles from its mouth.

We sighted an elk while ascending the ridge between the Eau Claire and Chippewa, from whence we descried Mr. Warren's barn, for which we steered our course, and struck the Chippewa within twenty rods of the Falls, and ferried over on the company's keel boats fastened together and covered with plank."

"Obtaining a guide from Mr. Warren, and an addition of three or four men to our force, we took the divide between the Chippewa and Red Cedar, crossed the outlet of a lake we called Cedar

Lake, fifty yards wide and three feet deep, with a fleet of canoes sailing around us, wondering at our wagons and hungering for provisions."

"The fourth of July found us at Lake Che-tack, with a dozen Indians in our camp, and feeling a glow of patriotism, the men with me must have an oration, and I being the only talker by trade, was selected as the orator of the day, and delivered, I suppose, the first speech of the kind ever pronounced in that valley. William Warren, my interpreter, explained my discourse to the Indians present, who said they understood the history of our revolution. Very little game was seen along the route, and that little between Black and Chippewa rivers, that being a kind of neutrally forbidden ground, between the hostile bands."

Messrs. Brunett & Warren were undoubtedly competent men to manage the business of an Indian trading post, but the projectors and capitalists who furnished the means to build the new mill, and construct booming works at the Falls, very soon discovered that in order to a successful prosecution of the business, some person more experienced, and possessing greater executive ability, must be placed at the helm. Five years had now passed, and no return for the capital invested had been realized, or seemed likely to accrue, and the company were anxious to find some responsible party to take the property off their hands. The death of Mr. Warren during the winter following the visit of Mr. Brunson, hastened the necessity for prompt action, and accordingly, early in the summer of 1844, the mill, with all their teams, tools, boats and fixtures, was sold to Jacob W. Bass and Benjamin W. Brunson, son and son-in-law of the Rev. Dr. aforesaid. The consideration was $20,000, payable in annual installments, with interest. The principal factor in this young firm, was Mr. Bass, who had been a peddler, kept a hotel, run the ferry at North McGregor, a successful merchant, was just married, and the young couple were as ambitious and determined to hew themselves out a fortune, as any couple with whom I ever became acquainted. Mrs. Bass came directly to the Falls with him—the only white woman there—and though a mere girl in age and appearance, possessed unlimited confidence in herself, and a great deal of family pride, that sustained her under privations and exile.

The new firm came into possession of a property, run down by mismanagement and constant disaster, without piers or booms, or any arrangement to secure a stock of logs, the mills and race out of repair, it required greater experience and more capital than they could command, although a year and six months of untiring exertion had overcome some of the obstacles to success. when in 1846 another operator in this losing drama, must be introduced. In order to do so, we must go back to the Red Cedar once more.

In the management of the mills referred to in the previous chapter, H. S. Allen had associated with him in the business, in 1842, G. S. Branham, and the firm had accumulated considerable capital, and during the winter of 1845-6, began to look about with a view to invest it in some larger establishment. Why they did not retain the property on Wilson's Creek, and the site on which the Menomonie mills and village now stand, is a mystery—one of the unaccountable mistakes, which even far seeing business men will sometimes make, by which the golden opportunity is lost forever, or, as in this instance, surrendered to another. After a thorough examination of all the numerous elligible locations in the valley, this company, having associated themselves with my brothers, Simon and George Randall, under the firm name of Allen. Branham & Randall, fixed upon the Lower Dalles of the Chippewa, as the best, and in fact the only place, on the whole river, where logs could be taken out of the current and held securely and safely, and cheaply handled during high and low water. The works at the Falls were even then the great obstacle to the improvement of this grand natural position. But they determined to go on, notwithstanding the opposition they expected to encounter from that source.

To avoid all immediate difficulty, their plan of operations was to erect a dam at the foot of the dalles half the distance across the river, thence a side or wing dam, on the smooth rock bottom, up along, near the raft channel, to the head or upper reef of rock on the dalles, and by a low, brush and stone (or gravel) dam, across to the east or south bank, which would raise a sufficient head of water, but would not interrupt the navigation for raft or boats. Booming capacity was to be obtained at first, in the eddy, where Ingram & Kennedy's logs are stored for their eddy mill, and inside the wing dam, and eventually, as the business became more developed, and their means more abundant, a raft and boat channel was to be excavated across the point where the mill formerly owned by Nelson, Hunter & Co., now stands—the channel so much talked of since, when the entire river for two miles in the bend thus relieved by the cut off, could be used as a safe reservoir for logs. This plan of improvements was fully matured by the aforesaid company, was repeatedly submitted to other business men, myself among them, and would be pronounced today, by a competent engineer, a feasible—perhaps the best method of improving those far famed dalles that could be adopted. Every arrangement was forthwith made to carry this undertaking forward. Allen &

Branham sold their mill on Gilbert Creek to Samuel Gilbert, Sen., father of Gen. Isham Gilbert, and came immediately over and commenced operations. A contract was made with the writer, who was then operating the Blue Mill, for all the dam plank and other lumber required, and means advanced to enable him to furnish it. Shanties, in which to board the men, and warehouses for their goods were immediately erected.

The peninsula formed by Half Moon Lake, being convenient and studded with pine timber, of suitable size for the purpose, was taken possession of, and the timber got out for a large mill. So much had been accomplished when spring came on, and the parties comprising the firm, having separate interests to attend to, relinquished operations for a brief period, as was supposed to be resumed again when those private interests were closed up.

Allen & Branham had a considerable amount of lumber on Gilbert's creek, to take down the river and convert into money. During the previous summer, (1845), Steven S. McCann and Jeremiah C Thomas —the latter since the death of Arthur McCann, having sole possession of the Blue mill, had formed a partnership and built a claim shanty near the site of the Eau Claire Lumber company's water mill on the Eau Claire river, the former, McCann, had also erected a cabin near the confluence of this stream with the Chippewa, for a warehouse, and another on the site of the American House in the Second ward of this city, into which he moved his family. These were the first improvements made in Eau Claire. This firm had no means to build a mill, but succeeded in putting a couple of logging camps up the Eau Claire for the winter, but running short for supplies had recourse to Simon and George Randall, who were prevailed upon to invest a considerable sum to help them through the winter, and found it necessary to look after it pretty sharp in order to secure it for use in the new firm of Allan, Branham & Randall, the principal of whom as before stated was down the Mississippi closing up the old business.

The historian can only speak of results, the causes which produce them are frequently beyond his ken. The fate of empires depends as much on the success of diplomacy, as on the force of arms, and the benefits of many a hard won battle have been lost to the victor by a short sighted policy in arranging the terms of surrender, and private operations are no exception to the rule. I suppose it is all right for men to protect their own interests against the competitive enterprise of others even if they have to make " the worst appear the better side. In the mind of H. L.

Dousman, there was just this question presented when he heard that H. S. Allen had concluded to locate at the Lower Dalles: "Every dollar I have put into that property at the Falls is a dead loss or that man must be induced to abandon that enterprise; aye, more! I must have the experience, the energy, and financial ability of that man enlisted for me, not against me." What agencies were employed, what arguments used, or what inducements offered to effect this purpose has not come to light. Perhaps Mr. Allen, naturally cautious, came to the conclusion that the undertaking was too great for the means at their command. Be that as it may, the first news that came up the river was that the whole project was abandoned. that Allen & Branham had dissolved, that the former had bought in with Mr. Bass at the Falls, and that the strong team of Allen & Bass would be able to overcome all the immense natural obstacles and disadvantages of that situation.

Dr. Williamson in his treatise on human volition, says there is no such thing as there might have been, but it certainly looks to me as though the situation and condition of a great many things on this river might have been very different had Allen, Branham & Randall gone on with their contemplated enterprise. One thing certainly might not have been, the ten years struggle to obtain a charter under which those works could have been successfully constructed, would have been obviated, and in all probability most of the lumber manufactured on the river would have been made here, where a safe and ample reservoir for logs might long since have been perfected, and millions saved to all lumbermen on the river that for want of these works have year after year proved a total loss, and brought many to the verge of bankruptcy.

CHAPTER VI

Satisfactory arrangements having been made between the partners in the late firm of Allen, Branham & Randall, for their separation, the two juniors', S. and G. Randall, took a half interest in the claim of McCann & Thomas, at the mouth of the Eau Claire river, and preparations were made to erect a dam and mill on the site of the Eau Claire Lumber company's water mill, and in October, 1846, the dam was completed, and the work progressing finely, under the firm name of McCann, Randall &

Thomas. Messrs. Allen & Bass, had also commenced expensive improvements at the Falls.

During the summer the writer had brought his family, which, until now, had remained in Iowa, to the Blue Mill, which he had bought of J. C. Thomas. Mrs. Randall had been reared in the bosom of the Methodist church, and regarded the loss of its privileges as a very serious drawback to her enjoyment on coming here. Since our marriage, some two or three years previous, I, too, had been identified with that church and its services. It was now proposed to do what we could for the interests of religion in this remote corner. Appointments to hold Divine service on alternate Sabbath's at the company's boarding house, in Chippewa Falls, and at the house of S. S. McCann, in Eau Claire, were accordingly made in September, of the year before mentioned, 1846, and continued until the setting in of winter, when a severe illness prostrated the writer, and the meetings were discontinued—the first public religious services ever held in this valley. Another little event of a social nature occurred also about this time which must not be passed over. Geo. W. Randall, of the aforesaid firm, having become satisfied that it is "not good for a man to dwell alone," concluded to "take unto himself a wife." Miss Mary La Point, formerly of Prairie du Chien, and brought up in the family of Mr. Brisbois, came to Eau Claire during the summer and made up her mind to relieve him of his disconsolate condition. Mr. and Mrs. McCann made a big wedding. Mr. Bass, at the Falls, had received a commission as Justice of the Peace, from our Territorial Governor, and was invited down to solemnize the nuptials; the throne of Grace was addressed, and the blessings of Heaven invoked on their union by the writer, and this was the first wedding that took place in Eau Claire.

Some time in the following winter another event not without interest, came to pass, Simon Randall, the other junior partner in the same firm, having suffered several years of isolation, had like many other young men among the early comers taken one of the maidens of the forest with whom he lived quite happily. She was a good cook, and kept his house in good order. Simon really seemed attached to her, but though of a hardy race she was not exempt from the conditions of her sex, and ere she became a mother, the "destroyer had done its work." Funeral services were held over her remains, and the bereaved invited to the consolations of the Gospel, by the writer, from 1st cor, xv 21, 22, and this was the first funeral service ever performed here.

The winter of 1846–7, was in some respects very remarkable; scarcely any snow fell, and so intensely cold was the weather that the water in the Chippewa, at the Falls, froze to the bottom, forcing it to overflow, in the same manner we frequently see small rivulets rise to the surface and cause a fresh layer of ice every night, and this was continued until every rock, island and tree on the Falls, were submerged with ice, lying solid in many places twenty feet in thickness from the bottom. I have never known this to occur since. This scarcity of snow extended the whole length of the river to its source, and would have proved ruinous to "long hauling" contracts, had there been any at the time, but Messrs. Colton & Moses, on Yellow river, for the Falls company, and the Hoosier Logging company on the Eau Claire, had bank hauling, and managed even without snow to get large stocks of logs for their respective companies. But if the winter was remarkable for want of snow, the spring was still more remarkable for absence of rain, there being scarcely enough to lay the dust through the entire months of April and May, and not a log floated in either the Yellow or Eau Claire rivers during the whole time. But on the evening of the 5th of June, after a foggy morning and a hot windy day, rain commenced falling, accompanied with most fearful thunder and lightning, unlike anything I ever before heard, or witnessed, and continued to pour down in torrents until eight o'clock the next morning, at which time the Chippewa had risen twelve feet, and was covered with logs, drift wood and the debris of piers and booms from the Falls, where a total wreck of all the costly structures placed in the river during the previous winter, to stop and hold logs, had been made; nothing was left but the mill, and its race and guard locks were completely demolished or filled with gravel.

More than ten thousand logs—the entire stock out of Yellow river was carried away, and the total avails of a winter's operations perished in this flood.

The supply of logs for the Blue Mill shared the same fate, and in my endeavors to save a part of my boom, I was taken out into the wild and surging current, on it as it floated away. I have been on many log drives and often placed in positions of extreme peril, but never has death stared me more directly in the face than while afloat on that frail boom—bent, crushed, and broken, between masses of logs and drift wood. I could do nothing with it, and on, and on, it went with the rapidity of a railway train, passing repeatedly under the branches of reclining trees. I lay flat on my face and clung to those strained timbers, well knowing that once in that boiling flood no skill in the art of swimming could save me from a watery grave, but as the fates would have it, my rickety craft shot like an arrow out of the current and went ashore at the eddy where Sherman's mill was since built, so being only a short distance from my brother's on the Eau Claire, I walked over and witnessed a more terrible devastation still. It was now nearly noon, but every log pier, and boom on this stream had, hours before, been swept away by the still fast swelling flood, and in one hour more the new double saw mill just ready to commence operations, was borne almost bodily away by the resistless current. It was a sickening sight and I hurried back to relieve the fears of my family for my safety.

A party of Geologists under the Superintendeence of Hon. David Dale Owen, had just reached my place at the Blue Mill as I returned; had camped just below, the night before and could go no farther until the water had subsided. The party had fitted out at Prairie du Chien, under the directions of the Secretary of the Interior, by authority of an act of Congress providing for a Geological and Minerological survey of the northern part of Wisconsin Territory, and had chosen this route to reach Lake Superior, in bark canoes. I regret that I cannot remember the names of all the party, but one name, besides Owen's I shall not soon forget, Dr. Gwyn, the physician, on account of his kindness to us under affliction. Six weeks before a sweet babe had been born to us, the alarm and exposure of its mother on this day together with the drenching rain, brought on an attack of croup. On being acquainted with the case the Doctor immediately prescribed for it, and was unremiting in his attendance upon it during his stay, and when he left we supposed the danger had passed, but on the evening of the second after, a relapse came on and the little sufferer's struggles for breath were soon over and we were a second time childless.

Not often does it fall to the lot of enterprising men to sustain so heavy a calamity as fell upon those two, young lumbering establishments at Eau Claire and Chippewa Falls. The savings, of years, of toil, and struggle, had been invested in these undertakings and now scarcely a vestige of all remained, and worse than all, heavy liabilities had been incurred for which there was no possible adequate provision to meet. Misfortunes almost always lead to dissolution in partnerships. It was so in this case. In fact nothing else could be done, as in the case with the company here in Eau Claire, capital to start again, could only be reached by taking into the concern some one with means, and as the crisis and panic of 1847, had made every one wary it was no easy matter to accomplish.

Mr. Bass withdrew from the firm of Allen & Bass at the Falls leaving Mr. Allen alone to bear the brunt. The logs that had been carried away were sold to the Hoozier logging company, before named, who contracted to gather them all up from the sloughs and river bottoms, and there being no money in the west at that time, the payments were made due in articles of farm produce, and amongst others one hundred barrels of mess pork were delivered at Lake Pepin, at seven dollars per barrel, transported too all the way from Rock Island. Flour was another item at $2.75 per barrel delivered at the same place.

Farmers of the Chippewa Valley, how would you like to grow wheat and pork now at those figures!

Mr. and Mrs. Bass removed to St. Paul then just starting into being, got hold of some land near the city, speculated in lots, lumber, and other property, and he is now one of the solid men of St. Paul. Allen had credit and used it to start again. J. C. Thomas came back to the Blue Mill, McCann took to farming on Eagle prairie above the Falls. Philo Stone and H. Cady took their places with S. & G. Randall, who rebuilt the mill on the Eau Claire the following winter, 1837–8. J. J. Gage, James Reed, and Capt. Dix bought the lower mill site, and erected a dam and mill on the site of the Eau Claire Lumber Company's flouring mill.

CHAPTER VII.

Some of my readers in this city having intimated that a more extended statement, or description, of the terrible freshet spoken of at the close of the preceding letter, (No. 6,) would be desirable, I will endeavor to give some idea of it by comparison and otherwise. Having carefully noted every great rise in the Chippewa and Eau Claire rivers, since that time, I hesitate not to say that in all places where their waters were confined between banks, within ordinary limits, they were full six feet higher than the highest freshet that has since occurred. All the way from the foot of the dalles down to the present Chippewa bridge, the water poured over the west bank of the river into the depression beyond, in sufficient depth to float the largest logs; and from Rev. Mr. Kidder's residence down to the present Pioneer block, logs and drift wood lay high upon the slope, being checked by the trees, while the entire flat between that bank and the river was many feet under water. The mark on some of those logs which I noticed at one time the ensuing summer, indicated that they were out of the Eau Claire river. The ground on which Shaw & Galloway's foundry and machine shop now stands, was at least ten feet under water. The entire farm of Mr. Yates, opposite the Blue Mill, was inundated, six to ten feet.

Some of the heavest timbers, and heavily ironed wheels belonging to the mill that was carried away at Eau Claire, floated across the bottom and lodged high upon the slope of the hill back of Porterville, the whole country from bluff to bluff being under water.

The Indians will now claim our attention. Many of the collisions between the hostile bands of Sioux and Chippewas, during the time covered by this history, have created so little interest among the white settlers, that it is difficult to obtain definite and positive information in regard to them. In most instances, too, these encounters are utterly unworthy the name of fighting. Nothing can be more dastardly, or better calculated to induce a mean, cowardly disposition, than their mode of conducting war—assassination or murder, better defines their treacherous, stealthy, fiendish butcheries than any other terms. In 1840, a party of Sioux were thus waylaid near the Red Cedar river, and entirely cut to pieces; and in November of the same year, a party of six, belonging to the opposite beligerant, was cut off in the same way. The following year, a large party of Sioux came up by invitation of the Chippewas to Eau Claire, where they held a friendly meeting, and smoked the pipe of peace. This was repeated in October, 1846, when 150 braves, all mounted on ponies, came up to the Falls, and thence to Chippewa City, and held a treaty of peace with their hereditary foes. Among them were the great Chiefs, Wabashaw, Red Wing and Big Thunder. Their first meeting took place at the Falls, about sunset, and was rather informal, owing to some misunderstanding as to the place of meeting. The writer was present and heard part of the Reception Address, and subsequently learned from Ambrose—one of the interpreters—the substance of what was said on both sides. The Sioux remained mounted on their ponies during the entire interview. The Chippewa Chiefs and braves were painted after their mode indicating peace, and the head Chief advanced toward their guests with a large red pipe, made of stone from Pipe-stone mountain, in one hand, and in the other a hatchet, which was thrown with considerable force so as to partially bury it in the earth; then raising the pipe to his mouth and taking a whiff or two, and turning the stem toward the Sioux Chief presented it for his acceptance. All this was done in silence; the Sioux Chief received the emblem of peace also in silence, smoked a few whiff's, bowed respectfully as he handed the pipe, reined his pony one step to the right, and waited the next salutation. The substance of which was, "Friends we are glad you have come, we are anxious to make peace with the Sioux nation. As you have seen us throw down and bury the hatchet, so we hope you are inclined to make peace." The Sioux Chiefs then threw down whatever arms they held, and declared their purpose to maintain permanent peace. They said their great father, the President, with whom they had never been at war, had requested them to conclude a lasting peace with the Chippewa nation; and although they had sold their lands on the east side of the Mississippi, they still wanted to hunt there, and were glad that in the future they could do so without fear. This was all done through interpreters; several of whom were present on each side, and closed every sentence they repeated with the expression of, "That's what we say."

The delegation met a much larger number of Chippewa Chiefs and braves the next day at Chippewa City where the ceremonies were still more imposing, and a dinner was served of which both parties partook. These demonstrations were so earnest, and seemed so sincere, that outsiders really supposed these hitherto mortal enemies had become fast friends. But in the summer of 1849, an event occurred that showed that one party to this treaty reposed very little confidence in the faith of the other. It will, however, be necessary to relate some intervening circumstances, before we reach this.

During the summer of 1848, a wealthy merchant of Galena, by the name of Bloomer, sent some agents up the Chippewa to select a site for a saw mill, and immediately came on with a large force and commenced operations The site fixed upon was the lower chain of Eagle Rapids, on the site of the present dam. The men brought along to execute the work, were mostly from the Wisconsin river, and at their head was the reckless and notorious Tim. Hurley, and another hard case by the name of Tim. Inglar, and several others of like temperament. To secure hay for the winter, some of these men were sent up on the meadows in the neighborhood of Vanville, and hence the name of Bloomer was given to the prairie and town.

Before winter came on, Mr. Bloomer got discouraged and sold the whole thing out to H. S. Allen at the Falls, and the project of building a mill on Eagle Rapids was thenceforth abandoned.

Bloomer himself returned to Galena, but his men were all turned over, with the teams and supplies to Allen, that is if they chose to stay, which most of them did. Hurley was married and built a house and saloon at the Falls, the first ever started in this valley, which soon became the headquarters of every gambler and hard case, in the upper valley, amongst others, a Frenchmen, named Martial Caznobia, who on the fourth day of July, of this year 1849 with a crowd of these fellows having imbibed pretty freely of "benzine," repaired to the wigwam of an Indian then camping near the Falls, wherein the Frenchman attempted some liberties with the Indian's squaw which was promptly resented, and drawing a dirk-knife, he instantly drove it to the handle in the body of the would be violator of his home.

The wound was a very dangerous one, bled profusely, and was thought the next morning to be positively fatal. It was Sunday morning, a great crowd assembled around, and at the Hurley House where Caznobia was supposed to be dying, when some one raised the cry, "let's hang the d——d Indian," and no quicker said than done. A rope was procured, and headed by Tim Inglar a rush was made for the Indian's residence, a noose was formed around his neck, the rope thrown over the limb of a pine tree, standing near the present site of the Union Lumber Company's Store, the weight of several of these desperate men was thrown upon the other end of the rope, and the body of the Indian soon dangled between heaven and earth, a lifeless corpse.

Mr. Allen remonstrated in vain against these outrages, well knowing it would involve the whole settlement in danger; and threatening demonstrations were very soon made by the Indians who assembled to the number of 1,500, determined to burn the place unless the murderers of their brother were surrendered to them. And only the commanding influence over, and great esteem in which Mr. and Mrs. Allen were held by their Chiefs restrained them. After much delay and full explanations had been made in which the offenders disclaimed any intentional wrong against the Chippewa nation, that it was caused by whisky, and they were sorry, now, the Chiefs and braves became somewhat molified, and agreed that the ring leaders only should be molested, and that they might be tried and punished according to our laws; upon which Tim Inglar, and three others surrendered themselves prisoners, and were placed on board of a boat to be taken to Prairie du Chien for trial. Eight Chippewa braves volunteered to escort them down the river.

But as the party approached that point on the Chippewa, " half a days march from the Falls," alarm and terror siezed the brave escorts, and nothing could induce them to go another rod, in such constant dread were they of the Sioux, who twenty months before had promised eternal friendship.

The prisoners however continued their journey to Prairie du Chien, and surrendered themselves to the Sheriff of Crawford county, to await an examination, but as there was no one to appear against them, they were discharged. They took good care, however, not to be seen on the Chippewa river again.

To the credit of "Hole-in-the-Day" and all the Chiefs and braves assembled at the Falls on this occasion to obtain redress for a flagrant wrong done to one of their people, it must be said they behaved with great moderation. All the young braves were forbidden under severe penalties to taste a drop of whisky during their entire stay in the Falls, more than a week, and no depredations upon any of the whites were permitted, the only levy made, being for sufficient food to subsist them until the difficulty was amicably settled, when they retired peaceably to their several abodes up the river, dinner having been served, and a few cheap presents distributed amongst them, by Mr. and Mrs. Allen.

Caznobia recovered and also left the country for the country's good.

CHAPTER VIII.

Previous to the year 1847, no person had located in this Valley with a view to farming. Each mill, and most of the families, had their potato patch and garden, while the business and principal dependance of every one was directly connected with lumbering, or hunting. But in the spring of that year, George Meyers from "Father Land," in view of the great cost of boating up flour, feed, and other heavy articles of farm produce, and the high price occasioned by transportation determined to avail himself of these advantages, and grow those articles up here. Messers. Allen & Bass, at the Falls, seconded his undertaking, boated up his farming implements, and otherwise assisted him to open the first farm in this Valley. With the whole country to choose from, he selected a most beautiful and fertile spot, about six miles northwest from the Falls, with both prairie and timber, watered by a lovely spring creek, and evincing both taste and judgment in his selection. George was a bachelor, but soon found himself able to marry, and finally sold his farm to William Henneman, who still resides on it, and who informed me this winter when marketing his wheat at this depot, that, although twenty-seven consecutive crops have been taken from it, a good yield is still obtained, even where no manure has been applied. German immigrants seem to know instinctively where good locations and rich soils are, and Henneman was soon followed by a large number of these frugal, industrious agriculturists, who settled in what is now the town of Eagle Point, and are among the wealthiest and best citizens of Chippewa county.

One of the difficulties experienced at this early day in selecting locations, was the absence of surveyors or government lines, not even township lines having been run in any part of the valley, and excepting the correction line between towns 30 and 31 north, nothing had been done towards surveying the land in this part of the State. This line commences on the shore of Green Bay, in lat. $45°$ 20, and strikes the St. Croix Lake a little north of the village of Harriman. It was probably run the same year that the line of the fourth principle meridian was completed.

This last line begins at the south line of the State, on the meridian of $90°$ 26, 42, and is supposed to run due north; was surveyed in 1847 by Mr. Henry A. Wiltse, who was considered a very competent officer, using Burts Solar Compass, and who made the survey with unusual care, for a standard meridian, from which the ranges of townships both east and west across the whole State are numbered. It strikes the shore of Lake Superior, fifteen chains west of the mouth of Montreal river; was double chained and very distinctly marked, but notwithstanding all this care, the northern terminus of this line is actually seven miles west of the starting point, as laid down in the best charts of Lake Superior, by Henry W. Bayfield, R. N. and I. N. Nicollet, of U. S. Topographical Engineers. Which position is correct is hard to determine, as all the astronomical calculations disagree, varying from fourteen seconds, to 14 1-3 miles. (Wis. his. col. vol. 4, page 361.)

The United States Government adopted the best method of surveying its lands, ever pursued by any government, perhaps; the "section," or mile square, with all its subdivisions, being undoubtedly the most convenient form in which public domain could be divided, and had the system first inaugurated for its sale and settlement, been equally wise and beneficent, the hardships experienced by pioneer settlers would have been greatly mitigated. But, on the contrary, the policy adhered to until within the past fifteen years, was fraught with the grossest injustice and oppression. In nearly all its provisions, most iniquitious discriminations were made in favor of the wealthy speculator, and against the poor, hard-working settler. Let me point out a few of its unjust provisions, which for more than fifty years were on the statute books of this free and enlightened government.

Only once in a lifetime could a man enter a single forty, and then he must make an affidavit that he had never before availed himself of that privilege! Gracious boon! If he only had the money and wished to buy up whole counties, or a whole State, there were no restrictions, oh no! No limits or restrictions could be imposed upon the greed of Land Sharks and speculators, but the toiling plebian who could raise but fifty dollars to secure an adjoining forty must look on and see it—with all the improvements he had put on it—gobbled up by some grasping shylock, because the law said that "no poor man could twice be the recipient of such supreme condescension.

Then, too, the preemption law was utterly void of any benefit to the poor settler; no income could be derived from his labor on the land, the first year, and many a hard-working pre-empter having money due him, that he thought he could command when it should be required to save his home, has been frustrated by some sudden revulsion in the financial world that locked up all the money, and saw all his hopes and toil disappear under the relentless grasp of some land shark. And only once in a lifetime could a man claim the benefit of this franchise. Such, and many other equally unjust provisions remained on our statutes for half a century, the out growth of a system of oppression more terrible than any ever before existing among men.

For more than twenty years the people of the Free States battled against these wicked enactments without avail. Twice was a bill got through Congress, extending the right of pre-emption from one to five years, and as often vetoed, and even the right to enter more than one forty was contested for years, and the restriction blackened the statute until 1842. And twice was the present beneficent Homestead Law, passed only to be vetoed by a pro-slavery President. The history of these things belongs to the history of this valley as a part of the great Northwest, whose interests and progress were continually warred upon, and its settlement retarded by laws which should have been so formed, as to afford every possible encouragement to the honest toiler, seeking a home in these outskirts of civilization.

From the time these lands were ceded to the government, as related in chapter two the Surveyor General for this District, composed of the States of Wisconsin, Iowa, and Minnesota, had been letting contracts, and advancing surveying parties in the direction of this valley and in August 1851, Congress having created a new land district with headquarters at Hudson, and the President having appointed John O. Henning register, and Dr. Hoyt receiver, some twenty townships lying along the river and extending up into the most exposed of the pine region, were brought into market. In the outside world this sale created but little interest, and very little land was sold, except that on which improvements had been made. The truth is that throughout the entire Northwest, the prices of all farm produce had been so low ever since the panic and crash of 1837, that there was really no money to pay for lumber, land or anything else. Until this year, 1850, this whole valley was without roads, mails or any regular communication with the rest of mankind. But the Territory of Wisconsin having became a State in 1848, the Legislature had authorized, and made an appropriation to lay out and open a road from Prairie du Chien, via Viroqua, Black River Falls and Eau Claire to Hudson, and during the fall of 1849, and winter of 1849-50, Judge Knowlton, who had the contract for performing the work, had so far succeeded in making the road passable, that Congress had established a mail route over it with post offices at Eau Claire, and Gilberts mill on the Red Cedar.

Geo. W. Randall was appointed Postmaster at the former, and Samuel Gilbert, for the latter place. The road aforesaid soon became quite a thoroughfare for emigrants going west to the more inviting and fertile prairies of St. Croix and Minnesota, hundreds of whom passed over this intricate and forbidding route, never dreaming of the splendid fortunes soon to be realized in such sterile regions as these sandy plains seem to be.

The mills throughout the valley had now several years, immunity from destructive floods, and were slowly recovering from previous misfortunes, every year strengthening their piers, booms and introducing new machinery and other improvements into their works, but the country still continued without any administration of law except when very grave questions arose, when the parties went to Prairie du Chien for justice, the whole intervening country still comprising a part of Crawford county. Disputes and personal assaults were however speedily settled by reference to mutual friends and the social condition of the settlements, notwithstanding the heterogenous complexion of the people, was daily improving; and many began to think that law was an unnecessary evil.

CHAPTER IX.

EARTH WORKS.

Near my former residence, in what is now the town of Lafayette, Chippewa county, on section eighteen, town twenty-eight north, range eight west, was situated the largest, and only considerable ancient and artificial mound, or earth-work, that I have discovered in this valley. The land was claimed by George Mishler in 1850, and was included in his farm, being one of the first improvements on Wolf Prairie, and one-and-a-half miles south of Chippewa Falls. It was in plain sight of my first residence on that prairie, subsequently known as the Bolles farm, and I was curious to know more about it. It was about twelve yards in length, by five in width, and five or six feet high, above the surrounding prairie. Near its base was a depression of from one to two feet below the ordinary surface, indicating its construction by human agency.

I had seen similar works in Illinois, and in the spring of 1837, made one, of a party who volunteered to assist in opening three, in the town of Rockwell, La Salle county. There were five of those mounds very nearly resembling the one above described, all within a stones throw of each other. The agent of the Rockwell company, Hon. Dixwell Lathrop, Walter Tyrell, an engineer engaged in directing the construction of the Illinois & Michigan canal, and several of their assistants, myself, and a few others, composed the party to open and examine those ancient sepulchers of an extinct race. As the ground was frozen, considerable labor was required to remove the surface, but we were amply remunerated, and our curiosity gratified by the relics and remains disinterred from these tumuli. In all, human remains were found some of gigantic stature, and every bone perfect, while others were very much decayed, and well formed pottery vases containing beautiful shells, stone or flint arrow heads, chisels, curiously wrought stone images, ect. Surrounding these relics were evidences in many places of decayed textile fabrics, evidently of course material, also the skins of animals, decomposed and mixed with clay soil that for unknown centuries had covered and pressed upon them. As no iron, copper, or lead was discovered, these works must have belonged entirely to the "stone age," and corresponded with the tumuli, found on Rock river, Circleville, in Ohio, and many other localities in the west being undoubtedly depositories of the dead. But I was somewhat disappointed upon opening the first named mound, which was done in the spring of 1852, as no human remains were contained in it, only flint chisels or axes, arrow heads of the same material, and very small shells, such as had in all probability once decorated the warriors, whose prowess was exhibited in drawing the bow, and directing these missiles of death. These were found in considerable quantities, buried more than three feet below the surface of the mound, and some of them were preserved for a long time with a view to their transmission to the State Historical Society, when there should be suitable facilities for communication. Some mineral specimens found near by, were also added but in moving to the pinery and back during the winter, the collections were somehow scattered and lost.

Why, or for what purpose these impliments and trinkets were secreted here, deep buried in the earth, will forever remain a mystery. The presence of human remains would readily account for it as people in all ages, even civilized people have buried treasures and valuables in the tombs of their former possessors, but without these, it is not easy to conjecture the object of their accumulation and concealment.

I have frequeutly passed over, and examined the "earth works," spoken of by Carver and Featherstonhaugh as vast, ancient fortifications, situated on the west bank of the Mississippi, between the village of Wabasha, and what used to be known as the grand Encampment, and must say that a great stretch of the imagination is required to make anything more of them, than the formations of natures own handy work.

And until further excavations shall disclose more convincing evidence of human agency in their construction, I shall be slow to accept their conclusions.

INDIAN CUSTOMS.

During the winters of 1848 '9 and '50, my residence was in the pine woods near the mouth of "Bobs Creek" at that time a locality much visited by the Chippewa Indians, several families with whom we established something like social intercourse, and learned some things of their domestic and social usages that may be new and interesting to my readers.

In February of our first winter's stay there, a young couple with their infant child, encamped just across the river. The child was sick, and the mother frequently came to get medicine for it, of Mrs. Randall, who soon took quite an interest in the young mothers anxiety for her offspring, but soon discovered that no skill could save it, and after lingering a few weeks it died. The young parents seemed almost inconsolable, but after a few days, came and bid us good bye, and went on with others of their band up to the head waters of the Chippewa, and we saw no more of them until summer, when they came down the river, landed their canoe and hastened to our domicil. Mrs. Randall's interest was very soon fixed on the bereaved mother, who to her surprise, carried what she supposed to be an infant child, and with feminine and maternal curiosity removed its coverings to get a peep at it, when not a new and living baby presented itself, but an image of the dead one lost in the winter.

How strong is a mother's love! what undying affection was exhibited by this untutored young mother! During all those weeks of toilsome march, and ever moving weariness she had carried the image of her lost darling. It seemed to be her only consolation under bereavement to carry near her heart the likeness of her lost loved one. How we wished to tell her that her babe still lived, and that she should one day meet it in immortal embrace fast by the throne of God.

This young mother said all good parents who lost children, carried with them similar memorials of their departed little ones. This image was carved in wood, and though very imperfect was still a tolerable representation of the infant we first saw with her. The woman and her husband were at our place when the Indian was hung at the Falls as heretofore related, and assured us we need not be alarmed, for no harm should befal us.

CHAPTER X.

From 1850 to 1854, few events of general public interest occurred in this valley. Emigration was directed mostly towards the young giant just growing up to the west of us, and California still claimed the attention of the adventurous.

Some changes took place in the proprietorship of some of the mills.

Perhaps some of my readers who have come here from the "Old Pine State," will remember the name of Captain Stover Rines, who figured so prominently in the northeastern boundary of the State of Maine war, as a tall and resolute captain in the army of defense in the winter o 1836-7.

Having removed to Janesville, in this State, some years previous, the captain made a trip up this river in 1848, and bought an interest with H.

S. Allen, at the Falls, and removed his family thither the following summer. He came, however, like many others, not to stay, but to make a "raise," which he did in a couple of years by inducing his partner to buy back his interest. Moses Rines, his brother, who had bought in at the same time, continued in the firm. Jacob Wills, brother of Sam. Wills of this city, who was for some years foreman at the Eau Galle mills, soon after became owner in the same property.

Some such changes also occurred on the Eau Claire. Cady sold his interest to a young man by the name of Swim, and Simon Randall sold his interest to a Mr. Pope, and bought out Captain Dix in the mill on the lower dam. These three firms continued to do business thus organized for the whole period named; the former under the name of H. S. Allen & Co., and the two Eau Claire firms with the titles respectively Gage, Reed & Randall, and Stone, Swim & Co.

During one of these years, an incident happened to the last named firm, so unusual in modern business affairs, that I cannot forbear mentioning it.

Like all other lumbering firms, these men used their credit to help them over the long winter months, when none of the avails of their operations could be realized to meet expenses. Among others who trusted them with goods, was a Mr. Sincere, of Galena, then in its palmiest days as the grand entrepot of lumbermen's supplies. This dealer had exacted the promise, that he should be paid out of the first raft that came down in the spring; but, as several others holding similar claims on the floating chattels must be paid also, Mr. Swim found it necessary to cut this creditor short, and ask him to wait until the next raft should come down, whereupon the obliging merchant procured a warrant under the laws then existing in Illinois, and threw his debtor into prison, and kept him there (although no fraud or attempt at fraud was alleged) until some of his partners went down and procured security.

The firm of Colton & Moses completed their mill on Yellow river in 1850, and soon after Alex. and Henry O'Neil with Mr. Lockhart from Prairie du Chien, erected the mill on O'Neil's creek, now owned by Stanley Brothers.

This period was marked by determined efforts on the part of H. S. Allen & Co., to procure cheaper transportation, and to relieve the rivermen from the terrible hardships of walking up from Lake Pepin after taking down rafts, there being only a trail or footpath, along the steep side-hills, and over the sandy plains, by which the raftmen in those days returned, weary and foot-sore, to the mills.

Two projects were started; the first was to build a steamboat of sufficiently light draught to run over the sand bars, or, as the boys termed it, "to run on a heavy dew."

Captain Matt Harris, of Galena, had been induced to venture up as far as the mouth of Red Cedar once, and to Eau Claire once or twice with freight and passengers on the steamer Doctor Franklin, when the water was high, but all the Mississippi boats were found to draw too much water for this river. It was, therefore, resolved to build one for this trade. But the science of boat-building, had not then reached the point of constructing a boat that would carry an engine of sufficient power to propel the craft against the rapid current, and yet float on six or eight inches of water; or, if the feat had been achieved, the builder of this first steamboat on our river—a Mr. Harlow, from Pittsburgh had not yet acquired the art. The boat, which, by-the-way, was named H. S. Allen, was a miserable failure, and could only run on the highest freshet, with any safety, and soon transferred to deeper rivers. But the year following another boat was built by the same company, with better success, though failing to meet the wants of the trade for more than a part of the season.

The other undertaking was to open a wagon road from North Pepin to the Falls. Some slight attempts had been made to start a town at this place, North Pepin, a year or two earlier, but the country back being entirely unsettled, its growth was very slow. Now, however, farmers began to stop their canvass-covered wagons on the best spots along the route to the Chippewa pineries, as the mills were called, and at one time this village was considered a very strong point. Col. Ben. Allen, a lawyer and speculator, located there, and with his aid, and Mr. Colburn's, at Dunnville, a stage line was started from North Pepin to Chippewa Falls, up one day, and down the next—through by day light, for $3. Cheap jolting, we should think now, for a new country.

Early in this period, one farmer located in what is now, Eau Claire county, the Rev. Mr. Barland who came first alone then with his amiable family, far in advance of any other agriculturalist, and settled on the farm, he and the family now occupy, on the Sparta road, two miles from this city. He held divine services at the mills, on stated Sabbaths for several years.

The Methodist Episcopal Church, too, always alive in the interests of religion, and ready with its perfect church machinery to promote its welfare in remote corners through its Wisconsin Conferance, sent a preacher of that order into this valley, in the summer of 1852, by the name of

Mayne, a young man from England, quiet, humble, and zealous, but un equal to the task of planting a Christian Church amongst so many opposing elements, as he found here; and his appointments, at the Falls and Eau Claire, were discontinued after a few months, but not before a boats crew of wild fellows, from the Falls while stopping over night at Eau Claire, had assailed him with stones and missles, while he was addressing a meeting held for divine service in the dinning hall of Gage, Reed & Co.

The mills on the Eau Galle and Red Cedar, during this period, were steadily advancing in wealth and improvements, being secure and able to defy the highest freshets, they had nothing to do but grow rich by silent profits, and persevering industry.

Far otherwise was it with the mill company at the Falls. who every winter spent large sums in erecting piers, renewing booms, and strengthening their works to secure logs, a charter granting ample privileges, having been obtained from the Legislature for that purpose, and so determined was the company to make all secure, that piers costing more than a thousand dollars each were placed in the river; booms with heavy iron fastenings were attached and every part of those vast structures seemed perfect, and impregnable against all freshets. The capacity of the mills was every year enlarged, and in the winter of 1854–5, a very large amount of logs were put in to supply the season's cutting; the spring drive was good, lumber sold readily and at a good price and all the affairs of the company seemed flourishing, but by a strange and sudden freak of nature all these hopes were cut short in a day.

But little rain had fallen from early in April until the sixth of July, when a dark cloud formed directly over the territory drained by the Chippewa, clearly visible from this place and the Falls. No rain fell here and only a little hail at the Falls, but dark masses of clouds could be seen, rolling and gathering from every direction into that one spot in the heavens, accompanied with fearful peals of thunder that made the earth tremble, and this continued for about thirty hours, appearing every moment as though it were coming right down upon us, but actually spending all its force in that single locality.

The consequence was a sudden and terribly destructive rise in the river, bringing down vast quantities of logs and drift wood, which drove with such force against those piers, that the channel was soon cleared of all obstructions, and more than seventy thousand logs, (twenty-five million feet) together with their piers and booms, were carried away and scattered all over the bottoms and amongst the sloughs of the lower Chippewa. The mill race, too, was badly damaged, and no more lumber could be made that year, which, when we consider that 100,000 feet was being manufactured every day before this unfortunate flood, and that every thousand feet was worth twenty dollars in gold, makes the loss very great.

"The last straw" it is said "breaks the camels back," and this was a very large straw which contributed very much to the final downfall of the company.

Previous to the winter of 1856, there had been, since the removal of Mr. Bass no adminstration of legal justice, in this valley. After the organization of Jackson county, these settlements were attached to that for judicial purposes, and as several grave offenses had been committed subjecting the county to great expenses to bring the offenders to trial, the necessity became imperative to form a new county, which was called Chippewa, and embraced all the settlements in the valley above the Red Cedar.

The act was passed in 1853, and a town and county board organized the following spring. The same Legislature also created the eighth Judicial District, and the new county constituted part of the same.

· One of the crimes referred to above, was wherein the party was accused of manslaughter in the first degree, was taken to Black River Falls for trial, but as the law creating the new District had just passed, he was discharged for want of jurisdiction, and strange as it may seem, was never again apprehended.

The first Judicial election is the new district, resulted in the election of Judge S. N. Full, to the bench of this circuit, who held his first court at Chippewa Falls, in January, 1854, the only attorney present, being our now distinguished and highly esteemed Judge Humphrey, who was unanimously retained for the people by the County Board.

CHAPTER XI.

The Rev. Dr. Brunson, of Prairie du Chien, whose able contributions to the State Historical collections, and other learned treatise mark his efforts as most thorough in research, reliable in statement, and clear in delineation. writes under date of June 26, as follows: "In your history

No. 9, you speak of an ancient mound. This reminds me of one I saw in 1842, between the Falls and Mr. Warren's, where Chippewa City now stands, and as it has a bit of history, I venture to give it:

"The mound, as near as I can recollect, was a mile or more south of Mr. Warren's. It was round, or nearly so, some thirty or forty feet in diametre, and four or five feet high. In the centre there was a hole resembling a rifle pit. It was this, that attracted my attention, and led to inquiry. There were a number of smaller ones in the vicinity, but I only examined this one.

"Michael Cadott, a brother of Mrs. Warren, told me that he was born in the neighborhood, his father being a trader, and his post some five miles below Warren's on the river. He was then fifty-two years old, which would take his birth back to 1790. His father told him in after years, that during his residence there, two years, the Sauks and Foxes came there from below, to make war on the Chippewas, the Sauks, from Sauk Prairie, on the Wisconsin river, and the Foxes from Prairie du Chien—and had their fight on the site of this mound, and the neighboring timber and brush. He said the pit in the large mound, and the pits in the smaller mounds, and some in the open prairie, were digged by the Sauks and Foxes, from which they fought till being repulsed they retreated, and never returned to fight the Chippewas again."

These mounds referred to by the Rev. Doctor, I have frequently examined exteriorly, but am not aware that any excavations have been made into or about them. It may be that the traditionary statements of Mr. Cadott have some foundation in truth, but I was inclined to think that these pits and mounds, and all the earth works, and tumuli found in the State, belong to a period more remote. And in support of my views will quote from the same learned author. Wis. His. Col., vol. 4, p. 225: "Early History of Wisconsin." "The earliest inhabitants of the district now included within this State, of whom we have any knowledge, were the ancestors of the present Indians of this vicinity, and from the best light I have been able to obtain upon the subject from Indian traditions, and from the earliest history of the country, the Dakota, or Sioux, were the occupants and owners of the soil, of what is now our entire State, together with Minnesota, and the northern parts of Illinois and Iowa."

This occupancy we can trace back for about two hundred and fifty years, and if the growth of trees on the mounds which indicate at least four hundred years to the time of the mound builders, be a true index, it is very strange that the Sioux have no traditions of them, as there would have been but one hundred and fifty years between them. This makes it probable that the time of the mound builders was farther back in the world's history than is generally supposed." If the date referred to by Cadott were the period in which these mounds were constructed, we should certainly find in and about them articles of European manufacture, but in scarcely any of them have any such articles been found. Carver always refers to them as the works of an extinct race, who, most likely, cultivated the soil and lived in towns and villages.

Having made frequent mention of this traveler and author, and premising that many, perhaps most of my readers, in this valley are not familiar with his narrations and the claim set up by his heirs to the ownership of the soil, on which we live, I trust I shall be excused for a more extended notice of him.

"The maps of the United States for nearly half a century (until within a short time past) had in the delineations of this quarter of the country always upon them certain lines, embracing a large district of territory, and denominated "Carver's Tract."

WHO HE WAS.

Jonathan Carver was a native of Connecticut, born in 1732, entered the British Army as an ensign, and rose to the rank of captain, a brave soldier a man of integrity and high moral worth, and possessing energy and enterprise.

He left Montreal early in the spring of 1767, attended by a small retinue of French and half-breed voyagers and soon found himself at Green Bay, where was a settlement of French traders, and a mission, went up the Fox and down the Wisconsin, spent some time at Prairie du Chien, also a French trading post, and wintered at Wabasha, and other points on Lake Pepin. The ensuing spring he ascended the Mississippi to its source, and his second winter was with the Cree Indians, to the west of Hudson's Bay, from whence he returned in early spring to Lake Pepin. It is proper to state that a share of the expense of this expedition was borne by himself, and he published the result of his observation in London on his return in which he gives an account of the continual wars going on between the Naudowisses as he calls the Sioux and the Chippewas. States that he was very successful in negotiating a peace, and that the principal chiefs of the former, paid great deference to him, and insisted on his returning to them to establish a trade with them. But not one word does he say of the grant of land which his heirs and legal representatives set up a claim to, as having been obtained from two of those chiefs, a deed, or rather a copy of a deed for which over their signature was produced, the original as was claimed being in Carver's own hand writing in which it was set forth on account of their good brother Jonathan's judicious conduct in acting as mediator between these two nations, and of their friendship and attachment for him. We the chiefs of the Naudowisses do grant to the said Jonathan, &c., the whole certain tract or territory of land bounded as follows: "Beginning at St. Anthony Falls, running along the east bank of the Mississippi river, to where the Chippewa joins the same, thence eastward five days travel, thence north six days travel and from thence again to the Falls of St. Anthony, on a direct straight line."

A map of the country as drawn by Capt. Carver accompanied this deed, the signature to which was for one chief a mud turtle, the other a snake or lizard, and is dated at the great cave council room, on the first of May, 1767. The names of no witnesses are appended.

Captain Carver died in 1780, and the only special interest to us which attaches to his narrative or the aforesaid deed grows out of the [claims and pretensions set up by one Rev. Doctor Peters, and a physician named Lettsom his legal heirs, who in 1806, went before Congress and made affidavit that this grant had been recognized by King George III, 1775, that a commission was granted, and means provided to enable Carver with 150 men to return to America and take possession of his domain, all of which was suddenly frustrated by the news of the battle of Lexington, and praying Congress by virtue of the British King's approval to renew the grant to them, Carver's legal heirs.

These claims were backed up by pertinacious arguments, and positive affidavits, but Congress could not see it, and the whole pretentious claim fell to the ground. Had their title been verified, certain Englishmen would have got possession of this whole valley, without advancing money on bond and mortgage to build a railroad through it, as certain other Englishmen have done by virtue of a certain other grant of lands, made not by the chiefs of the Naudowisses, but by their great father, Uncle Sam.

CHAPTER XII.

Chapter 10 closed with the commencement of Judge Fuller's first court in this the Eight Judicial District, at Chippewa Fall, in January, 1854. The County Board appointed Samuel Allison, a competent young man from Louisville, Kentucky, Clerk, and Blois Hurd, a mill wright then residing at the Falls, Sheriff. Much time was consumed in organizing and adopting rules for the court and bar. Grand and petit juries had been drawn which included nearly all the elligible citizens in the county. Very few civil cases were on the calendar, and those unimportant. But the criminal list presented several indictments for grave offences, two for assault with intent to kill, others for selling liquor without license and for selling the same to Indians.

H. S. Allen & Co's, root house was taken possession of by the sheriff for a jail.

To the aforesaid indictments, all the accused plead "not guilty," and demanded time to procure counsel, which being out of the question at this term, the court advised the offenders to withdraw their plea of "not guilty," and plead "guilty," which most of them did, when suitable fines were imposed on some, and fatherly admonition given to all, and the prisoners were discharged.

Some other ludicrous things transpired at this first term over which it is better to draw "oblivious veil," than to burden history with mistakes about which "the less said the sooner mended."

Before the close of the term the clerk complained of illness, which proved to be a milignant type of typhoid fever, which in less than a week finished his mortal career. He was a young man of genial disposition, agreeable deportment, and highly esteemed by all who made his acquaintance.

In several respects the summer of 1855, was very remarkable. The spring opened very early, and the trees put on their summer green several weeks before their usual time, but during the month of June, three heavy frosts occurred that killed the grass on the prairie perfectly dead, so that it dried sere and crisp, the leaves on the bushes, and young trees were also killed, and the whole country took on the appearance of autumn or early winter, and the fires raged on the prairies and meadows as though the season had actually come for such conflagrations. These frosts extended over the entire northern portion of the State. It would be reasonable to suppose that these blighting frosts, and the forbidding aspects of the country occasioned thereby would have a depresing effect on emigration, but other powerful causes were operating to overcome these natural, but seldom occurring objections, and from early spring till winter, immigrants continued to pour into this valley by hundreds and thousands, and speculation in real estate began, for the first time since its settlement, to get possession of the people.

Perhaps no people in the world have suffered so much in the desire t grow suddenly rich, as the early settlers of Wisconsin. Of the causes which led to the sudden mania to get rich by entering government lands in 1855-6. I will advert to a few. The sub-treasury doctrines of "Old Bullion," and the insane prejudice against banks engendered by the terrible revulsions of 1837, and the hardships imposed upon enterprise and industry, by the almost total absence of the circulating medium, had reacted on the public mind, and given place to some sort of "free banking system," in almost every State. The drain of capital and labor which for several years had constantly depleted the means and working energies of the people to fit out adventurous spirits and enterprises for California, had now fairly begun to return the loan with interest, and to furnish what was supposed to be a reliable specie basis for the aforesaid banks.

The Crimean war, which for thirty months cut off western Europe from its hitherto never-failing supply of grain from the stepps of Russia, suddenly advanced the price of wheat, and set all the grain dealers, and some of the bankers to speculating in American flour, and cereals, and thus in the space of a few months, forcing up the price of wheat to quadruple its former value. This, of course, advanced the value of the land it grew upon, and every farmer in the west wanted more land, and instead of paying his debts, rushed into speculation in wild lands.

There was one other cause which powerfully stimulated the mad spirit of speculation. Corrupt, gambling politicians had a year or two previous, under the plea of patriotism, and a pretence of rewarding the soldiers, who had fought the nations battles, got a bill through Congress granting land warrants of various denominations to all officers and soldiers who had entered the army, during any of the preceeding wars of the republic—mostly of those who went to Mexico. These land warrants passed immediately, and usually for a merely nominal consideration into the hands of brokers and land sharks, and went to swell the absorption of the public lands by a class whose object was not to settle upon and improve them, but to hold them until the improvement of adjoining lands, the opening of highways and other public enterprises should quadruple their value.

Vast quantities of these warrants were sent to agents in this valley, to be located on the choicest spots; some with instruction to secure pine lands, others wanted "timber and prairie well watered," and large tracts of the best land in the valley were thus absorbed, which greatly retarded actual settlement, and increased the hardships of that other class, whose object was to acquire a home and a competence by honest toil.

Another class of agents were also here during the summer in question

(1855), locating State and school lands, university lands, and others still selecting "Fox River Improvement lands."

Such agents, while faithfully discharging their duties to the State usually have an eye out for some fat sinecure or private speculation of their own. The party in power at the State Capitol at this time contrived to find places for a very large number of these delegates in different parts of the country and among them W. H. Gleason and R. F. Wilson, who with compass tripod and chain as the ensigna of their especial position, carefully examined every locality on the Chippewa, with a view to lay off a village or found a city as future developments might determine. The rapid influx of settlers and successful operation of the lumber business, certainly warranted the undertaking, and these gentlemen, not only evinced discrimination and sound judgement, in selecting the site, which included the lower point at the confluence of the Chippewa and Eau Claire, but were very fortunate in negotiating with the owners, J. J. Gage and James Reed, for a half interest in the town plot which by agreement was to be immediately surveyed by the first named parties, and which was recorded at Chippewa Falls, the then county seat as the village of Eau Claire—the first in the valley, with the names of W. H. Gleason, R. F. Wilson, J. J. Gage, and James Reed, as proprietors.

Early in the summer of this year the mill owned and operated by Stone, Swim, George Randall & Hope, on the site of the Eau Claire Lumber Company's water mill, was sold to Carson, Eaton & Downs, of Eau Galla, who immediately repaired and remodeled the mill, substituting reaction, spiral or center vent water wheels, for the old fashioned flutter wheels, the new inventions and improvements in saw mill machinery, and a large amount was also invested in the purchase of pine lands on the tributaries of the Eau Claire.

The season being late, very little was done to improve the new village, until the following spring, two or three adventurous spirts were sanguine enough to invest in lots and commence business. Adin Randall came from Madison here, and commenced the erection of the Eau Claire House, E. E. Shaw and Henry Huntington, opened a store on a small scale, and Mr. Chapin M. Seeley commenced the erection of his dwelling house which, early in the following spring was finished—the first plastered house in Eau Claire. At the extra session of this year, 1856, the Legislature divided up Chippewa county, creating the counties of Eau Claire and Dunn, with county seats at Eau Claire and Dunnville respectively; attached however, to Chippewa county, for judicial purposes for one year.

One event occurred at the Falls, or rather at the Blue Mill, early in the spring of 1855, worthy of mention. A man named Frank Donaldson, a fire eater, from Missouri, went from French Town on Sunday morning in company with Batisette Demarie to the Blue Mill, where after drinking all day the two quarreled, and the former shot the latter dead. Deceased was a young brother of Mrs. Allen. The murderer was arrested, but there being no secure prison escaped, and has not been heard rom since.

CHAPTER XIII

One other circumstance occurred in the year 1855, to cause an influx of speculators to this region. In August and September, a large amount of the pine lands in this valley, not heretofore offered, were brought into market by the government, and as money was plenty and speculation rife throughout the country, operators in this class of wild lands were attracted in considerable numbers to their rivers. Little did they dream of the long tedious years to follow, when the taxes must be paid, and agents remunerated, year after year to look after and care for them, without any possibility of realizing from the investment, or many would have been less eager to possess such wild and remote domain, and in hundreds of instances these annual assessments could not be met, and tax-title deeds accruing, gave opportunity for another and more fortunate class of operators to invest in them. But those who were able to carry such heavy drafts upon their resources, of course realized handsomely in the end, as they had the choicest selection of land from a vast area, and of course took the cream.

The actual settlers and mill owners looked on with alarm and consternation at this absorption of the pine timber, and made strenuous efforts to secure all their means would possibly afford ; and in order to forestall others, many choice tracts were pre-empted by their employees who soon found it necessary to realize on their investments, to cover a loan made by their employers, to whom they deeded the land for that purpose.

The firm of H. S. Allen & Co., at the Falls, were less fortunate than some others in their efforts to purchase at the public sale at Hudson, on this occasion. In addition to the severe losses caused by the terrible freshet which fell alone on the Chippewa as related in chapter ten, the company sustained another reverse, through the faithlessness of one of its agents. At considerable expense in exploring the lands about to be offered and making selections the company took early and prompt measures as they supposed to have the necessary funds on hand to enter such lands as was deemed requisite for the successful prosecution of its business. A highly esteemed and trusted clerk, by the name of Murphy, was sent down the river to make collections and report at Hudson on the day of the land sale. Mr. Allen was there, and through the courtesy of other bidders was, being an actual settler, permitted to take such lands as he chose at the minimum price, and only needed the funds Murphy had collected, to secure all he coveted, and in painful suspense awaited the arrival of every steamboat at that point, in expectation of his coming, but that young worthy had very different views and having received from Mr. Wills, and collected from other parties, some six thousand dollars of the company's money took himself to parts unknown, and no clue to his whereabouts has yet been found.

Twenty-seven years had now elapsed, since Street & Lockwood erected the first mill in this valley, and during all this time, the settlers had not exercised that dearest of all rights, to an American citizen—the right of suffrage. A constitution had been adopted, and the territory in which we lived had become a State; Governors, Lieutenant Governors, Senators, Assemblymen, and other State officers, had been for years chosen by the people in other and more favored sections of the State, but no assertion or recognition of our rights to participate in such elections had been made. The election of town and county officers (the board being one and the same), at Chippewa Falls in 1853, had created very little excitement, being managed by a few individuals and resulted in the election of E. A. Galloway, chairman Wm. Henneman, and Henry O'Neill, supervisors; H. S. Allen, treasurer; B. F. Manahan, clerk of the board. The other officers were appointed.

This board designated Eau Claire, Menomonie and Dunnville, as election precincts, but no general election for State officers, Senator and Assemblymen, were holden in this valley until the fall of 1855. Candidates for the Assembly had electioneered here in 1854, but no election was held.

In the election of 1855, the famous Gubernatorial contest between Barstow and Bashford, was participated in here, and produced the still more famous or infamous bogus, Bridge Creek election returns. The

Twenty-eighth Senatorial District chose a member for the first time this year, 1856.

In the absence of party organization, local interests had much to do with the nomination of candidates for Senator. The term was for one year only, and the St. Croix politicians conceded the choice to Chippewa, and two aspirants were soon found for the position on the Democratic side. The first was P. M. McNally, an Irish lawyer who came from Hudson to Chippewa Falls, the year previous, and had some supporters at the former place; the other was W. H. Gleason of Eau Claire, both were young unmarried men, having very little property interest, but high aspiration and a great deal of pluck.

Amongst the Republicans, it was difficult to find any one in this part of the District willing to accept the honor

At the Democratic convention held at Hudson, McNally came out ahead and was declared the unanimous choice of the party, and for some time it seemed as though there would be no one to compete with him for the honor, but, in time, local interests and the self respect of influential business men began to develope an unlooked for opposition. Captain William Wilson, of Menomonie, was after much persuasion, induced to allow his name to be used in the Republican convention as a candidate, and although he personally made no efforts to secure it, found himself elected by a handsome majority. The friends of Gleason, it was observed almost every where, not only scratched McNally but worked hard for Wilson on election day, so that no test of the strength of the two political parties was determined by it in this district but outside it was considered a Republican victory, and the 28th has always maintained a strong proclivity for these principles.

County officers for Chippewa county were chosen at the same time, and although the extra session of the Legislature had passed the act, creating the county of Eau Claire approved October 6th 1856, and only a month intervened between this election and the election of county officers in the new county, special pains were taken by a few influential parties at the county seat, to elect certain candidates for offices, in the former county, very distasteful to a majority of its electors. This and some other things which occured, growing out of the separation, and a feeling of rivalry which soon began to develope itself, is adverted to in the first number of the American Sketch Book, from which I take the liberty to extract the following comprehensive description of Eau Claire, and its enterprising citizens at this time:

"This year, (1856), the country round about began to rapidly fill up with farmers. Merchants and mechanics located in the village. Gage & Reed sold out their entire interest in the mills, pine land and half the village plat to Chapman & Thorp. The Presbyterian church edifice, the first in the valley, was commenced this year, as a mission church, under the supervision of the Rev. Mr. McNair, to whose energy and persrverance its establishment is mainly due. Messrs. Chapman & Thorp, entrusted their interest during the first year to the supervision of Gilbert E. Porter, an energetic young man from Michigan, now a prominent citizen, and formelly mayor of the city. The Eau Claire House was erected by Adin Randall, and the Bank of Eau Claire went into operation under the free banking law; W. H. Gleason, president; C. H. Gleason, cashier. The former, since so conspicious as Lieutenant Governor, of Florida, was at that time a young man. A little romance is connected with his adventures here, or rather in this valley. In his peregrinations while in the service of the State, he had some where along the stage line between this place and Black River Falls, become much interested in a young lady, beautiful, intelligent, and agreeable, and withal very much inclined to favor his suit, which he pressed with much earnestness whenever he could make an interview convenient; but the lady having friends at Chippewa Falls, a place that already began to look with distrust and jealousy upon the rising young sister village, she concluded to spend the summer there. The young bank president found he had a powerful rival, who, having the advantage of continual proximity, eventually carried off the prize, and the lady became Mrs. James A. Taylor, of Chippewa Falls, instead of Mrs. Wm. H. Gleason, of Eau Claire. How slight a cause may have induced the choice between these two suitors for her hand, and how widely different might have been the life of all these parties had she chosen the other. This was not the last of the rivalry between the two young villages, nor the last instance in which the first named village won the prize. But long and bitter as the struggle for rights and privileges has been between these interests, and often as Eau Claire has suffered defeat, she has kept right on in the even tenor of her way, gathering fresh strength from fresh opposition, and though unable to command all the advantages of her position, has overcome obstacles which seemed at times unsurmountable.

In the year 1856, the Eau Claire House was completed by Adin Randall; Daniel Shaw & Co., located at Shawtown, (now the Fourth ward); Ingram & Kennedy bought the site for their first mill, and the race was projected to connect Half Moon Lake with the Chippewa river, which converts it into a safe reservoir for logs, and the year following the village of West Eau Claire was laid out and recorded by Adin Randall. A strange composition of reckless energy, of daring and enterprise, with a want of punctuality and an adaptation of means to ends, was this same Adin Randall; with many good business traits, he lacked some element of success that made him always unsafe, and lost to him the confidence of the business community. Two church edifices were also erected during the year 1857, the Congregational (also a mission church), on the West Side, and the Catholic on the North Side, where a town had been laid out by Augustus Huysen, and W. T. Galloway. A weekly newspaper, the Eau Claire Free Press, was started in October of this year, also another bank, called Hall & Brother's Bank. Both banking institutions were banks of issue. But the terrible convulsions in the financial and commercial world which commenced this year, came with crushing effect upon these young lumbering establishments, just struggling into life; even Chapman & Thorp, who brought a capital of quarter of a million into their investment, were reduced to great straits, and only the aid of powerful friends in the east saved them from bankruptcy. A new Land District had been created by Congress, and W. T. Galloway, appointed register, and N. B. Boyden, receiver. A large amount of the choicest pine lands in the State were brought into market, and offered to the highest bidder, but scarcely any were taken, even at the minimum price of the government. Discouraging as the prospects were at this time, Chapman & Thorp bought the entire interest of Carson & Eaton in the Eau Claire mill, pine lands, water power, &c., for $125,000, and set about building a steam mill on the site of their lower mill. The low price of lumber, which prevailed for the ensuing three years, so depressed the business that little progress or improvement was made; but this state of things was not without some benefit to the country, for many people, seeing no other way to live, betook thmselves to the soil, and the farming interest, hitherto very much neglected around this locality, now became suddenly developed. From a few hundred bushels of wheat in 1857, the first ever shipped from Eau Claire, the shipment had increased to 150,000 bushels in 1861, and now amounts to more than 390,000 bushels annually from the county. So it will be seen that this city has some solid commercial advantages aside from its lumber interests. But with the exception of the single item of wheat, all other productions of the farmers, naturally seeking a market at this point, find a ready sale at the hands of the lumbermen. A market is consequently near at hand, and the best of all markets—the home market. It is the meeting of these two great industries at this point, and the exchange of their products that constitutes the main traffic of Eau Claire—a trade that has constantly increased so far, and will continue as long as the pine lasts and is manufactured here. Before this fails, we hope the enterprise and good sense of our capitalists and manufacturers will induce them to build up other manufacturing industries instead."

CHAPTER XIV.

MENOMONIE AND DUNN COUNTIES.

"History," says an old authority, "is the record of wicked men's deeds and other men's misfortunes," and it follows that a community that cannot lay claim to some conspicuous examples of this kind is pretty destitute of material out of which to make an interesting narrative. The reader has probably observed that since 1845, little reference has been made in these columns to the locality which constitutes the subject of this chapter; the cause is mainly attributable to the dearth of stirring events of the character named.

A brief visit with some of the earliest settlers, and enterprising business men, calls up a few reminisence of the past which will interest the reader.

To the visitor of to-day, witnessing the vast resources and accumulation of capital, now wielded by the firm of Knapp, Stout & Co., running as it does well up into the millions, it may seem almost incredible that twenty-nine years ago the company commenced business with a cash capital of only one thousand dollars, and a few "traps," and their own indomitable energy and perseverance; this has been accomplished not by speculation and the adroit, lucky turning of fortunes wheel, but by actual creation of so much wealth added to the store of human comforts, using only the advantages supplied by natures abundant and common storehouse.

The presiding genius whose active vigilance, sagacious foresight and untiring industry, planned, guided and controlled their extensive operations through every struggle and undertaking is undoubtedly Capt. Wm. Wilson.

That class of reformers (not political) who maintained that in the allotments of life, if a husband and wife discover that they have not found "their affinity," and consequently their happiness, the connection should be dissolved and other attachments formed until the desired end is attained, may or may not be correct in theory, but however untenable such views may be in regard to marriage, it is undoubtedly true that in business relations, and the choice of an avocation, when one finds himself unfitted for, or continually unfortunate in the affairs of life, he may well conclude that he is not adapted to that kind of employment, and something else will lead to success. So thought Captain William Wilson, when, after trying his hand at contracting on public works, steamboating, and various other avocations, resulting only in disaster, he wended his way, solitary and discouraged, up to that little, old, one-horse flutter wheel saw mill, where twenty years before, Street & Lockwood had manufactured, and Jeff Davis had run away the lumber to rebuild Fort Crawford.

Able friends in Fort Madison, Iowa, had promised assistance in case he found an opening that promised a sure return, but when the time came, as the case often is with the unfortunate, for actual disbursement every one failed him, but they were willing to induce some one else to assume a risk that they were not disposed to undertake. John H. Knapp, a young law student from the "Old Bay State," was fixed upon as the responsible substitute for their assurances, and well did he fill the bill. Mr. Knapp brought into this partnership a young, healthy organization, good business qualifications, an ambition that rejoiced at hardship, an unspotted reputation, and what at that time was almost as difficult to obtain—one thousand dollars in cash.

In the former number reference was made to the purchase and tranfer of the aforesaid mill and fixtures from Mr. Black & Son, to this company, which commenced operations in July, 1846, under the firm name of J. H. Knapp & Co.

Since the departure of Allen and Branham, with their families, no females, or, only one, Mrs. Fanny Vail, had been bold enough to seclude themselves and undertake the hardships and privations of such an isolated abode. But Mrs. Wilson determined to share with her husband all the difficulties that the situation imposed. One other lady and her husband, Mr. and Mrs. Bullard, came up at the same time. The reader will remember that at this early day there was no means of ingress or egress to any part of this valley except by the the river—the "keel boat" propelled by men with poles, going back and forth on the "running boards" the lower end of every pole being furnished with a steel pointed, iron socket, which was thrust against the bottom, while against the other end pressed with all his might if need be the shoulder of the "living engine." whose duty it was to drive the boat over sand-bars and rapids to its destination.

On the first trip up the Red Cedar, the river being low and the boat heavily laden, got aground four miles below their destined home, and these ladies with their children, took the foot path winding along the side hills, and over the steep rocky bluffs to their new homes.

Of the many amusing incidents related by these ladies of their first experiences in their secluded and nearly embargoed domicil, I can find room for only one. Soon after their arrival, Mrs. Blois Hurd came with her husband, who was a mill-wright, to reside at Gilbert's mill, three miles below, and for some months, was the only woman residing there—a beautiful intelligent lady, but whose health was very delicate. Near the close of a day in September, Mr. Gilbert, (the old gentleman) came up and requested the immediate assistance of one or both of these neighbor women, for Mrs. Hurd who had been taken very ill. How they were to get there, was now the difficult problem to solve, to walk three miles over the difficult, intricate foot-path, after the fatigues of the day, was too much for their strength. Their husbands were ready to accompany them, and a bright thought seized one of the party, a raft with oars all on, "ready to pull out," lay just below the mill; to "tie loose" was only the work of a moment, but not one of the men had ever run those rapids, or knew how to handle a raft, but in high glee away floated the party, their hearts full of benevolence, and their heads with novel ideas of traveling; down they went with wonderful speed, and hair-breadth escapes from wreck, over the first falls, but on the second chain, where the intricate channel wound along between great boulders, the necessity for the guiding hand of an experienced pilot soon became painfully apparent, which was immediately intensified by the bow running high and dry upon a rock, the whole craft turned and twisted, the stern was forced down by the rapid current, and threatened to break up the whole thing, that a moment before floated so gaily. No boat was near, night was coming on, the water was deep all around them, and there they were inextricably fast, nothing now remained but to wade ashore, and cautiously they followed Mr. Gilbert, supporting each other, as waist-deep in water, whirling and eddying between the smooth boulders, they made their way to terra firma, and climbed the steep bank to the trail, and in their wet garments, drabbling in the sand, walked on to the residence of the sick lady, after again getting wet, by fording Gilbert's Creek. This we should consider, practicing benevolence under difficulties.

The social condition of these settlements was soon after improved by better means of communication, and the addition of other families, and a pretty widow, a Mrs. Clare, who however was not long permitted to wear her weeds, for the following April, 1847, Esquire Bass was sent for, from Chippewa Falls. who gave the legal sanction to the desire of Mr. William Whitcomb, for her to take his name, the first lawful marriage known to have been consummated there.

But two years later, in 1849, when Thomas Pierewell and Margaret Scott found that it was not well to dwell alone, and could only be happy united, all form and semblance of law and its power to gladden their hearts, had taken its flight from this valley, so they fell back upon their inalienable rights, and a written contract much after the Quaker style, setting forth their avowals to love, cherish, and cleave to each other until death should them part, was duly signed, witnessed and delivered.

Even down to 1855, when the company's chief clerk, Mr. S. B. French, and Miss Virginia Bullard, were married, no legal or clerical sanction could be obtained this side of the big woods, and Captain Wilson was dispatched to Hudson for the Rev. Mr. Thayer, to tie the silken knot.

CHAPTER XV.

MENOMONIE AND DUNN COUNTIES—CONTINUED.

Most men, like Ortogrul, when he saw in a vision, the avenues of wealth floating towards him, one a foaming mountain stream, the other a ripling rill, if told to choose between them, would say as he did, "let the golden stream be quick and violent;" But not all men would be so wise as he. when looking again he beheld the former dry and dusty, while the latter increased in volume, and, with returning consciousness, "determined to grow rich by silent profit and persevering industry,"

Whether the members of the firm of Knapp, Stout & Co., had read and profited by Adison's ideal type of the true method of accumulating wealth, is not essential to our purpose; but we see in the slow, cautious onward steps of this now opulent Company, a remarkable instance and exemplification of the "Spectators" rule for becoming rich. In one essential particular, this company inaugurated a new and better system. Hitherto every mill Company on this river, had sold whiskey to their men, and at the expiration of the term of service, almost every one found himself in debt. Their employers justified themselves on the plea, that these men would have liquor, and if they did not keep it for them, a "saloon would be started at their very door," and they might as well or better do it, than for some worthless scape grace of a gambler to get the profits of the trafic. And every invoice of goods ordered by any of these establishments included as the first item, from one to fifty barrels of whisky, "Goodhues" best, and a curious record was, the account against one of these old soldiers at the end of the year, running about thus :

1st. 3 drinks, 25 ; 1 plug tobacco, 75 ; $1.00. 2nd. 1 pint whisky, 50 cts.; 6 drinks, 50 ; $1.00. And so on month after month.

Not after this fashion did J. H. Knapp & Co., commence their operations in this valley, and although repeatedly told, that the business would not pay without the profits of whisky, they paid not the slightest attention to the warning, but neither dealt in strong drinks, themselves, nor allowed others to bring it upon their premises, if they could prevent it, and it is due to this stringent policy in opposing intemperance, that so few crimes have been committed in that locality, it being a notable fact, that the Circuit Court Calendar exhibits no instance of a capital offence being charged against any persons in Dunn county, since its organization, in 1857.

The only murder that is known to have been committed on the Red Cedar, since the death of McCann, was the killing of William Wickham, in 1850, by an Indian known as the brother of the "Big Scoundrel."

For five years the company kept the one little old mill running day and night, carefully husbanding its earnings, paying off old claims against the property, and accumulating means to build a new and larger establishment on the main stream, and in August, 1851, had the satisfaction of cutting lumber in this great mill, then the largest and best appointed of any on the Chippewa waters ; the mill-wright was the well-known Mr. Downs, who introduced the Stearns water wheel, and all the modern improvements of that time.

In 1848, another mill was erected on the Red Cedar, about half way between this mill and the mouth, by Messrs. Hurd, Bullard & Co., and with good financial management would have done a good business. It is now owned by the Menomonie company. The partners in this company residing at Menomonie, are in some respects lessfashionab than most men of affluence, being blessed with large families, and to provide for their education together with the children of other families, and to secure religious instruction as well, a school house was erected in 1854, and the services of the Rev. Joshua Pittman were engaged to fill the position of both teacher and preacher, an arrangement which continued some four or five years, and was probably the first school opened in this valley. It was succeeded in 1856, by the regularly organized district school. The first meeting held in this place, or in the county for divine service, was in the summer of 1852, by the Rev. Mr. Mayne, before mentioned. During the summer of 1855, most of the pine lands on the Red Cedar were brought into market and considerable quantities sold to non-resident parties, one of whom was the Hon. C. C. Washburn, who also took some 12,000 acres on other branches of the Chippewa at the same time. h latter entries were sold in a lump, the year following, first to Morrison & Woodman, and by them to Messrs. D. Shaw & Clark, father of Dewitt C. Clark, of Eau Claire. In order to make the former available, Mr. Washburn erected a steam saw mill at the foot of Nine Mile Slough, on the Chippewa, and about the same distance from the confluence of the Chippewa and Red Cedar. This was in 1857, and about the same time Mr. Downs erected a dam across the Red Cedar, and built a mill at Dowsnville. These last named establishments were rather sickly. Starting into being just at the inoportune moment of that terrible year of crushed hopes and broken promises, of fruitless endeavors and financial ruin, neither ever recovered from the staggering blow, and a few years later these mills and the pine timber land belonging to them were sold to the more staple company at Menomonie. In the spring of 1849, Perry Curtis and his brother opened what was afterward a large farm, near the Eau Galle mill, in company with Carson & Eaton who furnished the means, and were to share the property equally. This was the first farm commenced in the county, but the next year Mr. Franklin Ames, from Massachusetts, selected lands near by on which himself and sons opened out farms in the following year, 1850, and the first district school in the county was organized here in 1856.

In March, of this year, 1856, the act was passed to organize the county of Dunn, with Dunnville for the county seat. The election for county officers was not held until some months later, and the first term of the Circuit Court was held in September, 1857. S. C. & E. B. Bundy were the first lawyers settled in the county, one of whom was elected district attorney.

Like many other new counties, the question soon arose for the removal of the county seat. A few parties had invested in Dunnville property, supposing it would continue the permanent shire town, but it made feeble resistance. And in 1859, under legal provisions for a vote of the people, a large majority were in favor of Menomonie, which had that year been laid out, and immediately began to assume a high position in the sisterhood of villages.

The test of executive ability, either in public or private affairs, is exhibited in making appointments to subordinate positions, and few business firms have discovered wiser discrimination, or been more fortunate in the choice of agents than Knapp, Stout & Co. In their early struggles a young smooth faced, long nosed, keen eyed man, a native of Prairie du Chien, was selected as foreman to take charge of the boating, and running lumber in summer, and in organizing logging camps in winter, driving in spring, etc., energy, decision, untiring industry and unswerving fidelity, soon won the entire confidence of his employers, who in 1860, offered him a fourth interest in the fast accumulating property, on favorable terms, and Andrew Tainter became a millionaire. And now his palatial residence out vies all others in the village in its interior appointments, its lawns, fountains, deer park, costly statuary, and in the taste and elegance of all its surroundings, evincing a degree of culture and refinement, which seems to any one acquainted with his rough and tumble early life, utterly incompatible with his, to say the least, not elevating associations.

But as success is the criterian, and touch stone by which all human estimates and conditions are determined, Andrew has won the highest consideration.

CHAPTER XVI.

CHIPPEWA COUNTY.

We took leave of H. S. Allen & Co. in the fall of 1855, at the land sale. Every interest and movement in the settlement, business, and social relation of the entire county were more or less dependent upon, or identified with this company, and affected by the heavy losses it sustained. In the summer of 1856, the surrounding country received large accessions of farmers; the village of Chippewa Falls was laid off; a dam was thrown across the Chippewa river at a point nearer the mill; a large three story hotel was erected on the site of the Tremont House (lately burned); the Presbyterian church edifice was commenced as a mission church under the indefatigable labors of Rev. W. W. McNair. Early in the spring of this year, Thaddeus and Albert Pound were employed by H. S. Allen & Co., as clerks, who came with their families from the Empire State, and located as permanent residents of the place. James A. Taylor was another clerk in the same establishment, who in the succeeding fall, in company with Frederic Bussy, started the first store not connected with the mill, at the Falls. As indicating the opportunities presented by a new, and especially a lumbering country, and as an evidence that merit and ability will be discovered and appreciated, no matter how obscure their possession, I will give an account of this last named person. Frederick Bussy was born in Prussia, emigrated to the United States just as this country became involved in war with Mexico, and immediately enlisted in one of our New York regiments, in which he served as a private until the close of the war, and was severely wounded in one of the terrible charges made by our troops at Molino Del Ray. After his discharge from the hospital at New Orleans, to which he had been removed until his recovery, he found his way up to St. Louis, where in the fall of 1848, Mr. Wills employed him, with several others also returned soldiers from Mexico, and sent them up to Chippewa Falls to do such work as they were able. As the writer was running a logging camp at Bob's creek, and needed men, Bussy was sent up to him. He could speak scarcely a word of English, and never had had an axe in his hands, was utterly ignorant of the work I had for any man to do, and after trying his hand at several kinds without success, he said he could cook, and wanted to try his hand at that. The cook I had required an assistant, so Fred took the place, and soon made me understand that if the wood was cut for him he could manage the business alone. This enabled me to put the former cook at some other business. Little did I think that this obscure and almost helpless soldier (Bussy) possesed business qualifications that would soon elevate him to positions of trust, and the management and control of extensive operations. But having mastered our language, he was found to be a good accountant, which secured him a position with the aforesaid company, and in 1856, commenced business with J. A. Taylor, as before stated. He was married the same year to Miss Galloway, a very estimable lady, and was elected county treasurer in 1858. The firm of Bussy & Taylor erected, or rather completed the

Gravel Island steam mill, which was managed with considerable ability until its destruction by fire in 1862. Mr. Bussy died in 1866, at Winona Minnesota.

Of the other emigrants to Chippewa county this year, the most prominent were Rodman Palmer, Elijah Pound—father of Thaddeus and Albert, James Woodruff, Mr. Waterman, Mr. Skinner, Mr. Fuller, Mr. Vanloon, I. P. Sheldon, A. Walker, Stephen Brown, Bonneville and Loveland, all well known citizens who came with their families.

As this year marks a new era in the social condition of this valley, it may be interesting before taking final leave of the old regime, to speak more at lenth of its peculiar aspects. Without schools, churches, and literary culture, the elements of social intercourse are very much restricted in a neighborhood, especially where several races and nationalities are represented ; balls being the only available resource from which all distinctions of race, color, language, family, or worldly position was utterly banished. Every winter several of these were given in different localities, some of which were grand affairs, and having frequently attended with my family at these gatherings, I will try to describe a grand ball of that period. It required about all the women in the valley to afford an opportunity, by keeping them constantly on the floor, for every man to get a partner for a single cotillion set, and accordingly, having sent out invitations to every settlement and family, the party giving the ball would send two men and team with conveyance to every lady whose presence was considered doubtful, and to these it was no use to make excuses, she "must" go, and nothing short of severe illness would induce them to leave the house without her. One of the long dining halls of the mill company is cleared of tables and most of its benches, and a motley group are assembled, many of whom are the dark-haired daughters of the forest, more, a shade lighter, are from Her Majesty's dominion of Canada, a few from the Red River of the North, (now Manitoba), and the rest from all parts of the country, and while the company are assembling, greetings are heard in half a dozen different languages, while an invitation to drink awaits every new comer of the men, and by the time the music strikes up several are too far gone to take part in the enjoyments. A survey of the room discloses about three gents to one lady, so there is no danger of any one of the ladies drooping as a "wall flower." It also discloses some half-dozen hard-visaged men, mostly from the South, with revolvers and bowie knives carried conspicuously about their persons, and who are ready to rope in and fleece some unsuspecting new comer, or to pick a quarrel with some one against whom an old grudge exists. For several years, Dan McCann, "Old Dan," as he is called, was the only hope of any terpsichorean assembly in this valley, as it was to the touch of his fiddle bow that every light, fantastic toe must yield active or passive obedience. He knew nothing of music as a science, but could play a number of marches, cotillions, and one waltz, very well by rote, and woe to the hapless ball or party that failed to secure his indispensable services. A marked feature of all such gatherings was the perfect equality manifested between all parties, their perfect freedom from envy and petty heart-burning on account of dress, family, or other distinctions; in fact, they were perfect free-and-easies, and being about the only social recreation, were regarded with much favor by all parties, and exerted a very healthful influence, the only drawback being the presence of the black-legs, who sometimes made things lively by promiscuous shooting amongst the dancers and into a crowd whenever a dispute arose at the gaming table and the opposite party took refuge among them. Such is the picture of the highest social enjoyment in the good old time.

When John R. Jewett, the English blacksmith, found himself safe and sound on board the good ship Boston, at Nootka Sound, Vancouver's Island, where for three and a half years he had been held a prisoner by Maquinuy, an Indian Chief, who, with his savage followers, had, by treachery in an unguarded moment, slain the captain and crew of a Newburyport northwest coast trading ship, saving only Jewett and one other man, which they plundered and destroyed, preserving all the iron about her forge, tools, and her blacksmith, whom they compelled to do their work, and to marry a chief's daughter, by whom he had two children— he bade good-bye to Maquinuy and all his chiefs, but not one word of regret at parting with his children.

When a mere lad I read Jewett's narrative, and could never refrain from denouncing him for the heartless, inhuman conduct, so destitute of paternal regard that he makes no reference to either his children or their mother.

In a preceding number I have stated that many of the earlier settlers took to themselves wives of the native population. The influx of white women during this and the previous year, '55-6, induced almost every one to discard these women, with a view to new, and socially more advantageous, attachments; but in no instance were the children forsaken, or their welfare neglected; ample provision, according to their means, being provided for their sustenance and education, and in most instances the mother also was cared for, indicating a higher appreciation of parental responsibility than the English blacksmith entertained in 1800.

The moral aspect of such connections, formed and dissolved as they were at the pleasure of one party, will present itself to every one according to their respective ideas of marriage, but no one will withhold their approval and highest commendation of the very few men whose family ties were strong enough to induce them to forego all social considerations and cleave unswervingly to the mother of their children.

Taking its rise in the timbered regions far to the north, where the chilling winds from Lake Superior prevent the melting of the snow on its upper branches until the ice is dissolved in the river at this point, the Chippewa has seldom broken up with an ice-freshet capable of inflicting much damage to piers, booms, and other improvements placed in its bed, but the spring of 1858 was an exception to former precedents in this respect, the ice breaking up for many miles above before its winter force and volume had abated, and coming down in jams of such crushing power that everything in its path was swept away; the new dam, several piers, a large share of the booms, and a vast amount of logs were mingled with the ice in one common ruin.

To a successful business man whose integrity has for long years never been suspected, or his ability to meet his obligations questioned, when on surveying his affairs he, for the first time, sees bankruptcy staring him in the face, is about as wretched a piece of humanity as the world affords. Innumerable expedients are conjured up to obtain relief, some, perhaps, not very honorable; in constant dread of some sudden disruption in his plans, his ideas become confused as to what will be right and honorable; at one moment he resolves to pay every claim as long as there is a dollar to pay with, and at the next, his wife and children engrossing his thoughts, he can not see them suffer; come what will, his first and last duty is to provide for them. But how shall it be done? Is there any way by which he can save his honor, and something that shall shield his children from want?

Such were the gloomy forebodings of Mr. Allen when, in the winter of 1856-7, he saw the tide of adversity bearing down upon the house of which he was the head, and threatening to bury every hope. Hitherto the company had met its obligations with reasonable promptness, but now note after note must go to protest, and soon judgments would nail every foot of land, and not a dollar then could be saved for the little ones. The company was now composed of H. S. Allen, Jacob Wills, Moses Rines, and E. A. Galloway. Rines held in his own right the title to a quarter-section of land upon which the city is now built, and considered that if any game was to be played, he held a pretty good hand. He was a drunken, worthless fellow, who never ought to have been in that position; he had kept sober long enough at one time to marry a beautiful and accomplished woman, and might have been happy but for his abandoned habits, but in self-defence she was soon compelled to leave him, and Mr. Allen also determined to rid the firm of such a burden.

That "there is a tide in the affairs of men" is so old that it need not be repeated here, but is very applicable, and no doubt H. S. Allen thought that for him it was fast on the ebb when he bought Moses Rines' interest in the firm for ten thousand dollars, and borrowed fifteen hundred of it to make the first payment, of a maiden sister, and mortgaged the aforesaid quarter-section to secure its payment, but whether he could discern through the darkening vista of coming events, the gleam of brighter skies beyond, is known only to himself, but to this single stroke of luck, tact, or good management, is due his present easy, perhaps I may say opulent, circumstances.

Of the many expedients to afford relief from the present pressure, one was resolved upon. A common stock company was organized, and one thousand shares of one hundred dollars each represented the property. Various parties from abroad were induced to take stock, which relieved the old firm in some measure, and in the summer or fall of 1857 the new company commenced operations under the name of the Chippewa Falls Lumber Company, H. S. Allen, President; one Jordon, Vice-President; a lumber merchant of Dubuque, Treasurer; John Judge, Secretary.

The old company went into liquidation, its liabilities being assumed by the new—a vast accumulation of interest-bearing debt. John Judge was a thorough business man, but was appalled by this immense burden; with a sound currency and hopeful times, he would have raised the company's credit and gone on, but after one summer's fair trial, the officers met by agreement at some place in the interior of Illinois, divided the earnings amongst them, and the poor stockholders were nowhere.

CHAPTER XVII.

In deference to the wishes of several friends, I will refer again to the forged certificates of the Bridge Creek election returns.

At the first election for State officers under the present constitution, held on the second Monday in May, 1848, the Democratic party carried the State and maintained its ascendancy, with a working majority in both branches of the Legislature, until this year, '55.

In the incipient organization of any government, the promotion of persons to positions of trust and official power, whether by the executive or the choice of the people, is usually attended by the appointment of a large per cent. of corrupt, faithless, and designing men to carry on the government.

The Democratic party seems to have been especially unfortunate in this State, and many unscrupulous demagogues found favor with both the executive and the people. In a strong political party long in power, it seems to be natural for such men to obtain places of trust and honor.

I state it as a matter of history and not as a partizan, when I say, and the record shows, that the party in power at this period in this State was fearfully corrupt, and its leaders and parasites seemed determined, no matter at what cost, to hold on to the offices, whether the people willed it or not.

The selection, management, and disposal of the school, university, and other State lands, afforded a pretext for the employment of a great number of agents, who, being scattered all over the State, even to the remotest corners, could always be relied upon to do any dirty work for the party when occasion required it.

The Democracy of this State had been compelled to go back on its early record and follow Judge Douglass in his squatter sovereignty doctrines; which alienated a great many of the most intelligent free-soil Democrats, and added to the glaring corruptions in every department of the government, both national and State, so demoralized the party that its leaders became very apprehensive of the result of the election in November, 1855, and determined to resort to fraud, if necessary, to carry it.

There are some people who consider an election a mere farce, the turning of a card and "repeating," ballot-box stuffing and forging election returns, just as legitimate a way to get into or hold office, as to be fairly chosen by the free suffrage of the people; and the Democratic directory at Madison, on this occasion, seems to have incorporated the worst features of these dangerous views into its policy, and resorted to any and all these methods, varying in different localities, according to circumstances, to carry this election. Having reliable and willing instruments in this place to do their bidding, it was deemed a safe point to operate in, if necessity required.

A member of the State Board of school lands came here from Madison a few days before the election, to inspect the work done during the summer by its agents, and the subjoined memorandum was drawn up as the outline of proceedings. "If Barstow received a clear majority, nothing was to be done but congratulate, etc. If Bashford received an overwhelming majority, nothing was to be done but to prepare to abdicate. But if a few hundred votes were necessary to overcome Bashford's majority, they were to be manufactured, and if new and unheard of election precincts were required, they too were to be manufactured as the safest way of multiplying votes." Such was the programme of proceeding, and special means of communication were called in that there might be ample time to carry out the dark plot.

Now, every one at all familiar with the subject, knows that if there had been any such voting precincts in the county as "Bridge Creek" and "Spring Grove," that it was the duty of the inspectors of election at those points to make their returns to the county board of canvassers at Chippewa Falls, but that board knew of course that no such precincts existed, and therefore no such returns would be entertained for a moment; the bogus returns, therefore, from these bogus precincts, were sent diractly to the board of State canvassers at Madison, and incredible as the statement may appear, that board actually received and counted these votes so informally and illegally returned, and declared Barstow and the whole ticket elected by a meager majority based on these forged returns, and drank their champagne and cracked their jokes over it as though they had done something smart. Already in the chair, Barstow retained his place and made a grand parade with a costly supper, to which all the magnates of the party were invited, and thought perhaps the fraud could be concealed, but on a writ of quo warranto sworn out by the opposite party, an investigation was had before the Justices of the Supreme Court, wherein it was shown, first, that the returns were informal and illegal; second, that no such voting precincts existed in Chippewa county as Bridge Creek and Spring Grove; and lastly, that although the two precincts purported to be fifty miles apart, and the certificates bore the same date, the two half-sheets of foolscap on which they were written fitted together so nicely as to prove conclusively that they had once been one and the same sheet.

No other alternative existed than for the Court to reverse the decision of the State Board of Canvassers, and declare Bashford the legal governor of this State, and the honest people began to hope that now we should have an honest, capable administration of the State government; but, alas for human hopes, bribery and the most venal corruption characterized the next two years, and it seemed as though the whole body politic was tainted with fraud and given over to work iniquity.

In March of this year, 1856, Congress passed the act donating in trust to the State of Wisconsin, all the alternate sections of land embraced within certain parallels along the lines of certain railroads therein described; one of which, commencing at Portage City, was to extend to Tomah, and thence to St. Croix county, and of course must cross this valley at some point, and almost everybody supposed that the road would be built immediately, and speculators were everywhere on the alert to know where that point was to be. Little did they dream that fifteen years must elapse, and the grant be twice renewed, before we should hear the notes of a locomotive whistle among us. But we learned to get along very well without it.

Some of the wildest and most visionary schemes ever thought of, grew out of this land grant, some of them disastrously affecting parties in this valley.

Byron Kilbourne, of Milwaukee, organized a company to take this grant and construct the road and placed himself at their head. Several million dollars were issued in stock, and a bombastic advertisement or manifesto, setting forth among other things, that the road would be built with very trifling assessments on the stock, that so rich and vast were the franchises of the road, that bonds could be negotiated to build and equip the road, and that whoever was lucky enough to secure this stock, would obtain its dividends without any assessments, and proceeded immediately on the assembling of the legislature, to put the stock where it would do the most good—that is, to bribe the members of the legislature, and the Governor, to confer the land grant upon that company. The downfall of such an organization could easily be predicted, and the sequel of its history was one of infamous swindling, and contemptible petty cheats and frauds upon the unsuspecting laborers employed on the work, and farmers and merchants who could be gulled. Various lines or routes were examined for this road, some crossing the Chippewa far down, and others above the Falls. Reports of these surveys would at any time be considered very uncertain data on which to base a heavy investment at a given point, but these or something still less reliable, gave rize to one of the wildest and most visionary speculations ever conjured up in the brain of the most reckless adventurer. In an extract from the Eau Claire number of the American Sketch Book, in a previous chapter it was stated that the Bank of Eau Claire went into operation this year, '56, under the free banking law, W. H. Gleason, President, and C. H. Gleason, Cashier. Its principal manager was C. M. Seley, a man of considerable experience in financial affairs, cautious and conservative in his operations, and at first inspired public confidence in the bank as a safe institution for deposit or exchange. The summer of 1856 was marked for reckless speculation, but most operators had learned by the following spring, '57, to go slow; not so, however, with the two young proprietors of half the village of Eau Claire; flushed with their success in the enterprise and the rapid sale of lots during the previous eighteen months, they felt strong for new operations. It has always been supposed that some motive not discovered on the surface inspired this transaction, but R. F. Wilson utterly denies any other incentive than legitimate speculation, but that any men who had ever possessed business tact and foresight enough to accumulate such a sum, should seize upon a random report made by some subordinate engineer, that "the Tomah & St. Croix railroad would cross the Chippewa at O'Neil's creek," and put twenty thousand dollars into lands at that point as a lucrative investment, seems almost incredible. But such is the positive fact, and a village plat was laid out and recorded as Chippewa City, a few lots sold, and a saloon or two started, and one-tenth of the sum then paid would to-day buy every lot and acre of their investment.

There were, probably, some other parties involved in this unfortunate and short-sighted affair, and coming just at the time of that terrible crisis in the west, when all values were tumbling, and all business operations paralyzed or utterly prostrated, this hopeless speculation proved very disastrous to all concerned. The bank soon became sickly, and eventually was compelled to go into liquidation, mainly on account, as Mr. Seley said, of the withdrawal of deposits so absurdly invested at the foregoing point.

The prevailing opinion at the time of this whole transaction was, that it was undertaken to spite Chippewa Falls, and with the hope of building up a rival town. If such was the motive by which it was inspired, little sympathy should be felt for the losers.

One other matter of public importance came up this year, '57, calculated to engender ill-feeling between these two struggling villages. A new land district was formed by act of Congress, the bill for which was introduced by Mr. Washburn, in the House, with Chippewa Falls as its headquarters, but just before it was put on its final passage, a motion was made to amend by inserting Eau Claire instead. The claims of each were asserted with great pertinacity by its respective friends, but it was finally agreed that its location should be designated by the President of the United States, who fixed upon Eau Claire. The Commissioner of the General Land Office took immediate steps to carry the law into effect, and the President appointed Dr. W. T. Galloway as Register, and N. B. Boyden as Receiver, of public lands at this place. The former established his office in the new village of North Eau Claire, just laid out by himself and Augustus Huyssen.

The principal persons who settled in Eau Claire this year were Rev. A. Kidder, of the Congregational Church, and family, Joseph G. Thorp and family, the young and genial Peter Wyckoff, Jackson brothers, John Wilson, Ingram and Kennedy, George A. Buffington, Dr. F. R. Skinner, W. P. Bartlett, A. Meggett, and many others whose names will hereafter appear.

CHAPTER XVIII.

Individuals are integral parts of a vast whole, and corresponding to the rise and fall of nations, of dynasties, in the history of the world, may be reckoned the rise, progress, and decay of influential organizations in larger communities, and a revolution or the downfall of a dynasty in a State are not more legitimately the subjects of history than the failure of a long-established mercantile or manufacturing establishment in a city or country; although younger, more energetic, or more fortunate men may succeed in their places and positions in both instances, a kind of mournful interest attaches to those who once filled so important a place in the affairs of this life but who must now subside into obscurity.

At the close of chapter sixteen, it was stated that the officers of the company known as the Chippewa Falls Lumber Company, which had succeeded H. S. Allen & Co., met at some place in Illinois and divided the summer's earnings; it would be nearer the mark to say that some of the officers had been dividing the avails of their operations through the entire summer, as fast as the lumber could be converted into money; the result was, nothing for the creditors or for the stockholders, but the men were careful to take themselves out of harm's way, if their creditors or an exasperated community should choose to seek redress. But for Messrs. Allen and Galloway, whose families were here, and who, having been members of the old firm, became special objects of "attachment" by their old creditors, but their devoirs were paid by proxy, and the U. S.

Marshal made it his especial business to hunt these two men down for several weeks, with a warrant of arrest, as though they had been guilty of some crime. And even the men whose wages remained unpaid, threatened violence to their persons, under the mistaken idea that large sums had been concealed, and it was with great difficulty that they could be satisfied to the contrary.

Before spring, however, all these difficulties were amicably adjusted, and the entire property was surrendered to the creditors. Andrew Gregg, an eminent lawyer, who had lately settled at the Falls, was appointed receiver by Judge Miller, of the United States District Court; the mill and fixtures were leased to Adin Randall, of Eau Claire, and as no freshet or other mishap occurred, was enabled to pay the rent, although times were so hard that there was little or no profit in any lumbering operations.

But this depression of the lumbering interests was not without its benefits, as it induced great numbers of operators to resort to farming, and in the fall of 1858 Chippewa county shipped the first wheat—about seventeen thousand bushels. It was handled in the interest of H. S. Allen, but not in his name, and was worth there forty-five to fifty cents a bushel; this marked a new era in the business operations of the county, and although the home market caused by the various lumber industries has been immense, the county has shipped more or less wheat nearly every year since.

A few noteworthy incidents have been omitted. A fatal accident occurred in the hay-meadow on O'Neil's creek, where the two brothers, George and Edward Warren, nephews of Mr. Warren, previously mentioned in these pages, were at work haying; the latter, with a rifle in his hands, was passing through a thicket, and by some means the trigger was caught by a twig, discharging the contents into his body in the region of his heart. He lived a few hours, and was greatly mourned, being highly respected by all who knew him.

In 1851 an incident occurred to the writer that may interest some reader. It happened at Frenchtown. I was running some cribs of square timber over the falls, and, as usual, the boys drank pretty freely, and being a little "set up," one of them took it into his head that he must go home right away—he lived in Illinois—and must have a settlement then and there. I asked him to defer it until the last crib was over, when quick as thought he caught up a loaded shot-gun and discharged the contents at me, the shot taking effect in and just above both knees, shattering the left knee-pan pretty badly, and inflicting serious wounds in the fleshy part of the right thigh. I was facing and hastening toward him with a view to wrench the death-dealing instrument from him, when it was discharged, and if the aim had been a few inches higher, some pen besides mine must have written the history of this valley.

As it was, Mrs. Demarie had me on my feet again and attending to my business in six weeks, but, my family being in Illinois, it seemed a very long, weary time. It was about this time that a party of Sioux warriors came up into this neighborhood, and after skulking around back of Frenchtown awhile, succeeded in killing old Jack, a superannuated Indian, who lived mostly in the Demarie family, and was very much esteemed. For a while the little community was in a state of perfect terror, but the cowardly perpetrators were as much alarmed as the others, for they fled so precipitately that they slipped the halters from the heads of their ponies where they fastened them, and I saw several that had been gathered by white persons. Another party of Chippewas were surprised and shot near Dunnville, the same year, but in the summer of '57 the Chippewas made two Sioux braves bite the dust near the same locality, their heads were cut off and set on poles, their faces "ghastly grinning" by the road, where it crosses Rock Run, in the town of Wheaton. Some time in the spring of this year an unfortunate homicide took place in Frenchtown, which created a good deal of excitement and consideration for the offenders William Wylie enlisted in the same New York regiment with Fred Bussy, was in every battle from the siege of Vera Cruz to the surrender of the city of Mexico, a brave soldier and a great favorite with his comrades wherever he was; he came on this river in 1849, and some years after married a Miss Warner, to whom he appeared to be very much attached, and very jealous of other men's attentions to her. One evening, as she was passing near a saloon, some fellow in liquor accosted her in terms deemed too familiar, and having heard her statement, Wylie the next morning sought the offender, and at one blow with a billet of wood crushed the skull of his victim, causing death in a few hours. Wylie surrendered himself to the authorities, was duly presented to the grand jury at the next ensuing term of the Circuit Court, but that conscientious body refused to find sufficient cause to indict him, and the ermined brow of Judge Fuller grew black with righteous indignation at the announcement, and calling this august branch of his court before him, gave them such a reprimand as they, if living,• feel tingling their ears yet. An examination of the case was subsequently had before a justice of the peace and the offender bound over, but on some pretext a habeas corpus was issued by Judge Mead, of Eau Claire, who released the bonds, so that Wylie was now free, and he soon took himself to parts unknown. But by what right this astute Judge issued such a writ is a question for "men eminent in the law," as the author of Waverly says.

On the 30th of April, 1868, Andrew Seitz was murdered by Charles Nether, two Germans who occupied a room over the Receiver's office, on Eau Claire street. A dispute about a small sum of money, while both were in liquor, led to the fatal deed; the offender being armed with a dirk-knife, inflicted a fatal stab in the left side of the lower part of the abdomen. At the June term of the Circuit Court following, Hether was indicted and tried, but the jury disagreeing he was convicted of manslaughter in the third degree at the next term. He was sentenced by Judge S. S. N. Fuller to four years and twenty days at hard labor in the penitentiary. Bartlett & Mulks for the State. A. Meggett for the prisoner. Eau Claire Free Press of Dec. 30, 1857.

A member of the legal profession who had practiced in the courts convened in this valley since the organization of this district, would undoubtedly find data for much legal disquisition, and many laughable incidents might be told, and one occurs to me that may interest the readers, if not told in legal phraseology. It was while grand juries were in vogue in this State, and when the terms for Chippewa county were in January and July. It was the winter term, twenty-three grand jurors, good men and true, had answered to their names, had learned the history of juries from the days of "Alfred" down, the vast conservative power and influence of grand juries, from the learned judge, and heard his charge "to present no man through fear, favor, or affection," and sworn to present all who were guilty of such and such offences, including bribery and all and every attempt of men in official positions to receive bribes or compound felonies; and having been properly locked up in a room, well guarded by a resolute executive functionary, they commenced their onerous deliberation, and then and there making inquest for the body and people of Chippewa county, ascertained that the District Attorney, the man whom the people in their collective wisdom had chosen to prosecute offenders and draw up indictments against those whose conduct was contrary to the peace and dignity of the State, was the man, the moral and criminal turpitude of whose offending made it incumbent on that illustrious body to present him to the court for illegally and feloniously accepting a bribe and compounding felony, to the great detriment of the people of the said county of Chippewa, and contrary to the peace and dignity of the State. His Honor was therefore requested to send a good lawyer to that well-guarded room, to embody the result of their investigations as disclosed by the evidence into an indictment, charging him with heinous crimes and misdemeanors, that he might answer before the law he had sworn to help execute, in that he had received certain sums of money amounting to one hundred and fifty dollars, from a certain German arrested for assault with intent to kill, held to bail before a justice's court, and released through the interposition of this District Attorney, on the payment of the sum aforesaid to himself and for his personal benefit. Such were the facts disclosed by the evidence before this jury, as stated by their foreman, when called before his Honor to explain the cause of so strange a request; the party implicated being present, who, of all the members of that bar, most shared his Honor's confidence. Here was a dilemma; no member of the legal profession in that court could be prevailed on to draw such an indictment, but how was he to satisfy that grand jury. He was equal to the occasion, however; and after the confusion of the moment had passed, delivered himself of the following peroration: "Gentlemen of the Grand Jury, we read in the Bible, 'Blessed are the peacemakers.' This man is a peacemaker; he made peace between the injured man and the wrong-doer by paying him fifty dollars out of the one hundred and fifty, and now they are good friends, and if for mediatorial services and influence he received the hundred, it is all right. The officer will attend you to your room. Sheriff, adjourn the court."

The mill property at the Falls continued in the hands of a receiver until 1862, leased to different parties, the last being Henry Coleman, a practical mill man, who had been employed as foreman under the old regime, and who was assisted by the new firm of Pound & Halbert, who this year bought the entire property, mill, lots, pine land, and personal property. This firm commenced business at a very opportune moment, when property was low, and the advance caused by the war and a better currency, with favorable seasons and a close attention to business, enabled them to rise at once to an enviable position in the business community.

SCHOOLS AND CHURCHES.

The first district school organized in Chippewa county under legal provision was in the town of La Fayette, In the fall of 1855, and Miss Irene Drake has the honor of teaching the first school. In the succeeding winter, '55-6, a public school house had been commenced but remained unfinished, and the school was opened in a private house. The school system in this State has been revised and improved since that time, and its provisions better nnderstood by the people. But, at that time and in that little district, the people were so tenacious or their ancient customs and old-time notions, that the proposition to levy a tax to build a school-house was strenuously opposed, notwithstanding there was a large amount of non-resident lands on which the assessment would fall. "Where we came from," said these patriotic citizens, "the house was always built by private contribution," but school-districts got bravely over those old-fogy ideas, as many a speculator owning wild lands there can testify.

The first house erected in the village of Chippewa Falls for district purposes was built in 1857 ; was quite a spacious building, and frequently occupied for religious services by various denominations too feeble to have a house of their own.

The Presbpterian church was completed in 1857, and the Rev. Bradley Phillips invited to become its pastor.

The Catholic church was commenced the same year, and, after a hard struggle and many delays, completed in 1859, since which time its pulpit has been well sustained.

CHAPTER XIX

The act for the organization of Eau Claire county provided that an election for county officers should be held on the last Tuesday in December, 1856, and that the town board of the town of Eau Claire should constitute the county board until the next annual election. C. M. Seley, Chairman; E. W. Robbins and M. A. Page, Supervisors. Adin Randall was chosen Treasurer ; C. F. Babcock, Clerk of the Board ; C. H. Howard, Register of Deeds. Political conditions had but little do with the selection of candidates, although in most instances two candidates were found for most of the offices. Mr. Olin was elected Clerk of the Court without opposition; but the contest between R. F. Wilson and Charley Howard, for Register of Deeds, was quite exciting.

The most important accession to the settlement of Eau Claire, this year, 1856, was undoubtedly Daniel Shaw; having bought extensive tracts of pine land on the Chippewa and its affluents, his next move was to make it available, by manufacturing the pine into lumber. The selection of a suitable point at which to erect mills and establish the seat of his business required the most careful consideration and mature judgment.

As the choice of any site on the main river involved complications in regard to its navigation, boomage, the storage of logs, etc., strong inducements were held out by the Falls company, just then erecting a new and expensive dam, and making other costly improvements, to invest at that point; but the evidence of previous losses by devastating freshets, was too apparent at that point to afford any encouragement to the capitalist or manufacturer. He pronounced the lower Dalles then as now the only point on the river where a reservoir of safe and sufficient capacity to store all the logs on the stream could ever be established, but the impediments to overcome were too great.

Half Moon lake afforded a perfectly safe place for a certain amount of logs, if there was any possible way to get them in there; to excavate a race or canal from the river to the lake and establish a sheer-boom at a suitable point above, to direct the logs through, seemed a practical operation but too great an undertaking for his means single-handed, but by associating his with the means of others desirous of establishing a like business, he hoped to succeed. Ingram & Kennedy, Smith & Ball, Adin Randall, and some others were parties to this association; a charter for a boom was obtained from the legislature, and the work of building, opening the canal, and getting logs up the river to stock the mills, were all pressed forward with hopeful energy.

But if Mr. Shaw or any of his associates could have just had a glimpse of the future that was before them, their hard struggles against fearful floods, destructive fires, the hopeless and crushing effect of the utter prostration of all business interests throughout the West for several succeeding years, and the near approach to bankruptcy to which some—perhaps all—of those firms must come before the dawn of a brighter day should inspire hope, it is very probable that they would have shrunk from the undertaking, and that the "West Side" would to this day have continued to be a region of scrub oaks and wilderness waste.

For, good reader, you who own lots and fine houses on that side, and you merchants who, by the labor and industry of others, are getting rich, and you lawyers who, by darkening counsel, involve your neighbors in legal difficulties that you may profit by their silly whims, and you well-to-do mechanics and laboring men, many—most of whom sit under "your own vine and fig-tree," what would it all be worth if it were not for those mills and booms that have cost so much energy and struggle?

SCHOOLS, RELIGION, SOCIETY.

Corresponding to the enterprise and indomitable energy in business affairs displayed by the early settlers of Eau Claire, was their zeal in the cause of education and the advancement of religion, and it is safe to say that a larger per cent. of cultured minds and well-educated people were found amongst the early settlers of this county than usually falls to the lot of new Western settlements.

The first school-house erected in the county was on the Sparta road, three miles from Eau Claire, in what was known as the Olin and Bebee neighborhood, in the fall of '57, but during the succeeding winter a house was erected and a school opened in the village of Eau Claire, in what is now the Second ward; the building is now known as the Universalist church.

The M. E. Church, ever mindful of the educational and religious interests in remote districts, assisted by local enterprise and some eastern educational fund, commenced, in 1857, the erection in West Eau Claire of a school building known as the Methodist Institute, which was for several years conducted with much ability, and in the feeble condition of the early district schools, was of great benefit to many young persons desirous of advancing themselves in studies not taught in the then-existing district schools, but since the establishment of graded schools on both sides of the river, being free to all and conducted with such marked ability, the Institute has languished and bids fair to become entirely useless.

During the summer of 1856, Mr. J. F. Stone erected a saw and grist mill on Bridge creek, at a point where the village of Augusta now stands, and the year following Sanford Bills and others laid out the village of that name.

The valley of Bridge creek exhibits some remarkable topographical features. The course of the stream is southeast to northwest, and from its source to its confluence with the Eau Claire river describes the boundary between two sections of country differing in a marked degree from each other in soil and character. Along its southwest bank for almost its entire length, extends a fine, rich prairie, broken here and there by gentle elevations, but uniformly fertile, the soil being everywhere a rich clay loam, coming clear down to, and even into, the bends of the creek; but just across the rippling stream, and lo! how changed the soil and its productions; very little timber grew naturally on the former side—only luxuriant grass—while on the latter, a towering pine forest stood proudly out to view, stretching along for miles in bold contrast to the flowering plain on the opposite side. Here was marked in bold relief the line between that vast prairie and nearly timberless region extending a thousand miles to the Black Hills of Colorado, and the great timbered region stretching unbroken away to the great lakes, and here to-day in the trade and traffic of the village of Augusta, we see the meeting of two great industries, equally dependent on and building up each other—the forest and the field kissing each other across this gentle stream, and crowning with plenty and comfort the labors of the farmer, the lumberman, and the merchant. And here, in this romantic spot, has grown up the beautiful village of Augusta; its proud temple of learning presided over by the talented young educator, Thomas Williams; its numerous churches, its comfortable dwellings, its sumptuous hotels, all lying in peaceful plenty, where, many years less back than this narration dates, the wild deer and wolf had their covert, and the red man of the forest had undisputed sway. But like all other Western towns and villages, the way to wealth and comfort has been through intense hardships, toil, and the most untiring perseverance, as a perusal of the following terse and expressive extract from the Augusta number of Mrs. French's American Sketch Book, pages 63 to 67, under the head "Nationality of the Valley," will inform us:

"The first settlers were New York and New England people, with an occasional foreigner, who at that early date had to migrate over new and almost unsettled country, on long journeys in covered wagons, stopping, when night overtook them, by some spring by the mountain side, or some babbling brook that would afford water for themselves and their cattle and horses, being weeks, and even months, on the journey. They were, with few exceptions, very poor, bringing with them barely enough to feed and clothe themselves until the first cabin could be built and the first crop gathered in. Industry and economy have repaid most of those old pioneers with beautiful homes, and surrounded them with nearly all the luxuries and comforts of the East. They were possessed with the determination that others had thus procured homes before them, and what others could do, they could and would do also; and they did do, as this narrative will show before completed.

One example might illustrate the many hardships that were endured by the first to open up this beautiful country. One, whose name I will not mention, came from Maine to seek a home in the then far west, and upon striking this county, made himself a claim in the shape of a pre-emption, and commenced improvements with nothing but his hands with which to labor. Every furrow broken had to be worked for, he giving hand labor to some neighbor that would exchange with him. After the land was broken it became necessary to build a fence, and nails had to be got without team or wagon. Well, what did he do but start on foot to what is now the commercial center of Eau Claire county, purchased a keg of nails, and carried them home, a distance of eighteen miles—making thirty-six miles of travel in the same day. Who is there coming now-a-days that is able to do this? Very few. I desire to follow this circumstance a little farther, to show what has been done. Another trial came. A hundred and sixty acres of land had to be paid for at a certain time, Could this be done? Only one way there was, and that was this: "My old father," thought he, "is in the East, and he can, by scraping together the earnings of a lifetime, help me out, and I will take care that he has a home in his old age." The message was sent back to his early home, and shortly after the much-needed money was received, the land paid for, taking, perhaps, all the old State-of-Mainer had accumulated through earlier life, thereby securing a home for both father and son. We will pass a few years and take another look at this western farm and family to-day. By calling at a splendid white house, surrounded by fruit trees, not nine miles from Augusta, you will find the same father and son, and the son's wife and family, enjoying health, wealth, and all the luxuries to be found in the West. He has all the wealth necessary to make him happy, and is carrying out that pledge to the gray-headed father, to the perfect satisfaction of all concerned.

The above is only an illustration of the trials and achievements of those who came in early times. All had their trials and hardships: none escaped.

In later years, Norway, Sweden, Germany, France, Scotland, and nearly all nationalities have contributed to help increase the population and improvements of our valley and country, these people being in the county a majority, and through our valley about half the population at the present time."

CHAPTER XX.

A perusal of the foregoing chapters, and especially the earlier ones, has exhibited to the reader the incipient struggles and maturer development of a community of lumbermen, whose principal business has been to build and manage saw-mills, and to conduct the manufacture of lumber.

A short account of saw-mills in general, and the progress of improvements in this branch of manufacturing industry, will not, therefore, be inappropriate.

To any one who has witnessed a first-class modern saw-mill in operation, having all the late inventions and improvements, and the wonderful facility, precision, and dispatch with which a rough log is converted into smooth, square-edged boards, the entire motive power of which is found in the restless energy of water, or by its conversion into steam through the application of heat, the statement may appear almost incredible when I say that three hundred years ago the saw-mill, driven by either water or steam, was utterly unknown, and when we consider their great utility, and the prominent part they now perform in supplying the wants of men, we are wont to ask, How did people live without saw-mills? How did nations fit out vast fleets, and make all the lumber required, by hand? Where and how was all the lumber manufactured that Spain put into the Invincible Armada?

Roman history speaks of almost every branch of industry, but it is silent as to the production of the lumber that composed the vast fleets of the Scipios, of Pompey and Julius Cæsar, of Mark Antony and Augustus.

The sacred historians of an earlier day, however, have told us that eighty thousand men were employed to hew out the timbers and boards for Solomon's temple, and for seven years they were thus employed. What a vast quantity of fir and cedar timber must have been wasted by those clumsy operatives, and how much time and labor could have been saved if some enterprising Yankee had been there to dam up one of the upper branches of the modern Nehrel Kasumych, put in a Leffel double-turbine water-wheel, or lay down a track and run up a forty-horse power steam-engine to the foot of Mount Lebanon, and with a double-rotary saw cut out all the boards and timbers in a week that several such houses required to ceil all their courts, and set up the posts and doors thereof. Some kind of saws were most likely used, even at this early day, as David laid the Ammonites under saws and harrows of iron, and the Greek historians some five hundred years later speak of saws set in frames across which logs of wood were moved back and forth until boards were made therefrom. Herod, too, rebuilt the Temple of God in less than half the time consumed by Solomon, and with less than a tenth of the force, and in a style, finish, grandeur, and architectural beauty far surpassing Solomon's. But his supply of lumber was mainly from the same forest, Mount Lebanon. We must infer, therefore, that great improvements had been attained in the manufacture of all wood materials required in building at this time.

Saws were the invention of a very early, perhaps of a prehistoric, period, and their use became largely identified with the civilization of the race, and to us it seems surprising that an instrument so easily adapted to machinery, propelled by wind or water, should be so slow in finding its way to public favor. But like many other labor-saving inventions, saw-mills incurred the most furious opposition from the laboring classes; in Germany, on the Rhine and Scheldt, where both wind and water were successfully employed to drive them, and in England, where a mob repeatedly destroyed every one that capital and enterprise erected, for more than a hundred years after its adoption in the American colonies. The first saw-mill erected in Massachusetts was in 1633, thirteen years after the landing of the May Flower. The same year a wind saw-mill was erected in New Amsterdam, N. Y. This latter mill was leased for one year, the rent of which was five hundred feet of boards, half pine and half oak, so it could not have amounted to much. Judge Mitchell, of Iowa, once defined tyranny as "too much law," which if we accept as true, will certainly denominate the early laws of the colony of Massachusetts Bay as outrageously tyrannical, for it was enacted by that body of sages that "If any of the towns people shall bring any logs or timber to the mill to be sawed into boards or plank, the owners of the mill shall saw it before sawing any for themselves, and shall be entitled to retain one-half the lumber for their labor, and if any man shall wish to buy any lumber, the mill owner or owners shall sell him as much as he may desire, for the country pay, at 2s- 6d. per 100 feet." [Mass. Hist'l Col., Vol. I]. What would our mill men think of such laws now?

The forests of the United States afforded not only a bountiful supply of building materials, but gave ample scope to inventive genius in improving the machinery for, and the methods of, its manufacture.

Before the application of steam power in propelling saw-mills, water power mills were almost exclusively used in America to make sawed lumber, and two principal elements entered into their construction, namely, the "wheel and saw."

The ancients seem to have been slow to apprehend the advantages of water as a motive power, and the invention of the best wheels, those that derive the greatest power from a given quantity of water, is of very recent date.

Less than fifty years ago, somebody advanced the idea that water, as it escaped through some opening in a flume where it was pent up, pressed, or "kicked," against the sides of the opening with the same force that it fell on the surface below, and a treatise on Natural Philosophy, of that time, has a diagram representing the principle by a hollow shaft with arms at the foot, also hollow; the whole filled with water, and issuing from extreme ends on opposite sides through small apertures; the "kick," or re-action, of the water on freeing itself from the tube, sets the upright shaft in motion. The principle once established, it was not long before scientific and practical men applied it under several different names, as "re-action," "center-vent," "double re-action," wheel, etc., all combining under various modifications the principle, that by its reaction against the surface from whence it issues, water set those surfaces in motion, and, by long and patient experimenting, inventors have probably ascertained precisely what amount of surface, and the best form or mould of surface, is required so that the greatest force may be exerted by the water in its passage through the vents, and several models have been patented, as the "Stearn's wheel," the "Rose wheel," and the "Leffel double-turbine wheel."

The old fashioned wheels were of two kinds, overshot and undershot, but combining the same principle in the application of the water's propelling force. The former were generally used where a great head of water could be obtained and the supply limited; and the latter, where rapid motion must be attained at the expense of water in larger volume.

These last named wheels were almost exclusively in use in all the mills on the Chippewa until about the year 1850, when in one after another, as they were rebuilt or remodeled, the "Stearn's," "Rose," or "turbine" wheels have taken their place.

Many of my readers can remember when saw-mills were all built after one pattern, a single upright saw set in a heavy sash or frame, the whole driven up and down by a flutter wheel twenty-five feet long, with a ponderous crank attached to a heavy pitman, at one end of which motion was given to the saw direct, and consequently the diameter of the wheel was so small as to secure rapid motion.

One of the drawbacks in using these wheels was their utter worthlessness in case of backwater, as no amount of "head" or fall would overcome the resistance offered by their immersion in dead water, while the re-action wheels work very well if there is sufficient head, though buried deep under water.

Another objection to the old wheels was that only a large volume and good head of water were equal to driving a gang of saws, while a moderate head with a Stearn's or turbine wheel will easily drive a double gang.

Well, good-bye to the flutter wheels. Ye did good service, and many a tired sawyer wishes for the return of the good old days when he took a good nap while ye were making a run! With the introduction of the new and more powerful wheels came the rotary saw, one of which for slabbing and fitting logs for a gang, will perform the work of half a dozen muleys, and with the aid of a Tarrant's log-turner and other improvements for handling logs and lumber, edging, butting, and forwarding to the raft shed, a vast amount of lumber is manufactured in a single day at some of the largest establishments in this valley, and no more gratifying sight can be presented to visitors who come among us than to take them to one of our first-class saw-mills, where from fifty to a hundred thousand feet of boards, plank, joists, scantling, and square timber are manufactured, sorted, and rafted in ten hours. And so well accustomed are the men employed in the different parts of the work, and with such precision does each perform the part allotted to him, that he seems a part of the machinery upon which he attends. But for this accuracy and strict adherence of each and every one to the duty assigned him, accidents would constantly occur.

CHAPTER XXI.

INVENTIONS.

During the war of the rebellion, the inventive genius of the whole nation was directed to improvements in the manufacture of arms, because war was the business of the people—engrossing their thoughts and absorbing their means and energies, and whether the old saw that "necessity is the mother of invention," is true or not, it is a well-established fact that many of the most useful inventions, those that confer the greatest benefits, have grown out of the peculiar wants and conditions of man;

being especially adapted to the pursuits and industrial development of the different races of men in the successive ages of the world. What but the strange, wild, ever-moving life of our American Indians, whose only highways were the rivers, could have led such unskillful, ignorant people—unskilled in the arts and manufacture of almost every useful thing—to construct so delicate, ingenious, and useful a thing as the bark canoe, requiring a degree of mechanical skill that it would be hard for our artisans to imitate, a craft so light a man can carry it anywhere, and yet so capacious and durable that whole families, with their effects, take passage in one of them? And who supposes that Whitney, the inventor of the cotton-gin, had he continued to live among his native New England hills, would have lost a moment's sleep or an hour's time, in working out the details of that intricate, but wonderfully useful, machine? But the enormous demand for fine cotton fabrics, and the fact just then ascertained that the soil and climate of the Southern States were adapted to the production of the finest fiber of cotton, stimulated a poor New England mechanic, who had gone down there with his tools and carpet-bag, to give to those arrogant Southrons an invention that at once conferred upon those States a commanding position in the commercial affairs of the world. The plow, too, that through all ages and in all countries, was little more than unshapely pieces of wood sharpened, and sometimes pointed with iron, was found utterly inadequate to the demands of our Western soils, and in 1836 began to claim the attention of practical, scientific men, for the first time in the world's history, and impelled by the necessity which the peculiar but fertile soil of the Western prairies involved, that long neglected but indispensable implement of husbandry soon underwent radical improvements, and became "a thing of beauty;" its polished, case-hardened, steel mould-board cleaving and flopping over the most sticky prairie loam to be found with as much ease as other plows would scathe a sand-bank. How much of the success and material prosperity of the West has been achieved by improvements in this one implement, we shall never realize, but in no other country in the world' not even in practical, inventive New England, can be found such perfect plows as have grown out of the demands of the great West. It is natural, therefore, to expect that the inventive talent of this valley should be directed to overcoming the natural obstacles in the way of, or in facilitating, the manufacture and transportation of lumber.

Every science employs certain technical terms or phrases peculiar to itself, and every branch of industry makes use of names and words which belong exclusively to that art, many of which require explanation in order to be understood by the general reader. A few instances of this kind will perhaps occur in speaking of our inventions, and their appropriation to the business of this valley.

Every person who has ascended the Mississippi, or any other shallow, sandy river, in low water, on a steamboat, and felt the shock as she ran on a sand-bar, must have some idea of the shape or form of the bar, which, in almost every instance, is a continually moving mass of sand stretching obliquely across the river, with a bold, bluff bank and deep water on the lower side, with a thin sheet of uneven depth spread out over the long, upper slope, everywhere getting shallower, until it reaches the very brink, where a perceptible fall is noticed, and the current slackened by its fall into deeper water, and any one who has observed the course of the boat as she feels her way along, endeavoring to find out where the channel is, has noticed that she ran along on the under side of the bluff bar, perhaps nearly across the river, the channel having changed to the opposite side in that short distance. Now, a raft floating down the river, guided with long sweeping oars, needs to be kept in the same serpentine channel, because the steamboat has taken the deepest water there is, and the only way it can be made to float over the next bar is to keep it up close under the bar above, until the draught of water will take it through, which is frequently a difficult task to perform, requiring the maturest judgment, skillful piloting, and rapid handling of the raft.

The reader will bear in mind that there is a shallow draft of water probably, over the whole length of this oblique sand-bar, and a constant tendency of the raft to drift down with the current on to the bar below, although it may be very thin, and whatever appliances can be brought to bear upon the raft to check its downward force, must be an important auxillary in guiding the raft; and for many years the raftsmen on this river felt the need of some such mechanical agency, which was at length found in the very simple, but immensely serviceable, contrivance called the "snatch pole." Who was its inventor, or precisely where (on what river) it was first used, I have not been able to ascertain, but its great value to the lumbermen on this river induces me to honor it with a minute description, as, by its aid in low water, fifty per cent. is saved in running lumber to the Mississippi.

The method, or art, of rafting lumber on the Chippewa is very much like that pursued on the Delaware, Susquehanna, Alleghany, and Ohio rivers. Cribs sixteen by thirty-two feet, instead of the old-style platform, is now the invariable shape of the first compact form of raft, into which the lumber is placed and firmly fastened by ironwood "grub-pins" inserted through two-inch plank, those on the under side, or bottom of the crib being called "runners," and those on the top "binders." The grub-pins are turned in a lathe, with the head on one end, which is neatly fitted into the under side of the lower plank, or runner, so as to make a smooth surface. These cribs are formed on ways, with rollers on which they rest, and when the crib is of the desired thickness—twelve to twenty courses, according to the stage of water—a strong lever, called a "witch," having a heavy iron clamp on one end, is placed over the end of each grub-pin, with a fulcrum bearing on the binder, by which means the grub-pin is drawn upward, thereby causing the runner and binder to be drawn together with great force, and binding the lumber between tightly together, when the grub-pin is securely wedged, and the crib is finished. The fastening which holds it to the ways is then removed, and away glides the crib into the water. Seven of these cribs constitute a string, and four of these strings form a Chippewa raft. The grub-pins are left standing, extend a foot or more above the binder, and by their aid the cribs and strings are united and bound together. By their aid "snubbing works" are erected on the raft by which it is checked and landed. It is, too, by means of these pins that the snatch-pole and line are operated to check the headway, and also in guiding the raft. This implement is about sixteen feet long and six inches in diameter at the thickest part, which is about three feet from the lower end. Upon the lower end a strong steel-pointed socket is fastened, and a band of iron, to which a strong ring is fastened, being driven down to within three feet from the end from which it tapers gradually to the upper end. A line called the "snatch line" is fastened to the ring, and lies coiled up near the stern of the raft, and as it approaches one of these intricate passages before described, and before the stern has passed the first-named bar, one of the oarsmen seizes the snatch-pole and, bounding into the water, hastens along the bar, in the direction desired to hold the raft, and by rapid movement thrusts the heavy steel point of the pole into the sand, holding firmly the other end at an angle of forty-five degrees, while the pilot, quick as thought, has the rope coiled around first one grub-pin and then another, as the raft passes on, continually checking its downward force, so that by the time the bar is passed the raft lies nearly still, under the bar. The man returns to the raft with the snatch-pole, and it is easily guided with the oars to the precise channel over the bar below, although involving the necessity of winding along a serpentine route that, without the aid of the snatch-pole, could not have been made, and the raft must have drifted hopelessly upon the bar, where the cribs must be separated and taken, at great expense, singly over or around, and down to some convenient place to couple up again. Sand-bars are the bane of navigation, either for boats or rafts, on all the Wisconsin tributaries to the Mississippi, and the bed of the Chippewa, for fifty miles from its mouth, is a constantly ever-changing mass of sand, bewildering the pilots and utterly defying all attempts at permanent improvement in its navigation, as several vast sand-banks slope down to the river at different points, and every high rise of water displaces immense quantities of sand from these banks, which floats along in restless masses, blocking up all the old channels, and mocking all human efforts to improve the river or make it a reliable and cheap thoroughfare for the navigation of boats or rafts. And right here I wish to remark that as the Wisconsin river, all the way from Kilbourn City to its mouth, is liable to the same obstructions and impediments as the Chippewa, no positive and permanent improvement of that stream will ever be attained by any means yet proposed, and that nothing short of a canal the entire distance will ever open the long desired and much talked of water communication between the Mississippi and the lakes by that route. And every dollar appropriated by Congress proposing anything short of a canal from Portage City down, is so much money thrown away.

CHAPTER XXII

INVENTIONS CONTINUED.

In the preceding chapters of this work, reference has frequently been made to booms, and presuming that most of my readers understand the meaning of the term, as used here in contradistinction to its nautical definition, as the main-, jib-, and studding-sail-boom, no explanation has been deemed necessary in regard to its signification; but the different methods of construction, using and fastening, together with improvements added by inventors in the structure and arrangement of certain kinds of booms, or booms for certain localities, as also a succinct account of a patent obtained for the same, will constitute the principal topics of this chapter.

In construction, the booms on this river are of two kinds, stiff and thorough-shot, and are adapted to two principal purposes, and designated as jam-boom and shear-boom. The former, as its name indicates, is a fixed obstruction placed in the river, or across some part or channel of the river, so as to effectually stop the logs, and retain them there until wanted for the mill, or to form into rafts, and is usually what is called a thorough-shot boom, and is formed of very strong timbers, coupled at the ends with six-inch bolts, or thorough-shots, the ends of two short timbers uniting with one long one between them; they are usually hewn on two sides, and the sections thus constructed are fastened to piers planted in the bed of the river at suitable distances to afford support, either by driving piles, if the bottom is sand or gravel, or, if rock, by filling cribs with immense piles of stones; ponderous chains being used for that purpose. Many such piers are erected at various points on this river, extending down from the foot of some island, so as to increase the storage capacity of a boom to which the island affords the starting point.

But the boom that guides or "shears" the logs out of the main channel of the river into those side receptacles, is a thing of very different construction, and to so construct and arrange a boom of this kind in a navigable river, where steamboats and rafts are frequently passing, that no delay or interruption shall occur, and at the same time direct all the logs floating in the swollen river, out of the rapid current into the side boom, has taxed the ingenuity and the resources of some of the first inventors of the age, and best business men of the Northwest. It will readily be supposed that such a boom must present a straight, smooth surface to the logs that float against it; that very strong supports of some kind must sustain it at different points against the powerful current, or it would trail with it; that it must be stiff, and of great strength; and, finally, that it must be flat, and wide enough for men to walk and work upon, to facilitate the forwarding of the logs, lest they accumulate by the pressure of the current. It must also be apparent to the reader that such a boom, or at least the lower portion, must have some contrivance by which it can be swung, or closed and opened readily; and this was the great difficulty, the grand problem to be solved—the opening and shutting of the gate so rapidly and securely that no detention should be caused to boats or rafts, and yet save all the logs. Long and sorely was this difficulty felt by those mill men on this river, who erected steam mills and side booms or reservoirs for logs below the Falls, with a view to shear their logs into such receptacles, before any successful process was presented by which it could be overcome. But genius and persistent effort have accomplished the desired end, and it will be the object of this chapter to set forth the wonderful invention to which it is due. It was not a new want, for on many other rivers it has been found desirable to arrest logs floating on their surface, and shear them into places of safety; and great losses had been experienced on the Mississippi river and other streams for want of such a gate. It has been previously stated that Daniel Shaw, in 1856, selected Half Moon Lake as a safe reservoir for logs; that he and other parties associated connected the lake with the Chippewa river by a canal, and established a shear-boom to guide their logs into said lake through the canal; but the manner in which this undertaking was first attempted was far from satisfactory. At a projecting point of rocks about one hundred rods above the canal, on the opposite bank of the river, a stiff boom, formed by fastening together three or more pieces of heavy square timber in consecutive lengths, was made fast to the rock and extended nearly down to the canal, where piers and sorting works were erected to facilitate the separation from theirs of such logs as were required to pass on. Chains attached to anchors supported this boom at short intervals, and at the lower end a windlass and chain forced it up so near to the shore where this artificial channel was opened as to guide most of the logs therein; but great difficulty attended the opening and closing of this swing gate by such an apparatus, to pass rafts and steamboats, and many logs went by before it could be closed by such clumsy machinery; moreover, when the water was high and logs running plentifully, the anchor chains were found insufficient and the windlass powerless to force the boom up against the strong current, so as to switch them out of the channel into the safe receptacle provided for them.

Adin Randall, one of the company, contracted with the association to perform the labor and secure all the logs for a consideration, and for two years struggled hard to comply with his agreement; but owing to the inefficiency of his machinery and arrangements, many logs were lost, and Half Moon Lake, as a depository for logs, bade fair to become a failure, owing to the difficulty of getting them in there.

But in 1859 a contract was made with James Allen and Levi W. Pond, in which those gentlemen bound themselves to perform what Mr. Randall had failed in a measure to do; care being taken, it seems, from the tenor of the agreement, to stipulate that the same machinery should be used, and by the same process as that employed by Mr. Randall. This contract was for a term of five years; but these men were not only skillful and practical operators in such matters, but scientific inventors, and by long and careful experimenting were enabled to work out the details of a boom moved and operated on very different principles, and to compel that very element against which they contended to serve them—a boom that would open and shut across the river independent of chains, anchors or windlasses, and without any external aid.

Grand and seemingly inconceivable as the idea must appear to the reader, that pieces of timber fastened together so as to form a slender raft several hundred feet in length might float in the river, securely fastened at the up-stream end to the shore, and that it would swing by itself up stream, and stretch itself obliquely across the river, holding itself against the headlong torrent and crushing masses of floating logs and driftwood as if firmly anchored to a rock-bound shore; yet the inventive genius of these poor, hard-working, but practical men not only conceived the thing, but reduced it to a positive demonstration. Mr. Pond informs me that, like many other inventions, the incipient idea was derived from a very commonplace circumstance; that in operating the windlass it was found convenient to use a scow at the lower end, and placed on the lower side of the boom as at first arranged, and that at one time a heavy strain was brought to bear upon the end up stream, which forced the stern or lower end out from the boom at an angle of thirty degrees or more; and by careful observation it was ascertained that the current set with such force against the side of the scow, held thus obliquely to it, in opposition to its force on the other side of the boom, as to very perceptibly move it up against the current. And right there was evolved the principle which only required development to produce a machine of immense value to the world; and in 1862 Messrs. Pond and Allen actually applied this principle in the management of their boom, by attaching wings or rudders at intervals along the lower edge of the boom, in such a manner that they would lie close by its side when necessary to open it for rafts or boats to pass, or could be expanded by a rope attached to the other ends, and extending to the upper end of the boom, where a windlass was employed to force the rudders out against the current, which, reacting against the pressure on the opposite side, held the boom and all the logs that came against it across this powerful current, and glanced or steered them with wonderful facility into the desired haven.

An invention involving so many nice adjustments, which could only be made when the water was high and logs running, required much time to perfect all its arrangements, so as to adapt it to all the varied circumstances and conditions of low water and flood; and as there were only a few weeks or months in the year in which experiments could be made, and as all these were necessarily open to the public, other parties copied it, and commenced using it before it was so far completed in all its parts as to warrant application for a patent. Want of means to prosecute it also deterred Mr. Pond from obtaining a patent on his invention; and when, with the aid of the Eau Claire Lumber company, such application was made, with models all complete, so much time had elapsed that a special act of Congress was necessary to relieve the applicant from the disability of not having applied soon enough, as, by the patent law, prior use of the invention for more than two years by other parties rendered it liable to objection; but, under the peculiar circumstances, Congress thought the two-year privilege enjoyed by all inventors ought in this instance to be enlarged, and, therefore, passed the act for Mr. Pond's relief. This, however, was in 1870, two years after the granting of the patent.

The association owning the boom upon which these experiments were made gave Mr. Pond and his associates two thousand dollars for the privilege of using his invention at that point, and certified to its practical worth and utility, saying, "It has stood the test of the highest freshets, is easily and cheaply constructed," and recommending it to all who have occasion for such an invention.

CHAPTER XXIII.

THE FOREST.

Next to the fertility of its soil, the great West owes its development and prosperity to the forests abounding near the sources of the grand river by which it is drained, together with those on the tributaries of the Great Lakes, and very much of the soil of Wisconsin would be utterly worthless and incapable of sustaining even the sparsest population, where are flourishing villages, were it not for the advantages derived from the near presence of a vast forest of pine, hemlock, oak, maple, and other valuable timber, in the northern and northeastern portions of the State. And though reference has frequently been made to the business of cutting and manufacturing this timber into lumber, in these pages, it is believed that a more extended and detailed account of these operations, peculiarities of the people engaged therein, modes of life, methods of prosecuting the work, face of the country, etc., would constitute an interesting chapter in this work.

A line drawn from the northern extremity of Lake St. Croix to Kilbourn City would describe the general course of the boundary between the prairie, or measurably timberless region, on the southwest, and the unbroken forest extending in the opposite direction to the great inland seas; varied, however, by occasional projections "of timber into the meadows," as the big woods on the Eau Galla, and the peninsular of pine woods on Robinson's creek. As we ascend any of the streams crossing this line, the soil along their banks becomes sandy, the grass and other vegetation stunted, black pine takes the place of oak timber, the beds of creeks and sloughs change from the sluggish, muddy appearance of the Western prairies to a clear, crystal sand or gravel, and the water a pure, limpid rivulet. These sandy plains are frequently of considerable extent, but, as before stated, partially covered with a certain kind of pine called "black Jack," are not the kind of soils on which valuable white or red "Norway" pine timber grows, but may be said to mark the boundary between the timbered and prairie regions of the Northwest. Bogs and abrupt, sandstone peaks and ridges are another indication of a characteristic change in the soil and its productions, but the soil best adapted to the growth of sound, white-pine timber is a damp, heavy, rocky clay. But the production of pine timber has not been solely dependent on the nature of the soil, although this is an essential element, but upon many concurrent circumstances; for no tree grows in our forests that has so many enemies as the pine. Towering in its best estate high above all other timber, the fury of the winds plays high carnival with its stately forms. The lightning, too, seems to delight in driving its shafts down its tall, spire-like top, and shattering its trunk by that subtle fluid that mocks all human control.

Many diseases fasten themselves upon this tree during the long centuries required for its maturity, and, like all other trees, suffers much from being too much crowded together, and as the feeble ones die out and fall against their fellows, many injuries are inflicted, causing decay that extends to the whole tree, sometimes affecting the "heart" and eating out the interior, year after year, as successive layers or grains are formed on the outside. Something in the soil, also, seems to favor this center rot, or, as the choppers say, cause the tree to be "hollow butted," for it frequently happens that over an area of forty acres, almost every tree of suitable size is hollow near the ground. In other localities, great numbers of trees will be found to be afflicted with "ring rot," where streaks of decay, in alternate and consecutive circles, extend around the tree, indications of which are pretty sure to be discovered on the outside, or bark, in the shape of "punk knots," and requiring long experience and mature discrimination to distinguish the sound from the unsound, for, like men, their outside appearance is often deceptive, and hence the pay of a veteran timber hunter, like that of experts in detecting other counterfeits, is very liberal. In many other respects the pine tree is liable to receive injuries that depreciate its value for lumber, where no rot exists. Owing to some peculiar characteristic in the tree itself, or in the soil on which it grows, or, as some say, to the force of the winds, the trunk becomes "shaky," the grains, or annual formations of wood, being separated, and destroying its value for any purpose as lumber. But the worst of all its enemies is fire, and when we consider the great length of time required to grow one of these stately evergreens, the wonder is so many of them attain a growth so perfect in size, symmetry, and usefulness. Some pine trees are of very rapid growth, while others mature very slowly. Of more than a hundred trees of a suitable size for logs, the consecutive annual grains, or rings, of which I have on different occasions counted, the indications were that a period of from one hundred and fifty to sixteen hundred years is required to grow one of these noble plants to full-size treehood. Only think of the tiny seed that floated heedlessly down from the lofty bough of some parent stem, when Christ was on earth, and nestling under the falling foliage of deciduous trees, found protection until the genial influence of spring opened the germ and it took root in solid earth, and through summer's heat and winter's cold, and all the dangers of its situation, in spite of storms and lightning's subtle shaft, the stem that was once so feeble that a breath would have wilted it, now stands before us a majestic tree, and all to provide the ungrateful children of men with lumber to build their houses. But the men who chop down these giant old trees regard not their age nor the lessons they teach, nor do they, nor the men who own the land on which they stand, nor those who manufacture their trunks into lumber, see anything but money in or about them; so much per thousand feet "stumpage," so much for hauling, and so much in the raft for sawed timber.

Each of these classes of individuals have their peculiarities, but in one respect are very much alike; they all require tools to work with, and the speculator in pine lands generally makes use of a pretty keen set. Their method of communication is sometimes very shrewd, and, like the Irish lover's dream, "always goes by contraries," so that outsiders are always in the dark as to their real meaning. The agent and timber hunter, however, is a free and easy fellow, aside from his business, and, unlike his employer, spends his earnings with the recklessness of a sailor. But the boys who chop, saw, haul, and drive the logs are a jolly, independent set of fellows, the old-line veterans especially, whose winters have all been spent in the woods, command big wages when they do work, but disdain most all other kinds of work, spending a few months of each and every summer in perfect idleness. But when the time comes for them to go up the river, in the fall, the highest wages are always given to these experienced woodsmen. These men plan or lay out the work for the ensuing winter, erect the camps, open the roads, boat up supplies, and make all necessary arrangements for the winter campaign, and with them everything is reduced to a perfect system; they require no "bossing," for every man knows his own business, and every man works without the presence of an overseer.

With the march of progress in all the various industries in this country, the logging and lumber interest has kept more than even pace, and as compared with the management of the same kind of business in Maine and the Canadas some forty years ago, the improvements are very great; and in no particular are they more apparent than in the mode of living, the construction of the camps being more house-like, with comfortable cooking and sleeping apartments separate; the tables being always well, even sumptuously, furnished, and the beds well supplied with blankets. In tools, bob-sleighs, and all other implements, there are marked improvements which enable operators in this business to perform a greater amount of work in a given time than formerly. And when these are combined with the wonderfully improved machinery and facilities for manufacturing logs into lumber, it is not surprising that the business is overdone, and that our pine forests are slaughtered with a rapidity and recklessness painful to contemplate.

Man's destructiveness is so prominent, and his disposition to appropriate what nature has already provided so greedy, that of all its bounteous provisions none are so unsparingly sacrificed as the trees which have required ages to grow, and the time has now come when the people of this valley should consider these things with a view to greater economy in the destruction of timber. In New York and Pennsylvania, in many localities, hemlock has taken the place of pine,—the latter having long since been cut away—and for many purposes is found to be a most excellent substitute. For scantling and all kinds of square lumber, hemlock might be used by our mills, which would save so much pine for future use. Large quantities of this valuable timber are utterly wasted, chopped and pealed for tan-bark, consumed in clearing land, and thrown down in felling pine timber, causing constant waste that our children will have reason to deplore.

CHAPTER XXIV.

Passing over a few years' time, and many important and interesting matters and events, to which I shall recur in succeeding chapters, I find it necessary to make an appeal to my readers, to the public, and to each and every individual in this valley who is desirous of having the locality in which he resides represented in that portion of the history relating to the war.

Isolated as these settlements were for most of the time prior to those stirring events—the grandest in the world's history—it would not have been strange if many beheld the approach of that terrible conflict with indifference, and a want of that patriotic ardor that characterized other and more favored sections. But it is believed that if all the facts could be set forth, of public and personal sacrifice, of heroic devotion, and persistent patriotic effort in that great struggle, exhibited by the people of this valley, it would not only compare favorably with the most loyal communities in the land, but make a valuable contribution to the history of the State. But the means are not at my hand to do justice to the subject; and without the aid of others—many others in all the towns and precincts who are in possession of interesting facts and data—to assist me in collecting them for this work, much valuable information, and many exciting incidents connected with the part borne by our people in the fearful contest, will perhaps pass into oblivion, unless collated in this homely narration. I therefore ask every officer and soldier who went from this valley to fight our country's battles, and every patriotic citizen who knows himself or herself to be in possession of any intelligence, serious or comic, facts, incidents, or accounts of soldiers or citizens, no matter how humble or obscure, if they were conspicuous for zeal, bravery, or self-sacrifice for the good of the country in the hour of peril, to communicate the same to me as soon as convenient, that it may be preserved to posterity as the heritage of a free and loyal people. More especially do I ask the attention of men in official position, town and county officers, postmasters, and all men who hold or have held positions of trust and honor in the towns, cities and villages of this valley, to aid me in making a full, fair and impartial record of the deeds of the brave soldiers who imperiled their lives, and of the sacrifices of the true men and women who sustained them through all the dark and wearisome days of defeat, and gloom, and doubt, that so long hung like a dark pall over our country's hopes.

It is not to individuals alone that I desire to do justice in these pages, but to localities also; a careful and just recognition of the claims and efforts of each of which will reflect credit and honor upon some neighborhoods that have made little pretensions, and are scarcely known in the Adjutant-General's reports, or in any records of the war.

In the beginning of the war, when no bounties were offered, and patriotism was the sole incentive to enlistments, many volunteers went from their homes in obscure places to the villages which received credit for the names enrolled there; and when it was found necessary to order a draft, the claims of such localities were utterly ignored, and the draft fell upon some communities already thrice decimated by voluntary enlistments.

Such was the fate of the little town of Lafayette, in Chippewa county, a town which, up to the commencement of the war, had never polled more than seventy-one votes, quite a number of whom were aged men, unable to bear arms, and yet actually furnished, in enlisted and drafted men for the war, sixty-five loyal soldiers, a large number of whom rallied under the old flag before drafts or bounties were thought of.

If any town or village in this State can show a better, or as good a record, I shall be glad to acknowledge it and make it enduring. Having been a resident of that little town when the war commenced, and personally acquainted with almost every person in it, the peculiar motives which induced some of those early volunteers to enlist, and many noteworthy incidents and circumstances connected therewith, are known to me; and though some may consider the trials and experiences of a private soldier unworthy of historical record, there are many I shall be happy to chronicle in these pages, as a just tribute to their services and sacrifices.

Born on a foreign shore, and in a land that had long felt the heel of the oppressor, were two young men who were in my employment when the tocsin of war was sounded. One, very young, ardent, fiery and impatient, had somewhere witnessed an artillery drill, and determined to enlist at the first call for men in that arm of service; and, taking up a newspaper one day, that announced the organization of the Second Wisconsin Battery, and a call for men to fill its ranks, he instantly gave me "notice to quit," closed up his affairs, and paid his own fare and expenses all the way to Racine, that he might share the perils and fight the battles of the country of his adoption. In religion he was a Catholic, and in politics a Democrat; but no braver soldier or truer patriot treads the soil of Wisconsin to-day than Tom McGrath. He served through the entire war; was in all the hard-fought battles in which the Second Battery was engaged, but escaped unharmed; and taking a fair Sucker damsel along with him on his return through Illinois, is now settled in a home of his own in Chippewa county, and a wholesome number of little Democrats surround his hearthstone and call him "pa."

The other was a man of maturer years; quiet and unobtrusive in his demeanor, but determined—almost obstinate—in his opinions. He was with me as foreman in several undertakings. He had spent several winters in the South; owned some good property in Bureau county, Illinois; had always voted the Democratic ticket until he saw the cruelties of slavery, and the party committed to upholding that giant wrong, when, said he, "conscience would not let me vote that ticket any longer." Though a man of few words, he often referred to the horrid cruelties and terrible sufferings of the negroes of Arkansas, and gave many instances he had witnessed, exhibiting a refinement of cruelty inflicted by their masters, which had burnt into his soul with deathless intensity; and powerless as he then was to afford relief, he had sworn on the altar of God, that if the time ever came in which he could do something to redress those wrongs, his life was none too precious to lose in such a cause, and, if necessary, should be freely offered.

True to his promise, when Captain Sherman called for men to fill up his company of cavalry, he unhitched the team he was driving from the plow, and hastened to enroll his name with the defenders of his adopted country. A transfer was subsequently effected to an Illinois cavalry regiment, by his request, and he soon found himself fighting rebel guerrillas in the same "Rackensack" neighborhood where, years before, he had felt his spirit sink within him because there was none to shield the oppressed and hurl back the oppressor. But now he saw that the day of recompense had come; and, whether called upon to scour the woods and ravines around Pea Ridge for guerrillas, or waste his strength in the malarious swamps of Mississippi, he never flinched or swerved from the line of his duty as a soldier; and when, in the third year of the war, when the great highway of the West had been opened, and New Orleans and Vicksburg were ours, and the bright rainbow of peace and promise encircled the western horizon, he was called to surrender the life so freely offered upon Freedom's altar, not a murmur escaped him; but he proudly declared, in a letter to a friend in Chippewa county, that "if he must die, he was glad to lay down his life in such a cause."

Oh, ye corrupt and truckling politicians, who pander to the prejudices of the ignorant, unfeeling and thoughtless multitude that yo may obtain place and power, think for a moment with what mighty issues you are trifling, and how many noble lives have been laid on the altar you would now desecrate with your vile pollutions and trickery!

William McFarland, the Irish-American patriot and soldier whose sacrifices are herein feebly recorded, was only one of that vast army whose "souls are still marching on." Inspired alike by the same high sense of justice and right, their lives were consecrated to the cause of freedom and the emancipation of their fellow men from the thrall of oppression.

I might mention many others who went from the same place. I might speak of young Stowe, who bade adieu to a fond and beautiful wife, who had committed her happiness to his keeping only a month or two previously, never to embrace her again; of the long, weary watching and waiting, and the blank despair when her hopes were finally crushed out; and of the whole score of heroes whose last farewell to wives and loved ones took place here, for the sake of the country whose welfare was identified with their own. And in every nook and corner of this valley similar scenes and struggles and sorrows were experienced, of which, if persons who feel an interest in this work would send me brief sketches, they would confer a favor, not only upon the author but upon every reader. And to every one who is in possession of any material facts, incidents, or other data concerning the war, the "Indian scare," enlistment, organization, partings and return of our soldiers, conduct and heroism in the service, imprisonment in Southern dungeons, and all their hardships and self-denial, are fit subjects for this work; and no matter how clumsy or illiterate any statement may be, it will be gratefully received by the author.

CHAPTER XXV.

From the claims I have set up to the loyalty of the people of this valley, when the war came on, it must not be supposed that all were equally zealous, or that none were found to oppose the measures of the administration in suppressing the rebellion. Inherent qualities of the human mind, as well as their education, cause men to see things in a different light, and to honestly differ in their opinions on all questions in which men feel any interest.

Next to the interests of religion, that of government should undoubtedly claim our attention. It is this interest in the policy of our government, and because we see things from different standpoints, that divides the American people into parties; but political parties in the United States have other and less philosophical reasons for organizing into opposing parties, besides more honest convictions in regard to the best policy.

The love of power, and the desire to obtain and hold office, too often becomes a controlling element in our elections. The Democratic party had so long held the reins of power and controlled all positions of trust and honor, before the war, that its adherents began to think that they had an inherent and indefeasible right to them, and fealty to party to be regarded as of paramount importance in questions of government. Whatever its leaders dictated was blindly followed by the rank and file, and no matter how iniquitous or unjust its measures might be, it was considered treason not to abjectly follow its dictates, and the early settler in this valley came with all the prejudice and blind subserviency to party that characterized its votaries elsewhere.

All deprecated the evils of slavery and seemed to regard it as the source of, or as threatening, overwhelming disaster to the country, but the course to pursue in order to avert it, involved the bitterest controversies: and, finally, as the question became one of peace or war, may be said to have marked the line between the enemies and the friends of our government.

In their eagerness to secure the united vote and influence of the slaveholders, both the Whig and the Democratic parties had, eight years before, gone down on their knees, and, in the basest and most abject servility, craved the privilege of stultifying themselves, of ignoring justice and the claims of manhood and freedom, and of doing any amount of dirty work for the party, for the sake of office, and as the Democratic party succeeded, its leaders supposed they could always win by such baseness, and then it was that the party, in this State, was compelled to go back on its previous record, and take up the refrain of the South, that "slavery was ordained of God, and that the negro had no rights that white men were bound to respect." And even the Church and the ministers of religion echoed these horrid sentiments with solemn and pompous arrogance, so that for a time it seemed as though justice, mercy, and truth had taken their flight from the earth, and there was none to shield the oppressed and hurl back the oppressor. But all good men of both political parties beheld this state of things with alarm and consternation; and assuming from the light of the past that further concessions to the slave power would only defer for a season, but could not avert, the impending calamity, formed a new party, feeble, indeed, at first, and seemingly powerless to grapple with an adversary so arrogant and powerful, but gathering such strength in a few years as to convince the world that justice, truth, and freedom for all constitute the only foundation of good government.

The insatiable demands and exactions of the slaveholding wing of the Democratic party became insupportable to a great many of the best men of the party, and the press, the rostrum, and the pulpit of the Free States soon recognized the necessity of a higher standard of political faith and ethics, and joined their fortunes with the new party as the only hope of salvation for the country.

But the most influential, perhaps, of all the agencies employed to reform public sentiment and mould the opinions and political thought upon a higher plane and into purer channels, were certain works of fiction, the most conspicuous of which was Mrs. Stowe's "Uncle Tom's Cabin," which, being dramatized, exhibited the awful horrors of the system of slavery to the most ignorant classes with telling effect.

In the Church, the most liberal and progressive sects were the first to plant themselves on the broad ground of freedom for all and exact justice to every human being, as the objects of "His care whose tender mercies are over all His works." And foremost among these in the great work of reform may be mentioned the Congregationalist, Universalist, and Methodist Churches, whose periodical literature had for several years previous been out-spoken in denouncing the horrid traffic in human beings as the sum of all villainies.

During the winter preceding the war, while the Southern States were busy taking themselves out of the Union, the prejudices of our people in favor of party as against country were sometimes painfully apparent. On one occasion, the writer dined at a hotel in Eau Claire, at which were present some thirty or forty of the business and influential citizens of the town and country, and adverting during the conversation to the attitude assumed by South Carolina, remarked that "it looks now as though, in order to save the country, we shall have to fight." When, to his astonishment, nearly a dozen of the most prominent who were present, from town and country, instantly replied, "If it comes to that, WE shall be found in some Southern regiment."

Three newspapers were at that time published in this valley, two of which, the Eau Claire Free Press, edited by Gilbert E. Porter, and the Dunn County Lumberman, edited by E. S. Bundy, were able advocates of the cause of freedom, but the Chippewa Falls Democrat, conducted by Joseph and A. W. Delaney, subject to the trammels of party, halted long between two opinions, but finally succumbed to circumstances and retired from the field, before actual commencement of hostilities.

Of the legal fraternity, as a body, not much can be said in their favor as self-sacrificing citizens and patriots. Hollon Richardson, of Chippewa Falls, (a Democrat), Hon. Pitt Bartlett, Horace Barnes, and Mr. Spencer, of Eau Claire, Col. E. M. Bartlett, then of Durand, and the Bundy brothers, of Menomonie, all gave their hearty support to the government under the new, or Republican, administration. Hon. Alexander Meggett, Democrat, prepared an able speech in defense of the war, extracts from which will be given hereafter. But devotion to the Democratic party had so long been the only passport to political preferment, that a very large share of the legal profession had staked all their ambitious hopes on its success.

Nearly every clergyman in this valley did honor to himself and the profession, by acts of loyalty and words of hope in the darkest hours of our country's peril. Rev. Bradley Phillips, of Chippewa Falls, wrote to his pro-slavery Presbyterian paper that its tone must be changed or the paper stopped. Rev. Mr. Kidder's voice was always for the Union, and for the war to uphold and preserve it. The itinerants of the M. E. Church, following the lead of the late lamented Dr. Eddy, of the Northwestern Advocate, boldly declared to their congregations that no man could be a good Methodist and uphold slavery.

A Christian minister, whose flock were politically divided, and whose living depended upon their united support, stood in need of a double supply of grace to enable him to act upon his convictions at such a time. Rev. J. O. Barrett, Universalist, of Eau Claire, was thus circumstanced; his parish was feeble, at best, and his congregation about equally divided in regard to the war, and the object for which it was waged; but his whole soul was in the cause of freedom and the Union, and he was recognized on all public occasions as an eloquent and powerful advocate of Republican principles and the cause of liberty.

A large majority of the Democrats here belonged to the Douglass wing of the party, and that statesman's speech in Chicago, after the firing upon Fort Sumter, caused many to pause in their mad and treasonable opposition to the government. But through the war, their sullen silence or half-suppressed groans, whenever news of success to the Union arms came over the wires, showed plainly where their sympathies were, as though they somehow realized that every shot aimed at the enemy was fired at their idolized party, and on the other hand, when misfortunes befell the Union cause, and during all the long, dark months of doubt and adversity, when the life of the nation hung in the balance, it was impossible for such men to conceal the satisfaction and delight with which every reverse of the Union arms was received. But who shall describe the agony, the bitterness, mortification, and sorrow of those weary, waiting months, to the anxious friends of freedom and the Union, as day after day brought new disasters, and the jeers, and ridicule, and triumph of its enemies were heaped upon them, with insolent and insufferable arrogance and effrontery?

Were all those sorrows and sufferings and all those sacrifices in vain; these terrible burdens and the lives of our sons, brothers, and fathers laid day after day and month after month, upon our country's altar, all for naught? But more fearful and agonizing still was the ever-recurring question, Shall wrong and injustice and oppression forever triumph? Shall slavery plant its heel upon all these fair fields, and curse forever with its blighting influence, the fairest portion of the heritage of man? Shall the bright escutcheon of American liberty be forever darkened by the awful cruelties of a system of legalized robbery?

CHAPTER XXVI.

In the preceding chapter the writer endeavored to portray the condition of the public mind, and the causes that led thereto, as the country found itself upon the verge of civil war; and also to point out in some measure the evils of a blind subserviency to party, rather than devotion to the claims of country, liberty and justice. The rancor and partisan hate which characterized much of the opposition to the Government in its struggles to put down the rebellion, and the fire in the rear, which, more than all other causes, protracted the war and encouraged the rebels to hold out, ought as a lesson of history to teach the American people that our supreme duty and devotion are due to the country, first, last, and always.

These views are nobly and forcibly set forth in the powerful war speech of Hon. Alex. Meggett, in August, 1862, referred to in my last, and delivered with great power to an immense audience, and published in the papers of that date; a copy of which he has kindly furnished, from which I shall make copious extracts, as expressive of the sentiments of all loyal men at that period, whether Republicans or Democrats, and especially of the earnest, patriotic and comprehensive faith of the speaker in the stability of Republican institutions.

Having introduced his subject with a few appropriate preliminary remarks, Mr. Meggett said: "After nearly half a century of peace—a period which has made for us a splendid and almost romantic history as a people—in an evil hour, goaded by a love of despotism and an insatiable desire for power, the viper of secession has reared its hydra head, and plunged its fangs into the vitals of the Republic. It were easy to indulge in speculations as to the causes which produced this untoward state of events, but this is no time for such reflections. They should be left to calmer and less perilous moments of our national life. Standing as we do on the very verge of destruction to the American experiment of free government on this continent, we, each and all of us, have far less to do with inducing causes than with the fact that danger is at this moment upon us. What seemed at first but a factious sectional resistance to the Federal Government, easy to be quelled, has come to be a powerful and gigantic rebellion against the Constitution and the liberties it guaranteed, calling upon us for the raising and expenditure of vast pecuniary resources, the mustering of millions of men, and the exercise of the highest military skill, to crush its mighty power and thwart its fiendish designs upon our once united Republic.

"And for what cause, we may well ask, is this worst of all wars waged? Has the Government become tyrannical, and trampled upon the sacred and guaranteed rights of those who wage it? Has it refused to enforce equal laws, and conform to the Constitution? Has it imposed unequal and grievous burdens upon them? Has it degenerated into a state of corruption and imbecility, so that it had become unworthy of their affections, refused to listen to their constitutional demands, and turned away from them when they sought its protection? No; not one of all these causes exists in the least degree; but on the contrary, against the public conscience, and yet in the spirit of concession, the majority have long permitted it to extend a special protection to their rights and peculiar institutions. Is it then a war without a cause? Yes! in every way. Yet it has a deep-laid design. It is a war between two diverse civilizations, between two diverse systems of labor. Strange anomaly! It is the old conflict which so often outcrops in history—that of aristocracy and class power against the people and right, waged for the first time under a free government. It is this old 'irrepressible conflict,' in which lust for power seeks to subvert public liberty and tyrannize over the masses. In short, it is a war upon the great experiment of free government upon these western shores, and it must be apparent to every reflecting mind that the triumph of this rebellion will determine at once and forever against the success of that experiment. * * *

Fearless and honest words in times like these are what we need, and it may as well be proclaimed first as last to the ear of every loyal citizen, that this conflict is waged for the purpose of destroying our government, and inaugurating upon its ruins a political system which must sooner or later sweep away the liberties of the people, and which, if established, will seek

> "'To bind, to loose, to build and to destroy!
> In peace; in war to govern; nay, to rule
> Our very fate, like some Satanic being.'

"Then let us rise as good citizens to a true comprehension of the work before us, for it is our own freedom that is endangered. Shall confederate minions triumph in such an inglorious cause? Shall the old flag, the historic emblem of just and equal government, fall before such a foe, to give place to an ensign symbolizing tyranny and brute force?" [Voices— "Never! never!"]

Up to this date the Government had not deemed it necessary to order a draft, and it was hoped the patriotic ardor of the people would fill up the ranks of the Union without resorting to such measures; and the speaker, after referring to the evils and hardships which such a necessity would impose, invokes the patriotism of his hearers in the following eloquent and stirring appeal:

"'Never let it be written in future history that Northern freemen were subjected to draft to fight for the preservation of their liberties. We today are making that history, and let us by deeds and sacrifices gild its pages with the living light of patriotic fire. Let it go down to posterity, that when the imperiled liberties of our country demanded action, sacrifices and blood, all was freely laid upon its altar. Let it be told with conscious pride, by those who come after us, that when the Republic was assailed by ruthless traitors, and about to perish, the people with spontaneous and patriotic devotion rescued it from danger, by heroic deeds of valor on every battlefield, and never for a moment faltered. In one loud and united refrain from every loyal breast, let the sentiment come forth by the love which its citizens cherish for it: 'The Union must and shall be preserved.' * * * *

When a government like ours is in danger, there is but one mode of making it effectual in the work of self-preservation, and that is by every citizen taking his stand fast by it in every position it may assume. We may not like the President's policy in regard to the negro, but I am one who believes that those whom we elect to places of trust, as a general rule, are the best judges, for the time being, of what should or should not be done. Hence, as true citizens, let us always stand where the Government stands, and give it all the force of our individual support."

Referring to the long-talked-of intervention of other powers, Mr. Meggott earnestly pleaded thus:

"The work, fellow-citizens, must be speedily done, or more fearful work and more onerous responsibilities may be imposed upon us. It may not be generally known to you, that nearly three years prior to the war of 1812, when far-seeing statesmen saw the approaching storm, one of the principal European powers sent one of its secret agents to Boston to see upon what terms New England would make a political alliance with it in case of separation from the Union, and to foment discord between its extreme sections. Now, is it less reasonable to suppose, as that same power contemplates with jealousy the rapid growth, national grandeur and increasing power and resources of this Western Republic, that it will lose so favorable an opportunity to humble it if possible. In every view of the case, then, fellow-citizens, we have no time to lose if we would avoid such a calamity, and successfully crush out this atrocious rebellion, and it can only be made successful by a war that shall demonstrate by actual and thorough conquest the superiority of Northern over Southern society and civilization—of free over despotic institutions. Such it should be, and by the help of the God of Battles such it shall be. It should be a war sanctified and made holy by our patriotic efforts to preserve and secure the perpetuity of the Union, and maintain the honor of the Old Flag. * * * Under its graceful folds, still adorned with every star of the Republic, hallowed with Revolutionary memories and still inspiring hope for the future, let us to-day, as loyal citizens, renew our vows of fealty to the Union of these States, and go forth to trample secession under our feet, and teach rebellious States that peace and safety for them lies only in the bosom of the old Republic." [Tremendous cheering.]

Are these lessons such as we should soon forget? Should not the memory of the scenes, sufferings and sacrifices still warn us to be ever watchful and vigilant? Are all those enemies, then so powerful and dangerous, now peaceful, loyal citizens, and worthy supporters of the Constitution and Union, that we should confide power to their hands? Or are many of them still as rebellious as ever, and as ready to wreak their hate and detestation of the Old Flag upon any and all Union-loving men?

CHAPTER XXVII

"Wisconsin in the War of the Rebellion," by Rev. Mr. Love, is undoubtedly the most reliable and comprehensive history of what the State and the people of Wisconsin did during that terrible conflict, to sustain the national honor and crush its foes; but full and complete as the above work is in all its details, their was one department which the author was necessarily compelled to leave untouched. Data were furnished him in regard to each company and regiment, from the time of mustering into service, from which his work was compiled; while all the patriotic exertions of the officers, and of the people, in filling up the ranks of the different companies of each regiment, and providing for their comfort; war meetings, speeches, and many incidents attending their enlistment and departure to the field of strife, furnish material for interesting local history which I have been very anxious to glean up and place before my readers. The faithful and indefatigable author above named, has, it seems to me, left little room for any one to add to the bright record of Wisconsin's heroic soldiers, from the time of their reaching camp to the final mustering out. But prior to that time, in most cases, not even the locality is given where the several companies composing each regiment were enrolled.

To follow each regiment to which the troops from this valley were assigned, through all their marches and sufferings, and recount their achievements and heroic conduct on hundreds of well-fought fields; through all the vicissitudes of those sanguinary battles and final triumph of our cause, however agreeable it might be to me to set these things forth, would, to a great extent, be only a repetition of what others have already recorded, and swell this work to much greater dimensions than it was at first proposed to extend it. I shall confine myself, therefore, to those events and circumstances relating to the initial experience of our soldiers and citizens in enlisting and organizing soldiers for the war, and the difficulties encountered therein.

On the 11th of April, 1861, Fort Sumpter was fired upon by the rebel batteries, and on the 14th day of the same month President Lincoln issued a proclamation calling for seventy-five thousand troops for three months.

One regiment was assigned to Wisconsin as her quota, and she immediately responded, this regiment being mustered into United States service on the 17th of May, and left for the seat of war June 9th. Such was the enthusiasm of the people, that in six days after Governor Randall issued his proclamation, the first regiment was enrolled and ready for service.

Vast numbers in every part of the State were ready to enlist, and many other companies were ready to report, among whom were the Dunn County Pinery Rifles, afterward assigned to the Fifth Regiment, Co. K, Captain William Evans, of Menomonie; C. A. Bayard, First, and J. A. Hill, Second, Lieutenant. The regiment was commanded by Col. Amasa Cobb, and was one of the first of three years' men to take the field; was mustered into U. S. service by Capt. McIntire, of the regular army, on the 13th of July, 1861.

Company K was the first, and, for a long time, the only, organized company from this valley, and owed its existence mainly to the zeal and patriotic efforts of the ladies of Menomonie, one of whom, Miss Eliza Wilson, accompanied the regiment to the field. Yes, the first war meeting that assembled in this valley to organize a company of soldiers to put down the rebellion, was called by the patriotic women of Menomonie, and apropos to the occasion, the Dunn Couty Lumberman of that date, then edited by A. S. Bundy, Esq., truly remarked: "There is no more convincing proof of the terrible earnestness of the whole people in this national struggle, than the heroism evinced by the women of the land."

Although this one company, the Dunn County Pinery Rifles, appears to have been the only one in the Fifth Regiment from this valley, I cannot forbear mentioning some of the many glorious achievements of this veteran regiment. It was this heroic band of Badgers that saved Wheeler's Battery and won the day at the battle of Williamsburg, that with the Sixth and Seventh Maine, and three companies of the Thirty-third New York, less than fifteen hundred men, withstood one of the most furious and terrible onsets of the war, made by six Confederate regiments, more than four thousand of the best chivalry of the South. The battle flag of the Fifth North Carolina was captured by the Fifth Wisconsin, in this battle, and on dress parade two days after, Gen. McClellan complimented the regiment in the handsomest manner, saying, "You have gained honor for your country, your State, and the army to which you belong. Through you, we gained the day, and Williamsburg shall be inscribed on your banner. * * * By your actions and superior discipline, you have gained a reputation which shall be known through the army of the Potomac. Your country owes you its grateful thanks."

But in this and the many other fearfully contested engagements near Richmond and at Antietam, the Fifth was terribly decimated. Captain

Evans was mortally wounded in the action at Golden Farms, Va., and more than half his company had fallen, by wounds and disease, during the first eighteen months of its service. Captain J. M. Mott succeeded to the command of the Rifles, but died of disease on the 26th of July, 1863.

Early in the summer of 1861, a recruiting sergeant of the Thirteenth U. S. Regular Infantry took rooms at the Eau Claire House and enlisted about twenty young men, among whom were Levi Hemingway and several others from Chippewa Falls.

The disastrous results of the "On to Richmond" campaign, in the summer of 1862, alarmed the nation and the people, and stirring appeals for men to enlist were the order of the day.

Receiving a recruiting commission from the Governor, Hollon Richardson, Esq., a rising young lawyer of Chippewa Falls, converted his law office into a recruiting station, and by great personal exertion and the assistance of a few friends, raised a company of men, which was incorporated in the Seventh Regiment as Co. A, of which he was commissioned First Lieutenant on the 13th day of September, 1862.

One of the greatest difficulties to be overcome after enrolling his company, was to procure sustenance and transportation. The river was very low, and no steamboats running; to march raw recruits one hundred miles to Sparta was out of the question. In this dilemma, Adin Randall, always patriotic and full of expedients, came to the aid of the young lieutenant and the country. An old ferry-boat that had given place to a better one, was soon repaired and at the disposal of the government. The ladies of the village had made a beautiful flag for the company, which was duly presented on the day of its departure. Provisions for the trip down the river were contributed by the loyal citizens, and away floated the scow, with the benedictions of a great crowd of friends and patriots resting upon its precious freight—a mixed company of different races and nationalities, but all burning with patriotic zeal and a determination to maintain the honor of the flag under whose folds they had set sail. With few mishaps, such as getting on sand-bars and short rations, the company reached the Mississippi at Read's Landing, from whence the government had made arrangements for their transportation to Madison.

Of the achievements of the Seventh Regiment under its four commanders, Van Dor, Robinson, Finnicum, and Richardson, as part of the Iron Brigade, I need not speak; its history is the history of the Army of the Potomac, and so long as great sacrifices, indomitable courage, and brave deeds are esteemed among men, the history of the Seventh Wisconsin Volunteers during the war of the rebellion will be regarded as one of the brightest on the pages of our nation's 'annals. And our young Lientenant comes in for a full share of the glory of its bright record, being promoted through all the gradations to the position of colonel, and breveted general for meretorious conduct at the battle of Five Forks, in leading the charge of his regiment, carrying its battle-flag aloft with his own hand as he cheered on the men.

CHAPTER XXVIII.

"THE SCARE."

I suppose the organ of caution or fear was given man as a very necessary element in his composition to guard against danger; but when suddenly or unduly excited, and especially from concealed or imaginary evils, sometimes leads to ludicrous misapprehensions or fatal consequences. The very fact that the danger is illy defined, or its point and whence it is to come hid from view, always invests it with indefinable dread, and causes what are known as panics. And panics, whether in monetary and financial circles, in an army or community, are usually fraught with very serious evils. Of the first, the Rhode Island Senator declared there was nothing under heaven so cowardly as five hundred thousand dollars, unless it be a million, which accounts for their frequent occurrence in the business world; and so often have the people of the United States been afflicted with this kind of "scare," that they expect about every ten years or so to be frightened out of their wits by some convulsion in financial affairs.

And the best disciplined armies in the world are subject to the malady. The first Bull Run was lost to us through a panic. The Bible often speaks of great armies suddenly stricken with dismay, and profane history everywhere abounds with instances of even well trained armies seized with unaccountable terror, just as victory was ready to perch upon their standards. But what shall we say when whole communities become paralyzed with fear; when the people in half a dozen counties, covering an area of hundreds of miles in extent, are in a moment seized with dread and fearful apprehension from unseen danger—from a foe whom no one has seen, and which in the very nature of things could have no existence.

Nevertheless, such was the fate of Dunn, Chippewa, Eau Claire, Buffalo, Trempeleau, Jackson, Clark and Monroe counties, on the last Sunday of August, 1862. A few weeks before, at New Ulm and other localities in Minnesota, bands of Sioux Indians, while feigning friendship, had fallen upon the unsuspecting settlers and committed the most horrid barbarities, murdering men, women and children, maiming and torturing those left alive and mutilating the bodies of their victims, and carrying terror and dismay into every remote settlement in the Northwest. Stories of these fiendish cruelties were everywhere circulated, and the timid caught up every whisper of news in regard to the Indians on our frontier, and every hostile indication was a thousand times magnified, until many really supposed that all the Indians on the continent were stealthily assembling in their neighborhood, prepared without a moment's warning to wreak their brutal ferocity upon our defenceless heads. Under such circumstances, the very atmosphere becomes laden with terror, and the slightest intimation of approaching danger is heralded in hot haste from neighbor to neighbor and from village to village, without any definite knowledge or tangible reason for their alarm.

In the early morning of the Sabbath in question, a dense fog rested upon the landscape in all the region named, and terror-stricken pedestrians in several localities, their vision strained to discover danger, imagined that stumps were armed savages and gopher-hills were forts, and forthwith the country was alarmed. Indians had been seen in the big woods with hostile intent; a thousand of the fiends were assembled in the big swamp on Mud Creek, and as many more at Point Bruley, on the Chippewa bottom. Sudden and improbable as such statements were, almost every one put faith in them, and ran to his nearest neighbor to know what he should do. People in the country rushed with frantic haste to the villages, carrying with them everything in the shape of weapons for offensive or defensive operations, while in the city everything was in a state of consternation and dread; but all were resolved to defend their homes to the last.

At Chippewa Falls Rev. Bradley Phillips was chosen captain of the army of defense, with headquarters at the church. Pickets were stationed at every vulnerable point, armed with rifles, shotguns, pitchforks, scythes and spades; patrols guarded the streets at every corner, and squads of men marched from point to point, where danger was most imminent; but the only enemy discovered was in the shape of sundry jugs of whisky, which before morning laid many a gallant soldier low on the field of battle.

At Eau Claire, the alarm being sounded early in the day, the churches were instantly emptied, and the worshipers, like the puritans of old, flew to arms, resolved individually, no doubt, that as "the earth is the Lord's and the fullness thereof," and as he had given it to them, his saints, to possess it, they would defend their homes to the last. A large body of citizen soldiers were at once enrolled, who, by virtue of a commission from the Governor some years before, appointing Wm. Pitt Bartlett, Esq., an officer in the militia of this department of the State, with the rank of Major, would rightfully be subject to the command of that official; but recognizing the extreme danger, and the necessity of greater military experience to give prompt direction to the forces, so ardent and yet so green, that gentleman deferred to the wishes of his fellow citizens in the selection of a veteran soldier to command the citizen brigade in this emergency. But where could such a person be found? He was here at the call of his adopted country. A German had joined his fortunes with Walker in his filibustering expedition against Nicaragua, and like him had lost, but unlike him had saved his head, and, imitating the exiled Whaley, came to the rescue of the beleaguered village with all the experience of a trained soldier.

E. R. Hantzsch was a rigid disciplinarian. The best troops in the world could accomplish nothing without discipline, and his first business was to organize and drill the command; and ordering all to report instantly, on Union Square, he was soon surrounded by a rabble rout, impatient to be led against the foe. Not so with the commander. He knew that discretion was the better part of valor; and after organizing his forces and appointing his subordinates, his next concern was to see that each and every detachment was well supplied with rations for the campaign.

Fine-cut to fill their meerschaums, and lager, were the principal items of inquiry with the German element; but whisky was the great staple with the river boys. Many ludicrous scenes and circumstances occurred in arming and equipping the different squads, and in posting them for the night; and as rumors of the enemy's approach were constantly coming in, confusion, alarm and insubordination were to be expected, especially when we consider that for many miles around the farmers, with their wives and children, had thronged pell mell to the village, and filled every nook and corner of every public house; and between squalling children, frightened mothers and half-sober men a pretty lively time was kept up. But the night wore away, and the morning revealed no enemy, save that subtle foe whose victims were laid hors du combat beside every camp-fire.

Many other villages were equally alarmed, and just as prompt to defend their homes; and all that seems wanting to make a bright page in our valley's history is the enemy.

CHAPTER XXIX.

"THE EAGLE REGIMENT."

Perhaps no regiment of volunteers was mustered in the United States service during the war, that performed more service, marched as many miles and did as much hard fighting as the Eighth Wisconsin.

It seems to have been constantly in motion; and being one of the first in the field from this State, and having the first company organized in Eau Claire, and that the company which furnished the live eagle, it will supply material for some interesting statements in this work.

Early in August, 1861, John E. Perkins, Receiver in the Land Office in this place, received a recruiting commission from Governor Randall, and being assisted by Seth Pierce, Frank McGuire, Thomas G. Butler and Victor Wolf, who enlisted, and several patriotic citizens, though without any offer of bounties, organized the first company of volunteers for the war from this county. It was composed largely of men from the country, and quite a number from Lafayette in Chippewa county.

Speaking of the battle of Iuka and Corinth, the Rev. Mr. Love says: "The eagle of the Eighth Regiment took a noticeable part in this battle. That eagle was originally captured by the Indian 'Chief Sky,' in the northern part of Wisconsin, near the Flambeau river, a branch of the Chippewa. The 'Eau Claire Eagles' brought him to the Eighth Regiment at Madison. Captain Perkins, afterward killed at the battle of Farmington, gave the name 'Old Abe' to the eagle, in memory of the services of Abraham Lincoln, and the bird gave the name 'Eagle' to the regiment. He generally rode on the banners of the regiment in all its marches, and manifested a singular sagacity. In time of battle he kept his place on his perch, upon the colors, and showed the highest interest and excitement, often jumping up and down, spreading his pinions, and uttering his wild eagle screams."

The name of the Indian, "Chief Sky," and the locality in which the eagle was taken, as given by Mr. Love, are probably correct; but it is proper to state that S. S. McCann, the old pioneer and soldier, bought him of the Indian at Chippewa City, town of Eagle Point, Chippewa county, and brought him to Eau Claire while Company C was filling up. Mills Jeffries bought him of McCann and presented him to the company, who immediately changed their title from "Eau Claire Badgers" to that of "Eagles."

The officers of the regiment were very anxious to appropriate not only the title, but the bird itself, to their ownership; but Captain Wolf and other company officers thought it was sufficient to confer the title upon the regiment, while the company should own and control the eagle; which they continued to do until the fall of 1864, when the veterans received a furlough home, when Captain Wolf, on behalf of the company, presented the noble bird to Governor Lewis, for the State of Wisconsin.

Captain William J. Dawes, who was severely wounded on the first day of the battle. October 3d, 1862, says: "The same volley that did the mischief cut the cord of Old Abe, who sat on his perch viewing the scene, and slowly raising himself on his broad pinions, floated off over the rebel lines until I lost sight of him. I was gathered up in a blanket and carried from the field, hardly knowing which most to deplore, our defeat, my own disaster, or the loss of our guardian ægis. Our broken regiment fell back and passed me, as I was slowly carried along, and raising my head to salute them, what joy filled my heart when I saw our noble bird in his proper place. And it was a sure omen of the terrible slaughter made among the rebels the next day. Our eagle accompanied us on the bloody field, and I heard prisoners say they would give more to capture the eagle of the Eighth Wisconsin than to take a whole brigade of men."

Captain Perkins, with his Eagles, was assigned to the position in the Eigth Regiment as Co. C, and was mustered into the service of the United States on the 4th day of September, 1861, under the superintendence of Colonel Robert C. Murphy, and immediately left Camp Randall for active service in the field.

At St. Louis, the live eagle created immense enthusiasm, it being the first Wisconsin regiment that had been ordered to that department. Its field of operations during the fall and winter was Missouri and Northern Arkansas. It was at the capture of Island No. Ten, in April, 1862, and for gallantry displayed in this campaign, General Pope ordered Island No. Ten and New Madrid inscribed on their banners. Up the Tennessee on the first of May, and on the 9th took part in the battle of Farmington, where Captain Perkins lost his life, and was succeeded in command by that veteran soldier and accomplished officer, Captain Victor Wolf.

On the 28th the regiment was brought into a hand-to-hand fight, to save a battery, and were complimented on the field for their bravery by Generals Plummer and Tyler.

The Eigth was kept continually moving, in Tennessee and Mississippi, thence back into Missouri and Kansas, thence to the siege and capture of Vicksburg, at Nashville under General Thomas, and finally, after the veterans had their furlough home, taking the eagle with them, and filling up their decimated ranks, were sent down the Mississippi to New Orleans and thence to Mobile, in the siege of which the regiment did its last hard fighting, losing two men at Fort Blakely on the 27th of March, 1865, and were mustered out at Demopolis, Alabama, the following September. The eagle still lives at the Capitol of our noble State, hale and hearty. During the war, the regiment lost in action, thirty-five; died of wounds, fourteen; died of disease, two hundred and one; died by accident, five; making in all, two hundred and fifty-five; twenty-one of whom, including Captain Perkins, were from Co. C.

Among the reasons assigned by General McClellan for delaying active operations against the enemy, in the fall of 1861, was the want of cavalry, and orders were immediately issued to the authorities of each State to recruit cavalry regiments to supply the want. In November of that year, Arthur M. Sherman, of Eau Claire, returned from Madison with authority to recruit a company for the Second Regiment, then filling up under the superintendence of Colonel C. C. Washburn. On some account or other, the undertaking met with less encouragement from the citizens than it deserved, and some even manifested opposition, and circulated reports that the government had countermanded the order for cavalry, and if men enlisted as such, they would not be mounted. But calling to his assistance some determined young men, among whom were Israel Burbank, Thomas J. Nary, George E. Grout, Len. L. Lancaster, and Milo B. Wyman, of Eau Claire, and James LeRoy, of Chippewa Falls, the company was ready with eighty-seven enlisted men by the first of January, 1862, and was mustered into the United States service soon after, and were mounted at Benton Barrack, Mo., in March.

The commissioned officers of the company, at first, were Arthur M. Sherman, Captain; Israel B. Burbank, First, and Thos. Nary, Second, Lieutenant.

Like most of the Western cavalry regiments, the Second Wisconsin was divided into batalions and scattered over the departments of the

Mississippi and the Tennessee, guarding railroads, fighting guerrillas, making raids into the enemy's country, doing provost duty, seizing cotton, and harassing the rebels generally. Stationed in malarious and unhealthy localities during the summer of 1872, the mortality from disease was very great, and much suffering was caused by their confinement in bad hospitals. Many amusing and some thrilling incidents are related of sudden attacks and hand-to-hand conflicts with guerrillas, while stationed in Missouri, Arkansas, Mississippi, and other Southern States. one of which is too good to be lost. Among those who came with Le Roy from Chippewa Falls and joined Co. L, to which our company was assigned, was a Frenchman, named Louis Blair, a first-class river pilot, both before and since the war. On one occasion, Louis made one of a party of six to reconnoiter a certain road leading from their post into the interior, just then infested by guerrillas, a strong party of whom came suddenly upon our little squad, some of whom escaped by flight, but Louis, being wounded, must surrender or fight. I will try to tell the rest in his own language as related to me during the past summer.

"I know dat guerrilla reb too well to tink dey keep dare word wid me if I surrender-r-r; and don't been all, I don't been made dat kind of stuff, an' I was tole him he might cut me up, but surrender, no sir-ee. A dozen of de cowardly villain den make for me, an' you see dat scar on my face, an' dat one on my neck?" Then, uncovering his back and breast, he showed scar after scar where great saber wounds had been inflicted. "An' dare, an' dare," said he, "dey cut an' gash me, an' all de time dey say, 'Surrender, you d—n Dutch Yankee.' But by an' by our boy was come, and den de reb he was shoot me right dare," pointing to another scar. "When our boy dey come, dey tink I was dead, but I don't been goin' die dat way."

The most severe fighting done by the Second Cavalry was with Gen. Grierson, in his great raid into Mississippi, in 1864. Its last work was done in Texas, where, at Austin, on the 15th of November, 1865, they were mustered out of service, having served four years lacking one month, and lost, in killed, wounded, and by disease, two hundred and eight of their number, thirty of whom were of Co. L.

CHAPTER XXX

At the beginning of the war, our valley contained numerous settlements composed mostly of Germans and Irish, but very few of the present extensive Scandinavian population had then located here, and those were widely separated, so that when the call was made for the Fifteenth Regiment, to be composed exclusively of that nationality, it was found a difficult task to enlist a company, and only one individual was brave enough to undertake it.

O. R. Dahl was educated at a military school in Norway, served eight years in the engineers with credit to himself as an officer in that department, but resigned and emigrated with his family to this country in 1853, found his way to, and was one of the first settlers in, the town of Bloomer, Chippewa county, in 1857, and encountered all the hardships and privations incident to all who removed to that remote corner during that terrible winter of '56-57. Called to mourn the loss by death of the mother of his children in 1861, he made such provision for them as he could, and immediately tendered his services to the government, and receiving a captain's recruiting commission from Governor Randall, he set himself to work and enlisted thirty-two good men for Co. H, Fifteenth Regiment, whom he took to Camp Randall, where, at the organization of the company, he was defeated by two votes for the captaincy.

But nothing daunted, he shouldered his rifle and served seventeen months in the ranks, until the battle of Stone River, when, for meritorious conduct, he was promoted to the position of First Lieutenant in Co. B, same regiment, and the next day appointed Topographical Engineer in the First Brigade, Second Division, Army of the Cumberland, and served in that capacity with the entire satisfaction of his superiors through all the subsequent campaigns of that veteran army; was in all its hard-fought battles until the 13th day of March, 1864, when, while making a military survey, and separated from the main army, he was taken prisoner, and thenceforth was subjected to all the horrors and sufferings that characterized the treatment of Union prisoners throughout the South, until relieved by the victorious Union arms in 1865. His sketch of the battle of Stone River, scenes of life in Southern prisons, and map of Chippewa county are his best published works of art. He is one of the one hundred and forty-four, out of one thousand and three men who made up the roster of the Fifteenth Regiment when it left Madison, who returned from that fearful struggle into which so many of our adopted fellow-citizens entered to save the nation's life. On hearing of his father's capture, his oldest son, Anthony, immediately enlisted and served in the army of the Potomac until the end of the war. The family are now residing at the city of Chippewa Falls.

SIXTEENTH REGIMENT.

Two companies were recruited in this valley for this regiment, the first company (G) at Eau Claire, and called the Chippewa Valley Guards, in November and December, 1861, under the direction of Captain John R. Wheeler; the other was consolidated with Co. I, and Co. H was recruited at the same place in November and December of the same year.

The regimental organization was effected under the direction of Col. Benjamin Allen, of North Pepin, and on the 21st day of January, 1862, was mustered into the U. S. service at Camp Randall, and after a few weeks drill left the State for active service, and reached St. Louis on 14th of March, and Pittsburg Landing, Tennessee, on the 20th; were assigned to picket duty on the 5th of April following, and at daybreak the next morning commenced the terrible battle of Shiloh, with our raw Sixteenth in the front ranks of the army, and during all that and the following day were constantly exposed to the enemy's fire, and sustained a loss of two hundred and forty-five men in killed and wounded. The regiment subsequently took part in the battle of Holly Springs and the second battle of Corinth, and soon after moved down the Mississippi from Memphis to Vicksburg, where, on the 5th of February, 1864, when three full companies from home, F, H, and K, joined them, and the veterans, having re-enlisted, were given a furlough home, and arrived in Madison on the 16th of March, 1864. Having re-organized and filled up its ranks, it was assigned to the First Brigade, Third Division, Seventeenth Army Corps, and left Cairo to join the forces of General Sherman in his Atlanta campaign.

During the summer and fall of 1863, steps were taken by the general government for a draft in all the States, under the act of Congress, approved March 6th, 1863, and under the call of the President for three hundred thousand men in October following, fourteen thousand nine hundred and thirty-five was the quota required from this State, but as the act contained the commutation clause, the result was that the government obtained eight hundred and eighty drafted men and substitutes, and $1,528,300 from five thousand and eighty persons who paid money rather than enlist.

The government soon saw the error, but to retrieve the damage resulting from so unwise a provision was no easy matter, as nothing could more effectually abate the enthusiasm and patriotic ardor of the people than this commutation of three hundred dollars for a soldier. In some localities, great sacrifices had been made to secure volunteers, for which no credit was given, and towns and villages already thrice decimated were called upon for the same number of recruits, in proportion to the original number of men able to bear arms, as districts that had done nothing, causing a great deal of dissatisfaction. Then, too, the poor man unable to pay the three hundred dollars, felt that great injustice was done him; and, however patriotic he might feel, he could not easily reconcile himself to the idea that his life must be pitted against three hundred dollars. Then, too, the term "conscript" soon became to be regarded as one of opprobrium, by many, and much prejudice existed, not so much against the service, as the manner of entering it.

Before this period, in the fall of 1862, John Klatt, formerly the ferryman at Chippewa Falls, who had enlisted with Lieut. Richardson, finding himself unable to do duty as a private, on account of physical disability, returned home, and having been educated as a soldier in Germany, his native land, determined to raise a company, which was assigned as Co. K, to the Thirtieth Regiment, and he was elected Captain. The regiment was officered as follows: Daniel J. Dill, Colonel; Edward M. Bartlett, of Durand, Lieutenant Colonel; Theodore C. Spencer, of Eau Claire, Adjutant; Edwin O. Baker, of Luna, Assistant Surgeon. Napoleon C. Greer was another one of its captains. This company was raised in Eau Claire county, with Charles Buckman, of Augusta, First Lieutenant.

This regiment, it will be remembered, was sent to chastise the Indians on our northwestern frontier. Rather an inglorious, but necessary, fatiguing, and hazardous campaign, attended with contant alarms and great hardships, and the boys were glad when they were ordered to report at Louisville, Ky., though still called to wage war against a contemptible and treacherous foe, for the guerrillas of the South were little less barbarous, and even more perfiduous, than the untamed red-skins of the wilderness.

It was immediately succeeding the depressed and unfavorable state of public feeling occasioned by the failure of the draft in October and November, 1863, as before related, that Captain John R. Wheeler, of Co. G, Sixteenth Regiment, returned to Eau Claire, to recruit its depleted ranks. Recruiting sergeants from all the companies previously organized in the valley, were also here, and it was necessary that the most active operations should go forward to obtain volunteers and avoid another impending draft. War meetings were called in every locality, and prominent citizens, with few exceptions, came forward with substantial aid for the families of married men who enlisted, while county and town boards gave assurance that no soldier's family should be neglected.

R. F. Wilson, chairman of the county board of Eau Claire county, at a public meeting, gave a positive assurance that he would attend personally to the wants of every soldier's family in the county. The clergymen of almost every religious denomination put forth extraordinary efforts at the various meetings called for that purpose, to arouse the patriotism of the people and procure enlistments, and the wonted enthusiasm was once more awakened. With such demonstrations, Captain Wheeler's company was soon filled up, and another, under the leadership of D. C. Whipple, who resigned the office of Sheriff that he might serve his country better in the field, was at the close of the year ready to report. The weather was terrible cold, and on their way to Sparta the men suffered intensely. The new company here elected their officers: D. C. Whipple, Captain; J. T. Tinker, First, and M. Grover, Second Lieutenant, and were mustered into the U. S. service December 31st, 1863, and soon moved to Camp Randall, uniformed, and drilled until February 26th, 1864, when, the regiment being complete, they were ordered South. Just before starting the men raised money and presented Captain Whipple a fine sword. Orderly Allen, afterwards Lieutenant, has kindly furnished an account of what the company experienced and accomplished from this time forward. He says:

"From the cold snows of the North to the balmy skies and peach blossoms of Vicksburg, was a pleasant change. After doing picket duty at Black River bridge for a month we were ordered back to Vicksburg, from thence north on transports up the river, passing Fort Pillow a few hours after the massacre by Forrest. Company H, and two other companies, were landed at Columbus to assist the colored troops in defending the fort against an attack momentarily expected from that chivalrous general, which, however, he failed to make.

"After two weeks of hard duty, we joined the command at Cairo, then preparing to join Sherman's army in Northern Georgia. From Cairo to Clifton, Tennessee, on transports, and thence by forced marches, three hundred miles across that State, Alabama, and Georgia taking position on the left of the grand army, before Kenesaw Mountain, June 10th, 1874. We suffered terribly during this march, and many gave out by the way, among whom were Lieutenants Grover and Tinker, who went to the hospital.

"From this time to the 10th of September, three months, we were constantly under arms, marching, skirmishing, and fighting, our first exploits being in the battles about Kenesaw, where we lost several men; then hotly pursuing the rebels night and day, until they took refuge in their trenches before Atlanta.

"We lay on our arms on the night of the 20th of July, the enemy strongly fortified in front, and just at break of day we were ordered to the charge. Grave doubts and fears were expressed, as there were so many new recruits in the regiment, whether it would not be better to put an old and tried regiment in our place, but after a short consultation it was decided to keep us where we were, for if the charge was made, the older soldiers who were supporting them would have no confidence in them, and they would lose all confidence in themselves. The result showed the wisdom of the conclusion. It was a trying moment when Col. Fairchild shouted the order, 'Fix bayonets, forward!' Out of the timber, down a ravine, up and across a field, over their works, driving out Hardee's veteran's and taking some prisoners, was but the work of a moment. Lieut. Col. Reynolds coming quickly up, said to the new men, 'You are all veterans now, boys.'

"The General commanding the brigade sent word to General Blair, saying, 'The Wisconsin boys did nobly,' but it was praise dearly earned. Colonel Fairchild, Lieutenant Colonel Reynolds, Captain John Wheeler, and many other officers wounded, but fortunately none killed. Co. H lost two killed and seven wounded. Captain Whipple particularly distinguished himself in this action, and a somewhat laughable incident occurred during the charge. So great was the excitement but little attention was paid to his efforts to keep the men in line with the colors, but finally becoming terribly in earnest, and shouting above the roar and din of battle, he sang out, 'If you don't know what line on the colors means, keep your eyes on that flag.' We held the works all day under fire, and strengthened them at night; but about noon the next day the enemy burst on our left, and was crushing that part of our army like an egg-shell, coming boldly on until they reached the works held by the Twelfth and Sixteenth Wisconsin, who repulsed them in six successive terrible charges, first in front, then in rear, and changing sides of their works as many times. Captain Whipple showed himslf the same hero here as the day before, but the strain was too much; constant fatigue and anxiety, and the suffering from his wound, sent him to the ambulance, and Orderly Sergeant Allen took command, there being no commissioned officer with the company. Being ordered to another part of the field by a forced march, Captain Whipple again joined us and assisted in repulsing several charges, but was soon obliged to go to field hospital, and E. W. Allen, just commissioned, took command.

"The final battles of Jonesborough and Lovejoy's Station closed the campaign, and with light hearts we spread our tents in Atlanta, September 10th, 1864. Our company was reduced from ninety to twenty muskets, so severe had been the work. Here we received a quantity of good things, pickles, berries, condensed milk, etc., from kind friends in Eau Claire, for which, if ever men felt grateful, we did. But we did not rest long. Hood had gone north and was eating our crackers, so we were after him again, and for five days and nights we chased him over mountains, rivers, and valleys, and then were ordered back to Atlanta again, where, for the first time in eight months, we received our pay, and voted for President, thirty-four for Lincoln and two for McClellan. That was the kind of men that composed Co. H." Writing of this campaign, Captain Whipple says: "Allow me to say a word for Lieutenant Allen, the youngest officer in the regiment. When commissioned, he took his place beside the older officers, performing his duty faithfully and bravely, and never missed a day to the close of the war." "On the 14th of November, we started with Sherman on his grand march to the sea, and a month of constant marching brought us to the gates of Savannah, where, after a short resistance, we marched, flags flying, into the city. Starting again, we took Pocotaligo, out on the Charleston railroad, which fell in consequence, and next, our company was at the burning of Columbia, then Cheraw, Fayetteville, Bentonville, and Goldsborough were taken, and, after a few days rest, waiting for our absent men to come up, a forced march brought us to Raleigh.

"When Captain Whipple, who had been sent home sick, rejoined us, how glad we were to see him! Here the war virtually closed. The fighting was over, but we were a long way from home, but marching was easy now, for every day brought us nearer our loved ones there. On to Petersburg, Richmond, and Washington, where, on the 23d of May, we took part in that grandest pageant ever seen in America, the grand review; Mrs. Sherman throwing bouquets at our tattered and worn colors. We were soon transferred to Louisville, Ky., where, on the 4th day of July, 1865, General Sherman took a final farewell of us, and a few days after we were mustered out, sent to Madison, received our final pay and discharge on August 21st, 1865, and with light hearts started for home, never more, it is to be hoped, to be called to take up arms for our beloved country against internal foes."

I have given the foregoing almost verbatim, partly because so few have taken pains to send me their war experience on paper, and because it is a concise narration of one of the most remarkable campaigns in the history of the world.

To close this, how happy I am to introduce another welcome communication, from the facile pen of the Rev. Dr. Alfred Brunson, whose interest not only in the history of the State, but in all that pertains to the honor and welfare of our country, is unabated, though his hand trembles with age as he traces patriotic thoughts on paper.

Prairie du Chien, Nov. 28th, 1874.

Thos. E. Randall, Esq.,

DEAR SIR—I read your numbers on history, etc., with deep interest. The twenty-ninth number is now at hand, but one thing about the Eagle, and the good service he rendered his country, you must have overlooked. You remember the Sanitary Fair got up in Chicago, towards the close of the rebellion, for the benefit of the sick and wounded. The Eagle, at the time, had a national fame, and to aid in raising funds upon that occasion, a picture of the Eagle was struck off by millions and sold for ten cents a piece, resulting in the receipt of over $10,000, which was applied to the objects of the Fair. By this means the Eagle contributed to the relief of sixteen thousand or more sick and wounded soldiers; more, perhaps, than any one man did, though it took benevolent patriots to make him so. When the Fair was gotten up, a friend of mine wrote to me from the State of New York, for one of Old Abe's pictures. How many thousands of others did so to their friends, I know not, but the incident shows the national fame of the Eagle.

Another incident: When that Eagle company was mustered into the service, and the regiment started for the front, an editor, speaking of it, alluded specially to the company that came from the pinery on the Chippewa, and said, "they are accustomed to camp life, are hardy, can endure the hardships of the war, and from habit can sleep on a saw log, if necessary." Respectfully yours,

ALFRED BRUNSON.

CHAPTER XXXI.

TWENTY-FIFTH REGIMENT.

Of all the regiments sent to the field from this State during the war, perhaps none did more hard fighting, or was more constantly in motion, than the Twenty-fifth Infantry. Recruited mainly in the river counties, between Lake Pepin and La Crosse, and organizing at Camp Solamon, in that city, on the 4th day of September, 1862, under the direction of Col. Milton Montgomery and Lieut. Col. J. M. Rusk. Its first operations were against the Indians in Minnesota. Co. G of this regiment was recruited in this valley by Virus W. Dorwin, afterwards elected its Captain, assisted by the patriotic citizens of Durand and vicinity, and its decimated ranks were frequently refilled from the same locality. Like the Eagle regiment, the Twenty-fifth was always in motion, and whether fighting Indians in Minnesota or guerrillas in Missouri, Arkansas, Tennessee, or Mississippi, or leading the vanguard at the siege and capture of Vicksburg, could always be counted on as a thorougly disciplined and reliable regiment; and when Sherman's grand army was organized for the Atlanta campaign, it shared in almost every one of the many hard-fought battles which led to the reduction of that stronghold and the march to the sea. The fame and efficiency of this regiment is due, no doubt, in some measure, to the able officers who commanded it; but no less so to the indomitable bravery of the fourteen hundred and forty-four loyal men composing its rank and file.

Three other companies were organized in this valley, all having their headquarters at Eau Claire. The first company, K, Thirty-sixth Regiment, was recruited under the call of the President for five hundred thousand men, in February and March, 1864, through the efforts of Captain Warren Graves, and Lieutenants E. A. Galloway and Joseph R. Ellis, all of Pleasant Valley, in this county, and nearly all the men were from the country towns in Eau Claire, Chippewa, and Dunn counties. It was a brave and hardy company of men, but the regiment was the most unfortunate of any that left this State, and of the eighty-eight men in Captain Graves' company, only one returned unscathed. W. W. Crandall, of La Fayette, Chippewa county, was neither sick, wounded, nor taken prisoner, while every other man in the company was either killed, wounded, taken prisoner, or sent to hospital. Captain Graves was wounded, sent to hospital, and died. Lieutenant Galloway was killed while leading an assault on the enemy's works. Many were taken prisoners in the deep railroad cut south of Petersburg, and suffered horrors a thousand times worse than death, in rebel prisons, and many painful circumstances grew out of the long suspense and almost hopeless uncertainty as to their fate.

One instance among many I will relate. Patrick O'Donohue, of Pleasant Valley, in this county, enlisted in this company, leaving a wife and a numerous and interesting family of children, mostly daughters. At the battle of Ream's Station, Va., on the 25th day of August, 1864, while in the deep railroad cut, he was taken prisoner but reported as killed, which painful news soon reached his family, and for many months he was mourned as dead, but in time vague rumors of his imprisonment in a Southern prison pen came, causing hope, fear, dread, and anxious solicitude to alternate in the fond hearts of his loved ones at home. Winter succeeded autumn, and still no positive tidings; nothing but dreary, desolate uncertainty and suspense, while he suffered not alone the terrible hunger and privations of Salisbury and Andersonville, but the ever-harrowing thought that all his efforts to communicate with his loved ones at home were unavailing. But this is only one of many thousand cases that occurred during the war, and reaching the loyal people in every hamlet and in the remotest corners of our severely-tried country.

To close this account of the Thirty-sixth, I will extract a few paragraphs from a letter addressed to His Excellency, Governor James T. Lewis, by the brigade commander, dated Nov. 1st, 1865, which shows what material the regiment was composed of.

"As your Excellency knows, this regiment came here new. They were rushed into the breach untried, in a campaign which has been fiercer and more bloody than Napoleon's.

"The Thirty-sixth made its debut in a battle of which the London Times says that England could not lose one-tenth the number.

"On reaching the field, the Thirty-sixth took up their position as steadily as the oldest, and in all operations in mass were undistinguishable for compactness and celerity from the best troops.   *   *   *
I determined to take the position across Hatcher's Run. The order to charge had just been given, when the enemy opened heavily on my right and rear, and advanced upon my main line in heavy masses. His forces enclosed three sides, and with worse troops the situation would have been menacing, and to crown all, a heavy body of rebels were thrown upon my rear (the fourth side). A swift face by the rear rank and wheeling, charged by the New Jersey brigade, cleared my right flank, but from the threatening body in my rear it remained for the Thirty-sixth Wisconsin

to relieve me. Captain Fisk threw them into line and dashed off the enemy. It was a short fight; that rebel brigade instantaneously crumbled and was destroyed, being mostly captured, to a number, with army colors and officers, three times greater than the Thirty-sixth. Having cleaned my rear, the regiment then returned to its place in line, and behaved equally well until their return to camp.

T. W. EGAN,
Brigade Commander."

In February, 1865, Professor Shadrach Hall, of the Methodist Seminary, West Eau Claire, received a recruiting commission, and, aided by the citizens and the powerful eloquence of the clergymen of Eau Claire, he enlisted a company, which was assigned to the Fifth Wisconsin as a body of new recruits at the time of its organization, and participated in almost every battle which immediately led to the fall of Richmond and the surrender of Lee's army, and when the charge was sounded for the assault on the rebel lines near Petersburg, on the 2d of April, 1865, the Fifth occupied the extreme front, and its colors were the first planted on the enemy's works.

And the last company organized in the valley was recruited by H. M. Stocking, of the Free Press, which was assigned to the Forty-eighth Regiment. Its scene of operations was first Missouri, and then the Indian Plains of Kansas and Colorado; replete with hardships, but the fighting was over. Nevertheless, this regiment was retained in the field until the 9th of December, 1865, and a portion until the following March.

CHAPTER XXXII.

Contemplating a chapter made up of stirring incidents and accidents in relation to the war and the action taken by our citizens and soldiers in it, and with that view having accumulated quite a number of items, which were carefully laid away for the proper occasion, and among them several letters from valued correspondents who have taken pains to furnish information for this work, but which in the changes and derangements incident to the season, got mislaid and cannot be found. I mention this as an apology to those who have so kindly lent their aid to assist me.

Amongst them was one, the loss of which I very much regret, giving an account of two friends who enlisted from the neighborhood of Durand, to fill up the depleted ranks of one of our brave regiments in the field, and of the bravery and self-sacrifice made by one to shield his friend from danger. How I regret that I cannot give the name of so gallant a soldier and comrade so generous!

It was in one of those fierce and terrible onsets, such as the chivalry made in the first part of the rebellion, when our boys were told to lie down and await the shock, that our two friends lay partly sheltered from the hail by a small log or stick, the one nearest, however, being exposed above and below, when, quick as thought, the one in the rear climbed over his fellow and placed himself in his friend's exposed position.

To the inquiry why he thus coveted a position so dangerous, he replied: "You have a young wife and many dear friends to mourn your loss, and to whom your life is valuable, but there is not a soul to mourn my death, no wife or children, parents, brothers, or sisters. Alone in the world, what is my life, compared with yours? Let me shield you with my body, that your life may be spared to the loved ones at home, and if one of us must die, let it be me." Pythias pleaded for the privilege of dying instead of his friend Damon, but here was a man who forced himself between his friend and a hail-storm of bullets!

The accounts thus far given of troops furnished from this valley, have taken cognizance only of organized bodies; from files of the Eau Claire Free Press, kindly furnished me by the Hon. G. E. Porter, covering the period of his editorship, and coming down to the spring of 1864, I am enabled to note the action and enlistment of several smaller and unorganized companies, and to cull from its columns many interesting events and circumstances connected with the war.

The following quotations are made with little regard to order and arrangement, as expressing the state of the public mind, and the feeling developed by the incipient and subsequent stages of the war.

FRIDAY, APRIL 19TH, THE WAR BEGAN.

The terrible fact now stares us full in the face, lovers of the Union must meet the sudden though unexpected responsibilities which devolve upon them. This is no time for crimination or recrimination. Every Union-loving heart will swell with emotion as it contemplates the unutterable baseness and dishonor of those who have inaugurated civil war, and we greatly mistake the tone and temper of all good citizens, South as well as North, if they do not firmly resolve to aid when duty calls, in executing a terrible retribution upon the rebels. Let the watchword be, "The Union must and shall be preserved."

THE WAR FEELING IN EAU CLAIRE.

There is no mistaking the deep and intense feeling that pervades all classes of our citizens in view of the exciting news from the South—the bombardment of Fort Sumpter.

The Union feeling is unmistakable everywhere, and we believe that when duty calls, this and adjoining counties will furnish as many strong arms and brave hearts as would the same number of inhabitants elsewhere.

STATE OF THE COUNTRY.

Dispatches from all parts of the country informs us that the hearts of the people are with the government. Impromptu meetings are held everywhere, and the united voice of the North cries out for vengeance. There are but two parties now—patriot or traitor.

The bombardment of Fort Sumpter and its surrender is given in this number of the Free Press, also the call of President Lincoln for seventy-five thousand men, and this:

"The Charleston (S. C.) Mercury boasts that 'nearly all the United States forts in the South have fallen.' Yes, and, we are sorry to say, like the poor man in the Bible, they have fallen among thieves.—[Louisville Journal."

A stirring call for an old-fashioned Fourth of July celebration follows, with a hope that the slumbering fires of patriotism may be kindled in this valley.

APRIL 26TH, 1861, PATRIOTS AROUSE.

There will be a meeting of the patriotic citizens of Eau Claire and vicinity, at Reed's Hall, on Monday evening, 29th inst., to get up a company to go and fight the battles of our country, under the call of the Governor for men to fill Wisconsin's quota in the armies of the Republic. Speaking and singing may be expected.

With one exception, this was the first war meeting in this valley, and in the local columns of the same date is "Three cheers for John Taylor," who had just returned from Milwaukee resolved to enlist a company for the First Regiment, and the editor adds, "Captain Taylor is just the man to do it."

The meeting came off according to call, N. B. Boyden, Chairman, J. G. Callahan, Secretary, and was addressed by Messrs. Barnes, Meggett, Davis, Bartlett, Barrett, Woodworth, Taylor, Porter, Whipple, Wilson,

Stillman, and McNair   Two bands discoursed martial music. Then come the names of sixty-one men who enrolled themselves as soldiers, amongst which I find the names of A. S. Bostwick, A. C. Ellis, Robert Lackey, John E. Stillman, J. D. McCauley, W. P. Bartlett, honored names still amongst us, but in the roll are many who, although the company as an organized body never left the valley, could not rest until—bearing their own expenses to the seat of war—they had joined themselves to the army of freedom and laid down their lives in fighting its battles.

War, too, has its poetic side, and here is a dignified specimen from the other side, found in the columns of the New Orleans Delta;

> Let Lincoln send his forces here!
> We'll lick them like blue blazes,
> And send them yelping back where
> They sing their nigger praises.
>
> We whaled the hungry cusses out
> At Charleston like the dickens;
> And not content with Sumpt-erous fare,
> They sha'n't e'en have the Pickens.

How like the White League bombast of to-day this sounds!

The company before referred to organized on the 10th of May, and chose for its officers Captain John Taylor, First Lieutenant A. S. Bostwick, and Orderly Sergeant A. C. Ellis.

It took the name of "Eau Claire Badgers." A noble looking body of men, says the Free Press, but just look for a moment at the next item, taken from the Mobile Advertiser, while speaking of Union soldiers: "Such men as marched through Baltimore, white slaves, peddling wretches, small change knaves, levied by Lincoln for the honor of being slaughtered by gentlemen." Vainglorious Southern Chivalry, how art thou fallen!

No provision having been made by the government for the sustenance or transportation of the Badgers, after an ineffectual attempt to support them by private contribution, they were disbanded, some returning to their homes, and others, as before stated, paying their own way, Captain Taylor among them.

AUGUST 22D, 1861.—FROM THE MADISON PATRIOT.

Miss Eliza T. Wilson is the "Vivandiere" of our Wisconsin Fifth. She is a fine-appearing, intelligent young lady, daughter of Hon. Wm. Wilson, of Menomonie, Dunn county, formerly of the State Senate.
   *   *   *   It is expected of her to assuage the thirst of the dying and wounded on the field of battle, and she is regarded as a sort

of guardian angel of the regiment. All honor to the vivandiere of the Fifth.

SEPTEMBER 12TH, 1861.

The Eau Claire Badgers (under the new organization, afterwards called the Eau Claire Eagles) took their departure from this place for Madison, preparatory to a campaign in Secessia, last Friday morning, on board the steamer Stella Whipple.

This was Captain Perkin's company. with the bird that gave the name Eagle Regiment to the Eighth Wisconsin ; the second organized company that left this valley. At West Eau Claire, in response to their call just before the boat drew in her plank, A. Meggett, Esq., on behalf of the citizens, bade them a formal and affecting farewell.

CHIPPEWA FALLS ITEMS.—A PATRIOTIC FAMILY.

We learn that S. S. McCann, who volunteered for the war a few days ago, has two sons and three sons-in-law in our country's service. Mrs. McCann, the 'Squire's lady, says they have one son left, and if the government makes another call for volunteers, he must go also. Such patriotism should be remembered.

OCTOBER 3D, 1861.—MORE MEN FROM CHIPPEWA COUNTY.

Lieutenant Luxton passed through this place from Chippewa Falls, on Friday last, with twenty athletic fellows to join the Milwaukee Tiger Rifles. Among them we noticed that bold pioneer, Stephen S. McCann. Mr. McCann has been in actual service, having served through the Black Hawk war, and came out with an honorable discharge. He is a man of undoubted pluck and patriotism, and although he has passed the noon of life, he could not turn a deaf ear to his country's call for "more men."

NOVEMBER 28TH, 1861.—THE EAU CLAIRE RANGERS.

Captain Sherman having enlisted forty men at Patch's Grove, his company is now accepted in Col. Washburn's regiment of cavalry, and will proceed at once to winter quarters at Milwaukee.

I should like to relate some of the affecting and also comical incidents of Captain Sherman's war experience, and that of his command, as told by himself, but will first mention a scene and circumstance in which he was an actor at which I was present.

It was in July of the year following (1862) that the Captain came home on a short furlough. To recreate and recover his health, he visited several places in the country around about Eau Claire, and amongst others a Sabbath-school picnic in the town of La Fayette. The young and anxious wives and many other friends of several members of his company were present and impatient to hear from their dear ones he had left down in Arkansas. In response to urgent calls, he commenced a little speech with a view, apparently, of setting forth the sufferings and wants of our brave boys in that malarious climate, and the horrors of Southern prisons which some of his company had experienced, but, soldier as he was and accustomed to affecting scenes and trying circumstances, he broke down, almost at the start, and burst into tears. So true it is that the bravest men are the most tender and sympathetic.

DECEMBER 19TH, 1861.—THE CHIPPEWA GUARDS TO DEPART FOR THE WAR.

This was Captain Wheeler's company, to whom the ladies of Eau Claire presented a beautiful flag, a grand ball being given at Reed's Hall, the Guards being formed in line by Sergeant M. E. O'Connell. Hon. H. W. Barnes made the presentation on behalf of the ladies in a most beautiful and patriotic speech, responded to for the Company by G. E. Porter, in the most touching and eloquent terms. Room for only a sentence or two of each of these addresses can be spared here. Mr. Barnes said:

"Bear in mind that this flag is entrusted to you as citizens and soldiers of Wisconsin. Let this prove to you how dear to the female heart is liberty—how sacred to her is the cause which you go forth to sustain."

In reply Mr. Porter said: "I can assure the fair donors, in behalf of these noble men, that while they have an arm to strike, no stain of dishonor shall ever pollute the fair folds of that beautiful flag."

CHAPTER XXXIII.

PEPIN COUNTY.

The reader has most likely observed that this curiously shaped piece or parcel of the territory of this State, embracing the delta of the Chippewa and a strip extending along its southeastern bank for thirty miles and along the northern shore of Lake Pepin, about the same distance, has received little attention.

From 1856 to 1857, it was included in the county of Dunn, from which it was taken, and organized by act of the Legislature, approved February 25, 1858. Being destitute of pine timber which was the object of the early settlers in this valley, no attention was paid to these lands for many years after the mills were erected in the lumber region on the several branches of the river, and at the Nalls.

The first house erected in the county, was built by John McKane in 1850 on the lake shore a mile and a half above the present village of North Pepin. He was a Mississippi raft pilot, not very circumspect in his morals, a great spendthrift and gambler, but having picked up a woman somewhere along the river to share his fortunes, an industrious and frugal housekeeper and manager, the two opened quite a farm and secured a considerable competence.

W. B. Newcomb another river pilot, was the next settler, who in company with John O'Conor and Benjamin Allen Esq., laid off the town or village of North Pepin in 1854. It was supposed by many at tha time that a flourishing city, would grow up at some point near the mouth of so large a river as the Chippewa and the proprietors of this village plot counted much upon it as the embryo city. Great efforts were also put forth to secure the trade and open up the country around to settlement and civilization. In connection with H. S. Allen & Co., a wagon road was opened to the Falls of the Chippewa and a stage line and mail route, were soon established. Hotels and business houses were soon opened; a State bank went into operation under the free banking law and the place only lacked a well settled and flourishing country, back of it to make it prosperous.

In 1857 U. B. Shaver started a newspaper there called the Pepin County Independent, and the year following, North Pepin became the county seat for Pepin county. Up to this time, little had been done in the way of filling up the country around with farmers, although much of the country was most excellent land for agricultural purposses. Shaver continued the Independent two years but removed to Wabasha soon after and the County was without an organ for some time.

In 1863 Myran Shaw published the Mirror which was succeeded by the Lean Wolf and that by the Durand Times.

Two brothers by the name of Hix, William and Samuel B., had settled near the trail leading up the Chippewa before the village of North Pepin was laid out, which comprised most of the country tributary to its business, but the energy and public spirit displayed by the proprietors in laying out and working the roads in different directions, soon had the effect to settle the country, and their prospect seemed hopeful. The landing for steamboats however was difficult in low water; the Lake being very shallow for a considerable distance from the bank, which was a serious drawback.

But other and still more potent causes were operating to defeat the hopes of this Lake Shore village. The country on the south side of the Chippewa was filling up with industrious and enterprising men, and it was soon ascertained that a shorter route could be opened between the Falls, Eau Claire, and the Mississippi on that side. Steamboats, too, of lighter draft were used to navigate the Chippewa, which in a great measure relieved the Falls and Pepin stage of any business.

A series of low water seasons had induced Perry Curtis and his associates to believe that the bottom lands of the Chippewa did not overflow, and in 1855 they laid out a town or village plat near the mouth of Bear Creek, three or four miles above the present village of Durand. A hotel, a store or two, and several dwellings were erected, but the long continued high water of the two succeeding years dispelled their hopes, the town site being under water for several months each year, and the project of building up a town there was forever abandoned.

But the distance from Eau Claire to the Mississippi was too long, and the demand for a town at some intermediate point on the south side of the Chippewa was too apparent to be long neglected.

Miles D. Prindle, a young man from the Old Pine State, came up the river in 1856, and after looking the ground over, secured the title to the land on which the village of Durand now stands, and laid out a part of the plat.

"Give me also springs of water" was the request of a Hebrew bride as she received her marriage portion, which embraced a south land domain; but Mr. Prindle says his town site was made up of just such marriage portions as Acsah coveted. It was upper and nether springs everywhere, but it had another advantage; no Chippewa flood would ever overflow it. Great obstacles were to be overcome in order to make his undertaking successful. A ferry across the Chippewa must be established; a steam saw mill to supply the wants of the surrounding country was essential, while roads extending in all directions were an indispensible necessity, which the young village proprietor must open to secure the country trade.

All this, and much more, was undertaken and accomplished by the enterprising proprietor and his associates, W. F. Prindle, George Ellsworth, and W. E. Hays, during those terrible years of failure and disappointment which followed the bursting of the California gold bubble of 1857. As the agricultural resources of the country became developed, Durand was found to be the nearest market to a large wheat growing country and quite a flourishing business was done in shipping that cereal to eastern markets. A boat yard was started by one of its enterprising citizens, and several boats and barges adapted to the Chippewa trade were built there. It was not a place holding out great inducements for the investment of capital, but by industry and economy the people of Durand have achieved reasonable success and surrounded themselves with a fair amount of the comforts and elegancies of life. In 1860 Durand laid claim to the county seat by virtue of a majority of the voters in the county and obtained leave to test the question at the polls which however was lost that year, but the next year the result was favorable to Durand, which was declared the legal county seat by judicial decision, rendered at La Crosse, in 1865, at the termination of a law suit in which the case became involved.

An elegant court house has since been erected, and the bitterness occasioned by the removal is fast disappearing.

A commodious graded school house and an elegant M. E. Church building are among the evidences of religious and intellectual culture.

Several other christian denominations have organizations in the village, among which is a live and growing society of Congregationalists, under the pastoral care of Rev. Mr. Kidder, heretofore mentioned in this work, whose labors in this Valley for the past twenty years have been identified with its highest religious and educational interests. Having been mainly instrumental in establishing churches in Eau Claire, Augusta, Van Ville in Chippewa county, Mondovi in Buffalo, he is now settled at Durand, as zealous in the Master's cause as at any period of his long ministry.

The manufacturing industries of the county are mostly located on Bear and Plum Creeks, on the former of which are a flouring mill, carding and woolen mill owned by Capt. V. W. Dorwin. These are near Durand, and on the former are flourishing mills for hard wood, flouring mills and various wooden ware manufactories.

Its citizens being largely engaged in agriculture, Pepin county has had few criminal cases on its calendar.

A most villainous outrage was perpetrated by a party of Sioux on the wife of one Bobert a German who built a cabin just below the present village of Durand several years before the country became settled. Having bound her husband, ten of the monsters violated her person before his eyes. Being a foreigner he knew not where to seek redress.

One other a most appaling case of murder occurred in the year 1866. Ira B. Wheeler living at a place on the north bank of the Chippewa river, known as Five Mile Bluffs, was murdered on the 24th of March, under circumstances that implicated his wife Margaret E. Wheeler and James E. Carter in the atrocious deed. They were immediately arrested but as the body had been concealed under the ice in the river and no positive proof of his death, or the manner of it being adduced, they were discharged; the parties continuing to reside as before, at the house of the missing man.

On the 12th of May following, the body having been discovered with marks of violence about the head, they were re arrested and committed for trial at the ensuing term. For greater safety they were taken to Eau Claire county, where she employed the legal talents of Hon. Alex. Meggett to defend her. Owing to some informality no grand jury was empanelled in Pepin county at the next term, and the parties lay in jail until the following March, when they were arraigned, but on the affidavit of the District Attorney, the case was removed to Dunn county, thence to La Crosse on the affidavit of the defense. Their final trial and conviction was before Judge Flint at the May term in 1867. Under the management of the able counsel, it was hoped that a confession of guilt on the part of Carter would clear Mrs. Wheeler, but on the trial their mutual accusations clearly showed that both were present at the killing and participated in the murder, and that both assisted in putting the body under the ice, and in concealing the evidence of their guilt.

The efforts of the able counsel were then directed to extenuating circumstances in favor of Mrs. Wheeler, with a view to lessen the time of her imprisonment. The virdict of the jury, however, was murder in the first degree, and the sentence, "imprisonment in the penitentiary for life." Alleging that the removal of the case from Pepin to Dunn county on the application of the prosecution was unconstitutional and illegal. She was remanded for a new trial on appeal to the Supreme Court, but failing to order her to be committed for safe keeping, Mr. Meggett obtained a writ of habeas corpus from court commissioner Hon. H. Clay Williams, under which Mrs. Wheeler was discharged, but immediately rearrested by the officers of Pepin county, from whom she managed to escape; assisted, as is supposed, by an old lover who took her to parts unknown. The story of Strang and Mrs. Whipple over again.

In September 1864 one Sloan, a resident of what is now the town of Seymour in Eau Claire county, was murdered in the village of Eau Claire by John Stoeplar one of its citizens. He was immediately arrested and held for trial, was ably defended by Horace W. Barnes and N. B. Boyden Esq., but the evidence against him was conclusive and the prosecution conducted by Mr. Meggett and W. P. Bartlett obtained a verdict of guilty of manslaughter in the second degree and the sentence was for five years imprisonment in the penitentiary; but before the expiration of the term he was commended by many influential citizens to executive clemency and two years of the term remitted.

One other horrid murder was committed at the close of the year 1868 in the town of Pleasant Valley Eau Claire county, John Hamilton drove the tines of a pitchfork into the brain of a son of Wm. Laughman which caused his death. It was a most uncalled for and brutal assult upon a young, defenceless lad and received the universal execration of the community. The perpetrator though defended by able counsel, Meggett and Barnes, is now suffering the penalty of the fearful crime.

CHAPTER XXXIV

In the foregoing chapter of this work, the reader has been made acquainted with all the principal business men and firms engaged in lumber operations, and the respective localities in this valley, together with many other individual improvements, and development of the country generally, down to the commencement of the war.

The recognized source of wealth and profit for all these firms was the pine timber standing upon the lands drained by the several streams and their affluents, upon which their establishments were located.

As each of these involved the necessity of placing piers and other obstructions in the stream, it was necessary to obtain certain privileges, either from the legislature or under the general charter law, in order that the placing and construction of such works might conform to legal restrictions.

Where two or more of these establishments were located on the same stream, as in the case of the main Chippewa, a conflict of interests soon became apparent, and bitter jealousies sprang up; so that in addition to the long season of drouth, quite as disastrous in holding back the supply of logs as the destructive floods by which they were succeeded, and the numerous other natural obstacles encountered in all new enterprises in a new country—the opposition of rival interests must be met or overcome at every stage of their advancement.

Their true interests lay in mutual concessions, forbearance, and assistance, because annual freshets were carrying away the avails of their labor and enterprise, and furnishing to the mills along the Mississippi not only a foretaste of the advantages to be derived from the manufacture of our wealth of pine into lumber, but a plausable excuse for putting in works at Beef Slough to save and secure the logs, more or less of which went adrift every year, for want of a safe reservoir near the mills.

Under a decree from the United States District Court for the District of Wisconsin, the vast property at the Falls, accumulated, or rather created, by the energy of H. S. Allen & Co.—proceedings in equity against the Chippewa Falls Lumbering Company having resulted in such decree—was sold at Milwaukee by the Marshal of said District in August, 1861. An association of several of the plaintiffs bought the property and subsequently sold it to the lessees, as heretofore stated, Pound & Halbert, who soon made their presence and power known not only in this valley, but throughout the State and the Northwest. The former lessee, Adin Randall, with the aid of French & Co., of West Eau Claire, erected a mill on the lower chute of Jim's Falls, with the usual dams, piers, booms, etc., which, with the mills on Yellow river at this time owned by Mason & Sons, and that on O'Neil's creek, operated by Lockhart, Manahan & Fair, constituted the mill or manufacturing interest above the Falls; while below were Bussy & Taylor, Gravel Island, Dole, Ingram & Kennedy, Daniel Shaw & Co., Smith & Buffington, McVicar Bros., and Stephen Marston, with their establishments of varied extent and capacity, all near Half Moon Lake, West Eau Claire. And the year following, 1862, Sherman Brothers commenced the erection of a mill at the Big Eddy, now known as the Eddy mill. And soon after, Charles Warner and his associates built the first mill piers, booms, etc., at Porterville.

The success of all lumbering operations up here depended at all times on the development and prosperity of the great agricultural regions to the south and west of us. Short crops and low prices for produce were as disastrous to the lumbermen as to the farmer. But there were other drawbacks to both these and all other industries throughout the West, one of which had always been the want of a stable, uniform currency, which, added to expensive transportation and inadequate markets, had retarded the settlement of the country, and crippled its industrial and commercial energies.

But now the war, and the necessities of the government growing out of it, had supplied both a market and a currency, sound, stable, uniform, and abundant, which gave an impulse to industry and the development of Western resources before unknown.

The passage of the Homestead law about this time also stimulated emigration, and capitalists saw at once that the pine lands in the Chippewa Land District, that had lain so long subject to entry, would now be a safe and lucrative investment, which, with the location of a large amount of Agricultural College scrip for our own and other States, soon absorbed vast areas of our pine land domain. From these demonstrations, it was very evident to the owners of these mills that the custom amongst them of exchanging logs, which had grown out of imperative necessity, and was in some respects very convenient, must soon be terminated; and at all times equally apparent that storage capacity for more logs must be provided at some point on the river for the mutual convenience of all, or the business must prove a failure.

Beyond all comparison the most eligible point on the river, a place seemingly fixed by nature for just such a reservoir, was the great basin above the Dalles and a little north of the village of Eau Claire.

To accomplish this it would be necessary to erect a dam across the Chippewa river at the Dalles aforesaid, which should set the water back and flood the low lands in the basin, slack the current of the river, and secure storage and conveniences for handling all the logs that would come down in any one year.

Such a dam would also create a vast water-power, and secure to the locality great manufacturing facilities. But before such work could be established, the river being a public highway, and its free navigation being guaranteed by the treaty of cession and constitutional provision, a charter must be obtained from the legislature granting to the party the necessary privileges, and guarding the rights of the public. So urgent were the demands for such an improvement, and so great were the benefits expected to accrue to the people of Eau Claire, that every citizen came to regard it as of paramount local importance; while the people of Chippewa Falls and the mill interest above that point could view the project only as destructive to the navigation of the river, and calculated to build up a rival village at the expense of the great interests involved above.

Being in the same Assembly District until 1866, and T. C. Pound, of the firm of Pound & Halbert, being elected to represent the people in that body the two preceding years, it was not deemed expedient to agitate the subject prior to that time. But in that year, the re-organization of the State into Assembly Districts, placed the two villages in different Districts, and the Hon. Fayette Allen, of Pepin county, was chosen to represent the Eau Claire interests at the ensuing session, 1867, Hon. J. G. Thorp, of Eau Claire, being in the Senate for the Thirty-second district. A stock company was organized, providing for a capital of one hundred thousand dollars, the outlines of a charter drawn up granting corporate powers, the right of domain, authorizing the construction of a dam across the Chippewa river at a designated point, with piers, booms, and all necessary works for securing and handling logs, and for manufacturing lumber, and imposing such restrictions, and providing for such locks, raft-slides, and channels, as would insure the unimpeded navigation of the river for rafts, steamboats, logs, and all other craft. Petitions numerously signed by the people of the lower valley, and a strong lobby force, were sent to Madison to assist in passing the bill. The services of Hon. J. C. Gregory, of Madison, a very able advocate, was engaged to argue the claims and merits of the bill before the committees, and strong hopes were entertained that it would become a law; but the opposition were vigilant and equally untiring in their efforts to defeat it, and when put on its final passage, it received a small majority in the Senate, while the Assembly was decidedly opposed. Such was the commencement of the great struggle.

CHAPTER XXIX.

As citizens of the world, caring nothing for country or locality, or the welfare and prosperity of one State or section, more than another, men would cease to be regarded as patriotic, and however philanthrophic they might consider themselves, without some special regard for the country of our birth, adoption, or wherein we have made our homes, its success and hapiness, we should scarcely be considered good citizens.

The sources of wealth and comfort or the means of subsistence are not equally distributed over the earths surface and aside from man's inherent selfishness, which usually induces a love for ones own, his home, his family. kindred, possessions, his town or city, State and nation, it would seem to be a natural conclusion that whatever resources have been bestowed upon any country (other things being equal as to health,' climate etc., would best serve human interests and contribute most to the welfare of that community by whom such resources are developed by being wrought into those fabrics or articles of comfort and convenience to which they are best adapted, in the locality, State, or country where they abound. Indeed we shall find by the briefest computation of the wealth, power, influence and progress of civilization and refinement amongst the nations of the globe, that in all countries where the internal policy of the government has persistently favored the exportation of the raw material, whether derived from the farm, forest, the mine or the sea,—such countries are always poor.

The support of government, education the church, humane and all other institutions which conduce to political and social advancement in a State, renders it imperatively necessary to raise a revenue from all the resources of its people whether natural or industrial, and the policy or necessity that precludes any community from the advantages to be derived from the manufacture of its raw products or takes them to a distant or foreign shore for that purpose, can only be regarded as a grevious blunder committed by its rulers or a sad misfortune of its natural position.

No wonder then, that the people of this valley who had borne the hardships and incurred the expense of first developing its resources, and of establishing homes in a corner so remote, should vehemently oppose any and all enterprises having for their object the carrying away of the timber cut from our pine forrests to be manufactured into lumber out of the State and in distant localities. More than half the value of our pine timber would be lost to us if taken to points on the Mississippi to be sawed. Strenuous efforts were therefore made to induce the capitalists who lately acquired title to large quantities of timber land on the Chippewa and its tributaries and were anxious to realize from their investment to take an interest in some of the mills here that required assistance or erect new ones and confine the manufacture to this State, but the want of some safe and capacious reservoir where logs could be assorted, and the conflicting local interests that defeated all Legislation necessary to insure that result, together with promised aid from the owners of mills on the Mississippi in the erection of works necessary to secure them in Beef Slough, not only deterred them from investing here, but secured an organization of means to carry out the latter enterprise.

And in the fall of 1867 an association composed mostly of lumbermen from Michigan, Fond du Lac, and Oshkosh, in this State, was organized with a nominal capital of $100,000, having their headquarters at Alma n Buffalo county, and for their object the establishment and maintenance of a shear boom at the head or entrance of Beef Slough and a cross or jam boom at a suitable point below, and the necessary works for sorting and handling logs.

Being flush with means and impatient to realize from their pine land investment, this company instantly set themselves to effect their object, J. H. Bacon, an ambitious and enterprising agent was sent forward to commence the work, while a strong lobby prepared to enter the Legislature and secure a charter granting the necessary priveleges on the Chippewa river.

At first all the mills on the river joined in the opposition to this gigantic rival as against a common enemy. Two of the ablest men on the river were chosen to represent the two Districts in the Assembly; in Chippewa and Dunn, T. C. Pound, and for Pepin and Eau Claire, Horace W. Barnes, who, aided by a strong lobby, defeated the bill on a direct vote in the Assembly; but another bill was subsequently introduced, a copy of an old Portage City charter changing the names of persons and localities—merely a working charter, it was claimed, embodying no specific privileges except corporate powers, but which was afterwards found to contain nearly everything asked for, and the work went on in spite of opposition.

Disastrous as the success of this new organization was considered by the mill men, a considerable class of our citizens favored the innovation. They were the class known as loggers who, while the mills on the Chippewa were the only purchasers of logs, saw themselves completely at the mercy of a dozen or twenty monopolists. What cared they whether cities grew up at Davenport, Clinton and Muscatine by the manufacture of our pine into lumber, instead of at Chippewa Falls and Eau Claire, if they could only get fifty cents per thousand more for logs with the promise of cash in the place of trade for pay.

But most of the mills were illy prepared for the new order of things. Subjected to annual losses by floods and short supply of logs for want of storage, few of them had been able to erect sorting works and keep sufficient force to sort out and pass the logs below going to other parties, and secure their own, and therefore had recourse to exchanging marks, as the practice was called. About fifty million feet of logs were contracted by the agent for the Slough Co., this year, 1868, and on the opening of spring, a driving force of 125 men was placed on the river, and a watchman at every boom and mill to guard the interests of the new company. A moderate freshet favored the drivers this spring, and it was well into June before the main force of the Beef Slough Company reached the Slough, who on their way down had cut or opened almost every boom on the river, and taken out, indiscriminately, whatever logs they contained. It seemed as though the agent of the new company aggravated every hardship by ruthless, unnecessary and arbitrary destruction of property and loud and bitter were the denunciations against him. It had been a doubtful problem even amongst the friends of the measure whether logs could be successfully driven over the broad sand bars of the lower Chippewa, and cost what it would its feasibility must be demonstrated now, or the stockholders, already assessed for the last dollar on their stock, would abandon the undertaking, the drive was therefore continued after the water got so low that the cost of driving was more than the logs were worth. But the drive was a fixed fact, and henceforth the Chippewa pinery must furnish its quota of logs for the mills and build up the cities on the shores of that great river whose tributaries span two thirds of a continent. The next session of the Legislature, 1869, witnessed a renewal of the struggle for charters, but it was a tri-party fight, with a leaning of the Chippewa Falls interest towards Beef Slough, and a final coalition of the two to defeat the Dells bill. It was not until the season of 1870 that the final charter for the Beef Slough company became a law, by which time the concern was completely bankrupt, and several of its stockholders financially crippled in the endeavor to sustain its credit; one of whom, Mr. Palms, of Michigan, informed me that in addition to twenty thousand dollars in stock he had actually loaned the company one hundred thousand dollars, more than fifty per cent of which will prove an utter loss.

Like many other western enterprises, the cost of this boom was too great for its earnings, and no dividends will probably be declared on the original stock. The whole concern, charter, boom, buildings and fixtures were leased to the Mississippi Logging Company, who will probably reap where the other sowed.

Although stoutly opposed and the establishment of those works much deprecated by a large share of our people as derogatory to our manufacturing interests, their existence has not been without its benefit, even to its most strenuous opposers. For in 1869 the Company at the Falls having planted some immense piers directly in the channel at the big eddy, just below paint Creek Rapids, a jam of logs of vast proportions was formed against them during the Spring drive, filling up the entire river for several miles with logs piled by the force of the current, twenty or thirty feet high, totally obstructing the passage of logs and rafts—and presenting a grand, almost sublime spectacle to the beholder—which jam, when broken in the July following, by the aid of two steam engines and a great force of men, filled the river for miles in extent with floating logs, pouring down in such rapid profusion, that any force the mills below could command was powerless to arrest their onward course, or secure a hundreth part that belonged to them. Millions on millions of feet of logs would have gone into the great river, and been lost in its thousand lagoons and bayous which were saved to their owners by the Beef Slough boom.

One paragraph more and the account of the Beef Slough and Mississippi Logging Company is done. They have been and are now using the Sheer Boom invented and patented by Levi W. Pond, the patent right being held by him and the Eau Claire Lumber Company—without consulting the patentees, alleging, it is said, that the patent is void by reason of prior use, and suit has been commenced by the patentees, requiring the said Booming and Logging Companies to show cause why the said Shear Boom now in use by them, should not be discontinued. The defendants will of course resist this action to the last extremity. The best legal talent in the State has been retained by the parties, and some curious developments may be expected to grow out of it.

The defense however seem to be aware of the hopelessness of their cause in the courts, and are lobbying in Congress with a view to abrogate the patent.

CHAPTER XXXVI.

To the people who may inhabit this valley half a century hence, this chapter may have some interest, but for the reader of to-day, especially the residents of Wisconsin who so recently during several succeeding sessions of the legislature, had their ears filled with discussions of the "Dells bill" until it became disgustingly wearisome, its rehearsal at this time can yield but little satisfaction.

Thoroughly convinced by the advantages of the situation, the hopeless condition of the entire lumber manufacturing business on the river without some safe storage boom for logs, and the great expense and difficulty of establishing such a reservoir at any other point, the people, not only of Eau Claire, but of Menomonie and the whole valley of the Chippewa below that point, together with many interested parties in other parts of the State, had come to consider the passage of this bill and the improvements contemplated under it, as the only hope of the lumber interest on the river. And the earnestness and determination with which the measure was so persistently supported by its friends, was a natural sequence of a position so advantageous, and the necessity for such a work.

Had the bill become a law, we could now determine something near what its results would be to the community it was expected to benefit, and to that by whom it was so strenuously and successfully opposed, as men of capital and business energy that were never known to fail in any undertaking were ready to invest in the enterprise.

As it is, however, the historian can refer the reader to little more than the successive steps of the struggle, and its final defeat at the hands of the Executive.

But it is safe to say that no merely local question ever arrayed the people of a state for and against it, or involved issues of greater moment, than the Chippewa Dells bill.

In the fall of 1869, Thadeus C. Pound received the Republican nomination for the office of Lieutenant Governor, and the Republicans of Eau Claire county, though not without many apprehensions in regard to the effect his election might have upon their long-cherished enterprise, voted solid for the man who of all others they most dreaded in the anticipated struggle to obtain the coveted charter; their patriotism outran all private and pecuniary considerations, incurring many bitter and ironical comments from their friends of the opposite political party.

By way of atonement and conciliation, however, C. R. Gleason, a Democrat, and a great favorite of his party throughout the State, was elected to the Assembly against V. W. Dorwin, Republican, with the hope of carrying the Democratic members in favor of the Dells bill.

Thadeus C. Pound, of Chippewa Falls, was born in Warren county, Pennsylvania, received a good academic and thorough business education, came to the Falls in the spring of 1856 with his family, and engaged himself as clerk in the counting-room of H. S. Allen & Co., whose subsequent failure paved the way for the advancement of the young accountant, after many vicissitudes, to his present high position and standing in the business community.

A leading trait in his character is the ease and perfect self-possession with which he approaches monied men and establishes himself in their confidence; even under depressing financial difficulties that would crush some men, he is always composed, and wins success where others would fail.

In the arena of politics, also, these qualities made him a formidable antagonist, whether in the canvass for the people's suffrages, or in the legislative hall as champion of any measure he wished to carry, or the opponent of any he desired to defeat.

Elected four times to the Assembly, and to the position of Speaker pro tem. in 1869, his legislative experience, his many friends, his elevated position, and his sleepless energy, quickened by intense personal interest, made him a powerful adversary in the struggle, which was renewed in 1870, to carry the Dells bill.

The bill was carefully drawn, so as to avoid all seeming possibility of injury or damage resulting to any party from obstruction to the navigation of the river, but the opposition to it was nevertheless stronger and more determined than ever ; and each party to the contest went into the legislature backed by a strong lobby, able advocates, an army of witnesses, and volumes of testimony for and against the bill. The rooms were thronged with eager partisans whenever it was considered by the committees of each house to whom it was referred, and the engrossing topic of conversation in every circle, was the bill to incorporate the Chippewa River Booming and Manufacturing Company at the Dells, in the county of Eau Claire.

The result of all this immense labor and strife is too well known to be repeated here. "Defeated in the Senate" came flashing over the wires, to the chagrin and disappointment of one party, and hilarious demonstrations of joy to the other.

But the end was not yet. The same necessity for the improvement still existed, and the hope of final success still animated the friends of the bill. One more effort was determined upon, and fiercer and more resolute still were the demonstrations in its favor, and still more obstinate was the resistance, in 1871.

But a favorable impression had been made on the people of the State at large. Those who had never taken pains to inquire into the merits of the case, began to think that anything so zealously and persistently striven for must, in justice, have claims upon the favor of the people. Rumor, however, soon furnished other grounds for this change in public sentiment, and for the fact that a majority in both Houses favored the bill. "Bribery and corruption, the demoralization of the representatives of the people," said Madame Rumor, "has done all this," and Governor Lucius Fairchild believed it and vetoed the bill, and the Dalles, with it great, natural basin, fitted expressly, it would seem, for the much-needed work, remains to-day just as nature formed it, without any of man's handiwork to utilize its advantages, while a costly and precarious substitute has been erected at Eagle Rapids, as the next best thing to do. It has this advantage over the Dalles, however; it serves the entire mill interest on the Chippewa, and obstructs navigation to a very inconsiderable extent, and if found to be permanent, and the works prove capable of accommodating the great interests they were intended to subserve, it may yet prove, all things considered, the best for all the varied and conflicting interests that could be done. A trial and test of the value of those works, and many other private improvements on this great stream, has not yet occurred. But let such a freshet as that of 1847, an account of which was given in the early chapters of this work, happen again, and I very much fear for the safety of any dams, booms, piers, or bridges on the Chippewa. We may hope and trust that it will never come.

CHAPTER XXXVII.

RAIL WAYS.

Reference has been made in the foregoing chapters, to a grant of land made by Congress in 1856, to be held in trust by the State of Wisconsin for the purpose of constructing a Rail Road from Portage city to the Mississippi at La Crosse, with a branch from Tomah to the St. Croix River. It has also been stated that the Legislature conferred the Grant upon an organization known as the "Milwaukee and La Crosse Rail Road Company, at the head of which was Byron Kilbourn; this last named branch being designated in the Charter of 1857 as the Western Wisconsin Rail Road. It probably had never occurred to the people of this valley nor to their representatives in Congress at the time the aforesaid grant was made, that we should ever need a road running transversely to this—down the river and on to the great prairie world to the Southwest of us—for, as it was then fashionable for the government to give away its lands to build Rail Roads, there is little doubt but a donation could easily have been obtained for a Road extending from Ashland on Lake

Superior, via Chippewa Falls, Eau Claire and Wabasha to Fort Dodge and the Missouri River in Iowa. Such a grant, for a Road crossing three great States would have found able advocates, and when built would have been one of the best paying roads in the Northwest.

St. Paul and Minneappolis were wise enough to see the point and secure a grant for the Sioux City road and are now reaping its advantages, while we have just begun to realize the want of a thoroughfare in that direction. Private enterprise will probably supply the want in time, but at the time of which we are speaking, the river was deemed altogether sufficient for the transportation of our lumber, and connection with the East of paramount importance; and the Hon. C. C. Washburn our Representative in Congress was instructed to secure the grant for this, the West Wisconsin Road, the route for which presented so many obstacles and so few inducements in regard to the value of the land and the prospective business over the road when built, that although ten years were designated in the act as the time for its completion no capitalists had been found up to the expiration of that period bold enough to undertake it.

Kilbourn and his associates had indeed sent out surveying parties who after making perliminary surveys for half a dozen different routes finally fixed upon the extreme Southwestern line, or the one nearest the Mississippi and farthest from the great business interests, it was intended to subserve—the lumber business—of any route examined, for the location of the Road.

In conformity with the act of Congress, the lands along this line were immediately withdrawn from market for six miles on either side, until all embraced in the odd-numbered sections should be designated on the official plats of the respective land-offices in the districts through which it passed, and greatly elated were the settlers along the line at the prospec t of immediate railroad facilities.

As an inducement to capitalists, these lands were exempted from taxation for ten years, but the prostration of all business operations, caused by the revulsion of 1857-8, and extending into several succeeding years, and the probable completion at an early day of other railroad lines to St. Paul, the objective point of this road, forbade all hope that a road would ever be constructed on that line. Another discouraging feature was that the company who were pushing one of these competing lines, held the franchises of this road by transfer from the old bankrupt company upon whom it was conferred. In view of this condition of affairs pertaining to the land grant, and the prospect of its forfeiture to the government, some of the business men of St. Croix, Dunn, Chippewa, Eau Claire, and Jackson counties, the most prominent of whom were D. A. Baldwin, Capt. William Wilson, J. G. Thorp, H. S. Allen, and W. T. Price, conceived the idea of a new organization to build the road.

These men, with their associates, were incorporated in March, 1863, by act of the legislature, with the title of the Tomah and St. Croix Railway Company, and held their first meeting at Durand, on the 9th of June following. At the next session, the legislature conferred the land grant upon this company, with the right of way and the privilege of locating the line on its present route. Congress was also memorialized to renew the grant, which was done, and exemption from taxes on the land until 1870 also granted.

It does not appear to have been the intention of the incorporators and stockholders in this organization to invest their means in the undertaking; indeed, few of them at that time had any capital to invest in any enterprise outside their regular business; neither did they expect to realize any benefits, except to secure the building of the road.

The only hope of achieving the object the company had in view, was to induce capitalists from abroad to take hold of the work, and the first thing to do was to survey the new route and obtain correct profiles, estimates of the cost of the work, topographical descriptions of the country, present and prospective value of the lands donated, and the business of the road when completed. To accomplish this required at least twenty thousand dollars, and one man only in the company was sanguine enough in his hopes of success to advance the money, and that man was D. A. Baldwin, of Hudson.

In the fall of 1864, he caused a surveying party in charge of a competent engineer to take the field, whose labors were continued for the year and all necessary examinations made—profiles, maps, estimated cost, description of the country, soil, timber, production, etc.

Armed with these vouchers, Mr. Baldwin, under the direction of the company, visited the Eastern cities and Europe, for the purpose of enlisting capitalists to undertake the work; and in the fall of 1866 succeeded in inducing four or five gentlemen from New York to come on and personally examine the route and inquire into the resources of the country. They could see no inducement to invest, and, being mostly financial agents only, made a most dismal and discouraging report to their principals.

At the next meeting of the Directors, the entire management of the concern was delegated to Mr. Baldwin, who was authorzed to contract with any party, and on any terms, that would construct the road, consistent with his interests. It was up-hill business, and he now began to realize that he had a good-sized elephant on his hands.

The principal railroad corporations doing business in the State were applied to; their means and energies were all absorbed and directed in the extension of more hopeful lines, and could afford no immediate aid. The apathy of Milwaukee in regard to this work has been the subject of condemnation by the press and people of this part of the State, and the advantages now reaped by the Chicago and Northwestern road are its natural sequences.

The Atlantic was again crossed, and two full years consumed in fruitless endeavor to find the right man. But his perseverance was equal to the occasion, and his efforts finally crowned with success.

Jacob Humbird, of Baltimore, was a successful railroad contractor; had lately returned from Brazil, where extensive contracts under the Imperial Government had resulted in a handsome fortune. To him Mr. Baldwin submitted his case, exhibited his profiles, estimates, acts of Congress and the Legislature; in fact, all the franchises of the road, and the resources of the country through which it was to pass, and a contract for all the work to complete the road was immediately drawn up and signed by the parties. It is reasonable to suppose that, under such circumstances, Mr. Humbird obtained very favorable terms; and, as the price of labor and every commodity was greatly inflated by the late war, it is not at all surprising that the cost of the work exceeded the estimates, or that its earnings should sometimes fall short of the interest, at least on the nominal investment.

The funds to complete the first thirty-two miles, to Black River Falls, were furnished entirely by Mr. Humbird, the payment of which, and all other sums due him for work under contract, is secured by a construction lien, or first mortgage, on the road-bed. Certificates were immediately issued by the Governor for the lands, and an eight per cent. loan effected in Europe, receivable in installments as the work progressed, and secured by bond and mortgage on both the lands and the road-bed. Before commencing the work, the name of the West Wisconsin Railway was assumed in accordance with an act of the legislature.

CHAPTER XXXVIII.

So long had the hopes of the people along the line of this road been deferred, that, in order to encourage capitalists to invest in the enterprise, a proposition was submitted to the legislature in 1866, at the time the right of way over the new route was granted, to authorize the several counties through which the road was to pass, to raise certain sums, by vote of the electors, as subsidies to the company when the road should be completed to designated points.

In Dunn county, the question submitted was for the county to guarantee title to the lands required by the road, which was promptly voted down, but in Eau Claire county the vote was for a subsidy of fifty thousand dollars in county bonds, which, according to the returns made at the time, November, 1868, was carried by a considerable majority. But when the conditions had been complied with by the enterprising Company, the County Commissioners refused the application for the bonds, on the ground that a judicial decision just then rendered in one of the courts of this State, declared the whole matter of subsidizing corporations, by counties, unconstitutional and void.

The demand has been renewed this year, and it is not at all improbable that the next application will be to Judge Hopkin's court for a mandamus to compel their issue.

The lands along the route of the proposed railroad, having been several years subject to private entry at the time the grant was made, some of the best locations had been taken by purchase or pre-emption, and in order to supply the deficiency, Congress, on the 5th of June, 1864, made an additional grant, the selections to be made by some person to be appointed by the Secretary of State (State Secretary) from the odd numbered sections for ten sections in width along the new line, the amount to be equal to the deficiency aforesaid, which accounts for the wide space occupied by the railroad company's lands.

Whether Mr. Baldwin at any time endeavored to raise funds to complete the road thus endowed, by placing the stock of the comwany on the market, does not appear from any records, and from the fact that quotations of West Wisconsin Railway stock never appear in financial statements, we may infer that either from choice or necessity he resorted to the sale of bonds as the only means of acquiring the necessary capital and the stock of the company was issued for other purposes than to cover or represent any considerable share of the actual investment.

On obtaining title to the lands, as the work progressed, another difficulty presented itself · they were liable to taxation, and as capital is always cowardly, it became dreadfully frightened, and in 1870, being unable to negotiate further loans on that account, Messrs. Baldwin and Humbird came before the legislature and declared that the work must stop unless the lands were exempted from taxation.

The road was now completed to Augusta, in Eau Claire county, and very impatient were the people of this and the St. Croix valleys for its immediate extension, and their representatives were instructed to support almost any measure that would insure its completion, and, with little opposition, the bill to exempt for ten years became a law— all the lands being included except those lying in Pierce county.

The work was now prosecuted with great energy, and in August following, the welcome sound of the locomotive was heard in Eau Claire, and, following the example of Black River Falls and Augusta, it was made the occasion of a grand ovation. Many substantial citizens of Milwaukee, Madison, La Crosse, Hudson, St. Paul, and all the villages along the line, Chippewa Falls, Durand, and from the surrounding country, responded to the invitation to help us celebrate the memorable event. A free dinner was provided for all, and Hon. Alexander Meggett welcomed the visitors, and set forth the industrial and commercial advantages of this valley in an able and appropriate speech, pointing out many remarkable incidents in its history and development, and hailing the railroad as the harbinger of still grander achievements. It was responded to by John Nazro, of Milwaukee, in a few pertinent and appreciative remarks, acknowledging the honor of the visit, and the interest the people of his city felt in our prosperity, and of the iron bands that now linked our welfare with theirs—eulogizing Messrs. Baldwin and Humbird very handsomely.

It frequently happens that those who assume to lead public opinion and represent the interests of the community, have at heart some petty scheme of their own, in which the great mass of the people not only have no interest, but upon whom its success inflicts positive injury. It is possible that such was the case with the parties who were instrumental in passing the bill to exempt from taxation the lands of the West Wisconsin Railroad Company. Certain it is that the people residing in the locality most affected by its provisions, were never consulted—the farmers along the old line, where the great body of the lands lay. But they soon began to realize its disastrous consequences, and the next year, 1871,

Trempeleau county was excepted from its provisions, and the asssessors forthwith included the railroad lands in the real estate list.

Regarding the law as a contract between the railroad company, its creditors, and the people of Wisconsin, the managers refused to pay the tax, and brought suit to restrain the county officers from the sale and transfer of their lands under the laws provided for that purpose upon non-resident and unoccupied lands.

Upon the trial of the case before Judge Bunn, the Hon. John C. Spooner, attorney for the road, urged the binding force of said contract, the illegality of the law of 1871 which excepted Trempealeau county from its provisions after having entered into and receiving the benefits of the contract, said the creditors of the road who had advanced the money to build it, had placed implicit faith in the people of this State, and that every sense of right, manhood, and honor, bound the people to shield the company against the imposition of such a tax.

Hon. A. W. Newman, for the defence, repelled the idea of a contract in the exemption law of 1870; said the people were sovereign and independent, that if one legislature made bad laws, it was not only the right but the duty of the next to repeal them; that this law was partial, iniquitous, and clearly unconstitutional, and its repeal demanded by justice and the rights of the people. Held that the assessment was legal, and the suit was dismissed with costs. An appeal to the Supreme Court was of course taken, and, after exhaustive argument, the judgment affirmed. But the foreign bond-holders, desirous of making this a test case, appealed to the United States Supreme Court, where the cause is to be argued on its merits.

In the meantime, a constant struggle is going on to effect the repeal of the law so obnoxious to the settlers near the location of those lands, who, by the removal of the line of the road, are so far away as to reap none of its benefits, and as the exemption from tax enables the company to hold the lands at a price far above what it would sell for if subject to assessment, it is natural that the law should be very repugnant to them. It is hardships like these that has brought the whole subject of railroad subsidies and land grants into public condemnation. The statement recently made by Mr. Spooner before a legislative committee, in his argument against the repeal of this law, that "two immense fortunes had been sunk in the undertaking," needs to be taken with a great many grains of allowance. The assets of the road are undoubtedly sufficient to pay the principal and interest of every dollar actually invested, and if roads like the Green Bay and Mississippi can be built and made self-sustaining without any land grant or other subsidy, it must be self-evident that the West Wisconsin, if built without any Credit-Mobilier steals, and run economically, will be able to meet all its responsibilities either with or without the "Potter" law. It has a ten-mile feeder running up to Chippewa Falls, built during the past summer, 1874, by a company organized in that city, with the aid of twenty-five thousand dollars voted by the citizens, and being chartered with the title of Chippewa Falls and Western Railroad, it may be considered the first division of an important work to connect this valley with the great timberless but fertile regions beyond the Mississippi. Extraordinary pluck and energy were displayed by the managers in accomplishing such a work at this time.

CHAPTER XXXIX

MINERALS.

The valley of the Chippewa appears to have received very little attention, so far, from the State Geologist, or from the parties sent out by the general government to make geological surveys in this State. The party under the direction of Hon. David Dale Owen, who ascended the river in June, 1847, before referred to in this work, did nothing more than collect a few specimens, examine the formation and ascertain the general geologic structure from what was visible along the shores and in the beds of the streams. This, and all other later surveys in the northwestern part of this State, seems to have been directed almost exclusively to the mineral regions of Lake Superior, the southern boundary of which, so far as known, seems to be the Penoka Iron Range, which, extending west in irregular ridges, constitutes the "height of land," or summit, between the lake water-shed and the Chippewa and other tributaries of the Mississippi. In the absence of more complete, practical, and detailed geological surveys of this part of the State, no accurate estimate of its mineral resources can be made. It is believed that iron ore exists in many localities, that scientific examinations, capital, and enterprise will develop into sources of wealth.

On the west side of the Chippewa, a little back from the shore, at the foot of an abrupt ridge, or bluff, and a little north of the correction line, between towns thirty and thirty-one north, are found, bursting out from the side-hill, quite a number of springs, all so strongly impregnated with iron, and perhaps some other minerals, that, though clear as crystal, the water is so disagreeable to the taste that no one can drink it. A little farther in the interior, surrounded by sharp pine ridges are several stagnant ponds, the waters of which filter through the earth and find egress by these springs. And near one of these ponds, on the top of a hill originally covered with thrifty sapling pines, I counted on a single acre more than a dozen trees that had at different times been blasted by lightning. What could have attracted to this particular spot, on so many different occasions, the destructive force of this subtle agent? The locality is some two hundred rods southwest of Bob's Creek.

The southwest quarter of the southeast quarter of section nineteen, town twenty-eight north, of range eight west, in La Fayette township, is, in the spring of the year, and during high water, a lake, or constitutes part of a lake covering a hundred acres or more, which usually dries up in summer. A considerable stream, taking its rise among the sand hills to the southeast, and flowing through a marsh, empties into the lake at this point. The bottom of the lake was originally a coarse, loose sand, now covered with a deposit from the inlet a foot in depth, perhaps more near its entrance. On removing this muddy deposit, a compact stratum of iron is found an inch or two in thickness, below which is a layer of sand succeeded by another of iron, and so on in consecutive strata of sand and iron, of varying thickness, to the depth of four feet, the iron in some instances being three inches in thickness and seemingly pure ore, but as it has never been submitted to scientific test, nothing can be positively known of its value.

These iron strata appear to have been formed by deposits from the water as it filtered down through the sand during time's slow processes; but whence the source? May not those red sandstone ridges from whence comes this inlet, be the depositories of immense beds of iron?

The Rev. Dr. Alfred Brunson, so well known and so intimately identified with every historical and scientific development in this State, writes as follows in relation to the prospective mineral resources of this valley:

THOS. E. RANDALL—MY DEAR SIR:—Our correspondence in reference to the Chippewa Valley History gives me quite a brotherly feeling toward you, and should I ever visit Eau Claire, I should have a strong inclination to give you a call, and should you visit our place I should expect a return of the compliment.

The recent accounts of the discovery of gold in the woods somewhere at or near the head springs of the Chippewa, reminds me of an incident or two touching mineral matters, of which, I presume, you will write, to make your History complete. I know not how precise you will be in confining your remarks to the precise limits of the valley, or whether you will follow the windings of the ridge which [divides the waters of your river from those of other rivers and the great lake, I am unable to decide, but presume you will claim every inch of your territory, especially if rich minerals are found there.

In 1843, when I was Indian Agent at La Pointe, on Lake Superior, an Indian of mixed blood presented me with a piece of pure silver (which I yet have) about the value of half a dollar. He said he picked it out of a rock on or near the divide between the waters that flow to the south —in true Indian style. He refused to give the least intimation as to the locality, but my impression is that he was a Flambeau Indian, and that the rock lies on or near the trail leading from that lake to La Pointe, which cannot be far from the track of the railroad now being built to Ashland.

There were two trails leading from La Pointe south—one to Flambeau, and the other to the St. Croix valley. It is possible that it was the latter, but my impression is that it was the former.

Now, as the enterprise of your valley men is equal to anything, it is possible that some one, taking this hint, may find the treasure. Another mineral that may be profitable, lies nearer your city. On my way from this place to La Pointe, in the summer of 1843, after leaving the Chippewa falls, our route was between the waters of the Chippewa and Cedar. At one of our camps, which, I think, could not have been more than forty or fifty miles from the falls, possibly not so much now, a young Indian in our company (no other Indian then being present) told my son, B. W. Brunson, now of St. Paul, and Mr. Wm. Warren, my interpreter, that we were near the "Red Pipe-stone" mountain, and offered to pilot them to it if they would not tell the Indians of it, for if they knew of his showing a white man where it was, they would kill him. He led them to the mound by one route and from it by another, and left at the mound a plug of tobacco and some other trifling article, to appease the Manitou, or Great Spirit, on account of the trespass on the sacred spot. This, he said, was the Indian custom in visiting that mound to obtain stones of which they made their pipes.

Of the specimen brought away, several pipes were whittled out with knives and carried along. This stone hardens on being exposed to the air. It admits of a glossy polish, like marble, and is impervious to the oil of tobacco from smoking. I should think it could be turned to profit for slabs or furniture, where red instead of white should be the fancy. The locality of this mound is difficult to settle. In looking over the map of the State, I see we must have traveled near the line between ranges ten and eleven, mostly in range ten, and should think the mound is in town thirty-four or thirty-five, in range ten. Respectfully,

ALFRED BRUNSON.

Pipe-stone mountain, referred to by the learned Doctor, or "Mountain of the Prairie," as Longfellow calls it in Hiawatha, is situated on the west half of section twenty-seven, town thirty-five north, of range ten west.

It is now owned by H. C. Putnam, Esq., of this city, who bought it of the government some time ago, after having personally examined the premises. His visit was made under the guidance of an Indian half-breed, who was quite as superstitious in regard to the desecration of the sacred spot, as was the one who attended the party of Dr. Brunson.

Mr. Putnam describes it as an oblong, irregular mound, rising two hundred and fifty to three hundred feet above the surrounding surface, sloping down from the summit on the north and west in irregular but not very bold declivities, but on the southeast in a concave form, as though a section of the hill had at some time lost its foundation and sunk, a third or more of its original size breaking off in a curved perpendicular line, and even now presenting a sublime exhibition of the convulsions of nature, well calculated to inspire awe in the savage breast. Before its upheaval, the mound appears to have been a mass of very fine red clay, which has hardened into a compact, nearly seamless, beautiful stone, well adapted to the purpose to which the Indians have applied it, and, no doubt, will be found far more useful and ornamental when the artistic skill of his less superstitious, enlightened successors, have opened the ways of commerce, and carved the easily wrought, but beautiful and substantial material into forms of elegance, adapted to the wants of civilization.

Small nuggets of silver and specimens of silver ore have occasionally been brought down the river by Indian and half-breed hunters, ever since the first white settlers came here, said to have been gathered on the rocky shores of some of the small lakes, on the head waters of the Flambeau, but nothing could induce those hunters to disclose the precise locality, and we must trust to time, circumstances, and scientific research to unfold this hidden wealth.

In ascending the Chippewa from its mouth, we discover the same sandstone formation that underlies the whole Mississippi valley, but the limestone with which it is overlaid disappears at Durand, above which, with a single exception in the big woods west of Menomonee, no calcareous rock is found, and the sandstone becomes thinner, more uneven, rising in places into irregular jagged peaks and ridges, between which the river has worn itself a winding bed, until we reach the falls, where, in a descent of twenty-two feet over the hardest granite, nearly vertical in its structure, it has scarcely made an impression on the obdurate rock in all the ages.

A few miles above this point, the sandstone formation entirely disappears, granite boulders disfigure the surface of the soil in many places, and obstruct the navigation of the river; a rock so hard as to be almost unmanageable for building purposes.

In town twenty-six north, range three west, in Clark county, on the head waters of Wedges creek, and near the source of the south fork of Hay creek, there rises suddenly to the traveler, right up in the midst of a dense forest of tall timber, a stupendous hill or mountain of pure crystallized sandstone, compact, fine-grained, white in some places as the driven snow, which glistened in the setting sun at the time I visited it in 1855 like polished marble. The peak rises about four hundred feet above the surface of the surrounding country, and seems to have been shot up to an immense height, as great masses that have fallen from its top and been detached from its sides, lie in great, irregular heaps at its base —beautiful in the confusion which surrounds them. See Webb's geological report for a more definite description of this striking instance of Nature's handiwork in the creation of a most romantic spot.

CHAPTER XL.

In looking over what has been stated in this work in regard to the seasons, I think of some things that have been omitted which may interest the reader and preserve the record of some of the most remarkable atmospheric changes, extremes in temperature and variations in the climate of this part of the State at a time when there were no newspapers nor newspaper reporters here to take note of them. Messrs. Allen and Brunette concur in the statement that the winter of 1837-8, and the spring of 1838, were very remarkable for extremes of cold and heat, of drought and flood.

Those of my readers whose memory reaches back to the fall of the first named year, will remember it as the one in which occurred the most remarkable meteoric illumination on record. An old fashioned January thaw, accompanied with rain, thunder and lightning dissolved the ice in the Mississippi, and enabled a steamboat to come up in "the middle of the winter," as a French flour dealer in Galena said when his monopoly in that article was broken by its arrival; succeeded by four weeks of the coldest weather ever known at that season of the year throughout the Northwest—marked the beginning of 1838. Spring came early, the month of March being cloudless and warm as June, but the most fearful storms of winds, hail, rain, thunder and lightning prevailed in April, May and June,—the temperature varying in twenty-four hours from zero to seventy on some occasions—and causing the highest water in the Chippewa ever known—such a freshet as if it were to occur now would sweep away millions of dollars worth of property, including every bridge on the river; and submerged every farm and mill on the Chippewa bottoms below Eau Claire to the depth of several feet. The Mississippi was also very high, flooding "Wabashaw's Prairie," where Winona now stands, with water ten feet deep

The winter of 1845-6, was in some respects a most uncommon one, preceded by a most lovely "Indian summer," lasting until near the close of November, it set in with a furious snow storm succeeded by a cold snap of such intensity as to close the Chippewa in a single night, almost its entire length. This cold term extended to the Gulf of Mexico, with terrible severity, closing the Mississippi at St. Louis and Memphis, causing immense damage to steamboats lying at the levee in the former city, when the ice broke up four weeks later.

After this first snow scarcely any fell during the winter here; what is still more remarkable, was the long thaw that followed, so warm that by the tenth of January, 1846, there was scarcely a speck of ice in the Chippewa. There was no rain, but the snow dissolved under the influence of the summer like sun breaking into the calculations of the loggers with ruinous effect. Just such a winter now would be better than a dozen Saginaw conventions to raise the price of lumber.

Directly the reverse of this, but quite as disastrous to loggers and business generally were the winters of 1842-3, and 1856-7, setting in early in November, they will ever be remembered as "the deep snow winters," snowing one day and blowing the next, almost the entire season. In the woods, heavy, compact snow lay on the ground everywhere, six feet deep, and in many places ten, while the prairies were piled with drifts that obstructed all the ways of travel, and hemmed in many an isolated new settler, and as effectually cutting off communication with the rest of the world for the time being, as though he were the only man upon the earth. Some of our more recent winters have been pretty severe on railroads in the Northwest, but one like either of those would well nigh bankrupt all the feeble ones.

But the winter that came on the earliest was that of 1873–4. Snow sufficient to make good sleighing falling on the twenty-fifth day of October and continuing until spring; it was, however, a very mild winter.

The religious and educational interests of this valley have, perhaps, received less attention in these pages than they deserve, and I think of some items which should not be lost.

The reader has already been informed that a large share of the settlers of Chippewa Falls were Canadian French, succeeded by another large percentage of Irish and German of the Roman Catholic faith, good citizens, and zealous Christians in their way, but not to be counted on when the claims of other sects are presented in the furtherance of any religious enterprise, which, with the hardships attending new and hazardous undertakings, the constantly recurring losses to which the mill company was subjected, and the struggles of every one to provide for his own, made the prospect for establishing a Protestant church there in 1856, look very discouraging. But in the summer of that year, Rev. W. W. McNair came up the river, charged with the responsibility of founding Presbyterian churches and erecting church edifices at that place and Eau Claire.

Of the Protestant population then at the Falls, not more than six or eight persons of both sexes considered themselves as even nominal Presbyterians, but amongst them were three sisters of E. A. Galloway, whose zeal and sympathies were immediately enlisted in the good cause.

The company of H. S. Allen & Co., of course, subscribed liberally, gave the building, lot, lumber, and materials, but under the constant pressure of business cares and liabilities, could bestow little attention on religious or other enterprises. The three sisters had little to bestow, but their hearts were willing and their hands active. Money was very plenty, and all around them were men whose earnings were daily squandered at the card table and saloon. Their only hope was to induce some of these men to appropriate a share of their means to a better object, even if the motive was inspired by no higher consecration.

The company was erecting a large new hotel; some of its largest rooms would answer for pleasant, social, evening parties; a dance in Chippewa Falls had never been known to fail in bringing "down the dust" from the stingiest pocket. Sham post-offices, fish pools, and grab bags may be by some considered a more innocent or less culpable method of raising money for a good cause, but these sisters secured good music, prepared generous plain lunches, charged a moderate fee, and induced almost every young man in the place, married or single, Catholic, Protestant, or Nothingarian, to contribute something towards the Presbyterian church, and the donors were all better pleased than they could have been at their usual haunts.

Shall any one say that the efforts and offerings of these ladies were less acceptable because "dancing" was a part of the social recreation at these gatherings?

At the same time, Mr. McNair was maturing arrangements for erecting a church in Eau Claire, which, through the liberality of the proprietors of the village and the earnest efforts of the ladies, the pastor, and the people, was completed the next year, as heretofore stated. Festivals were frequently held by the former to raise the necessary funds, an account of one of which I find in the Eau Claire Times of November 7th, 1857,—a spicy little sheet of Democratic proclivities, the first newspaper issued in this valley, the first number on the 21st of August, 1857—from which I make the following extracts:

"At about ten o'clock the signal was given for supper, and about one hundred and fifty individuals sat down to the daintily spread board."

A pretty large crowd, we should think, even no *w*, for a religious festival.

"After the cloth was removed, speeches were made by N. B. Boyden, Esq., A. Meggett, Esq., and Rev. W. W. McNair."

A few extracts from the many good things in Mr. Meggett's speech, seem appropriate here. He said:

"We are met here, my friends, to contribute of our substance that the first temple of religion reared in this valley may be appropriately adorned and it may be, as we have participated in these scenes and witnessed the arrangements made by fair hands and willing hearts for our enjoyment, that present admiration rather than reflection has crowded from our minds all thoughts of the transcendent importance of the work before us.   *   *   *   *   Man is eminently a religious being, and though often departing from the immutable principle of right, his loftiest aspirations, his tenderest emotions, his finest feelings and sublimest conceptions, have their foundation in, and are most intimately connected with, his religious nature—the avenue through which you must approach him in order to wield the power of revealed truth, if you would save him from the grossness of sin and secure to him the joys of a pure and holy life. Without religious culture his whole life is a moral waste, a desert unrelieved by a single oasis of virtue and high-toned thought and aspiration. * * * Nothing could argue so well for the character of our people as the early erection of a temple of worship under circumstances so disheartening, but now the work is nearly completed, and to you, sir, its pastor, who have watched over it from its first inception, we, as a community, owe a debt of gratitude we can never pay."

"Appropriate toasts followed, by the speaker, Mrs. Thorp, N. C. Chapman, and Mr. Porter, responded to by Rev. Mr. McNair."

Like all other people, the early settlers of Eau Claire who had contributed of their means to erect this first church, had their preferences in regard to who should occupy its pulpit. Rev. Mr. Kidder, from the city of New York, had removed to the village while the church was in process of building, and, during the absence of Mr. McNair, preached in the new church before its dedication. A Congregationalist of the more advanced and liberal school, a classical speaker and earnest worker, he soon became a great favorite with all the people of more advanced thought and liberal Christian views. And, naturally enough, as their means contributed largely toward the building, they claimed the right to ask that Mr. Kidder be installed its pastor.

Considerable bitterness grew out of this question, but it was finally arranged that Mr. Kidder should have a church on the West Side—a Congregational church, which, notwithstanding the prostration of business and the decline in the price of lumber, went forward under the superintendence of the pastor, who had already organized a church, and by persistent encouragement, economy, and energy its completion was accomplished.

As usual in the settlement of new countries, quite a number of Universalists, and others of the more radical religious element, had found homes in Eau Claire, but for a long time no effort was made to ascertain their number or strength. Some time before Christmas of the year 1858, Mrs. Edwin Wilkins issued a card inviting all Universalists and other liberally inclined religious people in Eau Claire and vicinity, without any distinction of age, sex, condition, or acquaintanceship, to meet at her house on the evening of that day to confer with each other in regard to their mutual religious welfare and future advancement, and to enjoy her hospitality. It met a hearty response from a large number of intelligent, earnest, liberal, Christian men and women, who, after mutual congratulations, organized a Universalist sociable, to meet once a week, for mutual improvement, and with a view to the establishment of a Universalist church. In July of the next year, 1859, Rev. Dolphus Skinner, of Utica, N. Y., came to Eau Claire on a visit to his son, Dr. F. R. Skinner, and held divine services on Sunday morning at Reed's Hall, and in the afternoon on the West Side. These were powerful discourses, and confirmed many wavering minds in the doctrine of God's impartial grace.

The sociables were well sustained, and quite a fund accumulated in its treasury, and in February, 1860, Rev. Joseph O. Barrett was engaged to minister to their spiritual wants. Services were held at first in Reed's Hall, but building lots were soon bought and exchanged with the East Side school district, whose house had become too small, and a house of worship secured.

The society was now considered very prosperous, united, and flourishing, but the war created dissensions, many of the ablest and most influential of the members removed to other localities, and now the house and lot are the only remaining evidences that such Christians as Universalists live in the city. Unfaithful pastors, however, are greatly responsible for this state of things.

Perhaps no Christian people ever struggled harder to establish themselves in a new locality than the Methodists of this city. Few at first in numbers, and still more feeble in point of wealth, their progress was at first very slow : their school, the "Wesleyan Institute," received no endowment, though it flourished for a year or two ; but the ministrations of that church are so well adapted to the religious wants of the masses, and its preachers have been so zealous and active, that seemingly insurmountable obstacles have been overcome, and two church edifices, one on each Side, have been built, and large congregations worship therein.

The Baptists, Catholics, and German Lutherans have each a church and sustain religious services in this city, and the Lutherans from Norway and Sweden, Rev. Ammon Johnson pastor, have two fine churches, one on each side, and the Episcopalians have commenced the erection of a fine edifice.

Eau Claire boasts of four flourishing graded district schools, and three denominational in a feeble condition, the greater advantages of the graded schools withdrawing their support.

In Chippewa Falls the authorities have divided the school fund between the Catholic and Protestant population, and each has a flourishing graded school at which their children respectively attend, but both are under the direction of the Public School Board and County Superintendent as district common schools.

CHAPTER XLI.

As long ago as 1850 a law was passed for the organization of Dallas county, the territory of which lies mostly in this valley and drained by the Red Cedar. Aside from its wealth of pine timber, much of the soil is very rich, which of late has induced many farmers to avail themselves of the homestead law and secure homes there. It was at first included in the eleventh judicial district, but subsequently, in 1865, was attached to the eighth, and in 1868, after several modifications of its boundaries, its name was changed to Barron, and it was attached to Dunn for judicial purposes until 1872, when it was detached therefrom and the year following organized for judicial purposes; the first term of court, however, was held in October last, 1874, but as there were no jury cases on the calendar, we may infer that the settlers up there are very peaceable.

Knapp, Stout & Co. have a mill at the outlet of Rice Lake, where a flourishing village has started up, and where, until recently, the county offices and the courts have been held, but by a vote of the electors lately taken, the county seat is removed to Quaderer's camp, some six or eight miles west and north of the former place.

Considerable dissatisfaction exists at this result, and the probability is that its removal is only a question of time, as several of the county officers refuse to recognize the decision of the vote.

The prejudice against the aforesaid company induced the settlers to vote for the removal, but this will probably soon die out and harmony be restored.

An important decision has just been rendered in the Supreme Court in suit brought by several non-resident holders of land in this county to set aside the sale of certain land for taxes, on account of illegality in their assessment. Held, that the assessment and sale was informal and void.

A portion of the lands donated by Congress, in 1856, for the benefit of the St. Croix & Lake Superior, now known as the North Wisconsin, Railway, lies in this county, and being drained by the Red Cedar, some of them have suffered from the depredations of loggers, for which suits are now pending to recover damages.

Repeated efforts have been made in the legislature, by the non-resident proprietors of lands in Chippewa county, to create a new county therefrom, comprising the pine lands, with a view to lighten the burdens of taxation, but so far such attempts have proved fruitless, owing, probably, to the fact that the resident population oppose the project. Fraught, as the present arrangement apparently is, with injustice, it, nevertheless, has its advantages in the laying out and opening roads through wild, uninhabited districts, so necessary to the lumbermen in getting supplies to their camps. A wise provision has been made by act of the legislature in granting ten per cent. of the proceeds from the sale of swamp lands in the county to construct bridges and open leading highways, which has been of essential benefit both to lumbermen and settlers on the soil, most of whom are homesteaders. It has been noticed, however, that for a road to derive any of these advantages, the lower terminus must be Chippewa Falls. A State road, authorized by the legislature in 1868, extending from Eau Claire, via Bloomer, to Ashland, is utterly ignored by the County Board of that county, not even the cost of laying it out being allowed to the commissioners appointed for that purpose. This is perfectly natural, and there may have been some irregularity in the survey or report to justify its action.

Many of the upper branches of the Chippewa are crossed by the line of the Central Railway, which, when completed, will develop extensive settlements, and it is hoped may open large mining operations in that portion of this valley. Loggers already find that road very convenient in transporting their men and supplies, and steam mills are going up near the track as fast as the road is completed.

The completion of this road and the North Wisconsin, obliquely crossing as they do the northeastern and northwestern sections of our valley, may develop its resources but will necessarily divert much of the trade and profit to other centers of business, which it seems as though the people of this valley ought to have secured.

Railways, too, have proved terribly destructive to pine timber wherever crossed by their tracks, as no method has yet been devised to prevent sparks [from the locomotive setting fire to combustible material, as it speeds along on its course.

These and the steam mills will undoubtedly destroy large tracts of our most valuable timber, and it will be much to be deplored if some of the railroads now contemplated shall pierce and destroy the pine forests whose destruction is already menaced, but which can be only accomplished by the agency of fire. The organization of two new counties may be expected to follow the completion of the Central Railroad, fifty-five miles of which are still unfinished. A branch road from a point called the Elbow to Chippewa Falls is contemplated, which time and enterprise may eventually accomplish; and from thence to intersect the North Wisconsin at some point in Barron county, with the Chippewa Valley road extended to the Mississippi, would place that city in a most enviable situation in regard to railway communication, without threatening any serious danger to the pine timber, in whose preservation every inhabitant of the Great West should feel an interest. True, it is now being cut off with alarming rapidity, but fire alone can stop its growth, and a healthy forest of pine timber may be cut over every ten years, if fire can be kept out.

There are extensive tracts of pine and hemlock timber that are and always will be utterly useless for cultivation, but being covered with thrifty growing timber will always be valuable, unless fires break out and consume them.

A growing forest of towering pine timber is one of the grandest sights in the world, and a standing monument of God's goodness and provident care, and next to the grasses and spontaneous fruit-bearing trees and shrubs, is, of all inanimate things, the most convenient and valuable, as so much ready capital to be appropriated by labor to human wants; mines of gold and silver offer tempting prizes as the reward of the toiler, and the rich virgin soil of the prairies promises abundant returns for the husbandman's labor, but none of these yield results so surely and in so little time—are not so immediately available—as a pine forest out of which to hew a fortune; hence, while the supply lasts, we may expect the business to be overdone.

Scientific experiment, inventive genius, and tireless energy have furnished facilities so ample and machinery so complete for the manufacture of lumber, performing an amount of labor so vast, so skillfully, and with such celerity, that it would seem that the supply of pine must be infinite or very soon fail.

A few examples will show the difference between the old and new machinery and methods in the manufacture of lumber.

The best work ever done by H. S. Allen & Co. with the old process and machinery—the mills having been enlarged since by the addition of only one small gang—produced a little over seventeen million feet of lumber during the season; now, with the same power but with new wheels, improved saws, and the most superior machinery produced by modern invention, the Union Lumbering Company annually turn out forty-five million feet of lumber of superior manufacture. Rotary and gang saws, patent log turners, self-setting carriages, machines for boring grub-planks, saw setters and saw filers, with many other labor-saving appliances are employed, and driven by this splendid water-power.

Experience has shown that lumber can not be manufactured and sent to market from mills above Chippewa Falls, so as to compete with mills lower down on the river, and one after another has succumbed to the unequal and adverse circumstances, until scarcely a crib of lumber passes over the raft-slides of the three great dams at the Falls, Paint Creek, and Eagle Rapids. What use may yet be made of the vast power which these two upper dams afford, time alone can determine; but so long as lumber must be rafted and run to market, the water power of the lower dam, at the Falls, will probably be used for its manufacture.

The city of Chippewa Falls is the headquarters for a very large share of the lumber, or rather logging, operations on the Chippewa; its future prosperity depends largely upon the permanence and stability of the booming works at Paint Creek and Eagle Rapids—works of immense strength, but the river is every where hemmed in between high banks, affording scarcely a cove, pocket, or lagoon where logs can lie safe out of the surging current, and have not been tested by such floods as have heretofore swept away in a day the earnings of years. Should these works prove efficient against such dangers, few localities in the Northwest occupy so commanding a position as the city of Chippewa Falls. Its citizens are noted for pluck, energy, and boundless confidence in the future greatness of their city.

No place, perhaps, has been so unfortunate in the destruction of its best hotels by fire. The first one, a large, three-story structure, erected in 1856, by H. S. Allen & Co., was destroyed two or three years later, rebuilt by Mr. Sellers in 1862, took the name Tremont in 1865, under the proprietorship of Messrs. Pierce & Upham,—men who know how to keep a hotel—shared the fate of the former in 1870, and the following summer saw a splendid five-story brick palace go up on the same site. It was erected by Messrs. Pierce, Upham, and William R. Hoyt, Esq., at an expense of more than one hundred thousand dollars, contained over eighty rooms, was lighted with gas and heated by steam, too costly and extravagant in all its appointments for such a place at that time, and when finished had completely bankrupted its projectors, and the property being sold by the assignee, came into the possession of George Winans, formerly a Mississippi raft pilot, who took possession of the house himself and probably would have made it a success in time, but during his absence in the winter of 1873 the fire fiend was let loose and this grand structure, the pride of the whole valley, fell a prey to its fury. Its loss was very much deplored, and it will long live in the memory of the people of this part of the State, as the scene of a very pleasant gathering in the winter of 1871-2, of the old settlers of the northwestern part of the State. It will probably never be rebuilt. Soon after, the Waterman House shared the same fate, but, phœnix-like, it has risen up from its ashes, and with the Central, run by the old indomitable firm of Pierce & Upham, and some new houses of lesser note, affords very good hotel accommodations to the city and business community.

In addition to the vast water-power afforded by the Chippewa, numerous dams have been erected on Duncan's creek, and two large flouring mills and two planing mills are in successful operation on this stream, owned respectively by H. S. Allen, McRae Brothers, and S. M. Newton & Co.

Besides many large business blocks and elegant private residences, the city boasts of having the most imposing court house in the valley, erected in 1873-4 at a cost of $75,000.

Presbyterian, Methodist, Episcopal, and Catholic churches, and two commodious graded school buildings, also adorn the city. The soil of the surrounding country is generally fertile, and is being rapidly settled by thriving farmers, who find an excellent home market for all their produce in the city.

Two weekly newspapers are published here. The Herald, published by Col. Ginty, is ably conducted, is the exponent of Republican principles, and has the public patronage. The other, called the Avalanche, is owned by an association and edited, at present, by a gentleman named Hollister. Its politics are Conservative.

With all these and many other advantages, with its present and prospective railroad facilities, and the growing importance of its commerce, the city of Chippewa Falls undoubtedly has a grand future before it. A thriving tributary village has started up in the town of Bloomer, known heretofore as Vanville, but lately changed to Bloomer.

Messrs. Smith, Brooks & McCauley have a flouring mill, saw mill, and shingle mill there, driven by Duncan's creek. The village is fourteen miles from the city, has a Congregational church, and a commodious graded school house.

In all that pertains to thrift and progress, Dunn county, during and since the war, is not a whit behind the most prosperous localities in the northwestern part of the State. An intelligent, enterprising farming population have secured homes in the fertile portions of the county, and many beautiful rural residences are seen in every township, and the village of Menomonie has an imposing court house, two Baptist and two Methodist Episcopal churches, one Congregational, one Catholic, one Lutheran Scandinavian, and an Episcopal church edifice in process of erection, two model graded school houses, and a great many beautiful private residences. In addition to their saw mills, the company of Knapp, Stout & Co. have an extensive flouring mill, a very large and commodious slaughter and packing house, and are extensively engaged in farming in the neighborhood of the village.

At Red Cedar falls, six miles above Menomonie, S. A. Jewett & Co. have a saw mill, and quite a village has sprung up around it. The mill was erected by the Gilbert brothers, from Gilbert's creek, just before the commencement of the late war. The present owners purchased a considerable amount of pine land on the tributaries of the Red Cedar in 1855-6, and have enlarged the mill to a second-class establishment. Its capacity is about eight millions per annum. Mr. Jewett is from Bangor, Maine, and is connected with the banking house of Jewett & March, of that city.

One newspaper, the Dunn County News, is published at Menomonie. It was started in 1859, by S. C. and E. B. Bundy, with the title of Dunn County Lumberman, and is now published by Hon. R. G. Flint. It is a sound Republican journal, and fully up with the times in all that relates to the welfare of the county and village.

The Barron County Chronotype is a new paper just established in that county, by S. C. Carpenter, but is now published by R. F. Wilson, H. C. Putnam, and Knapp, Stout & Co.

CHAPTER XLII.

So important a public measure as the passage of the "Dalles bill," in the shape of an amendment to the charter of the city of Eau Claire, and becoming a law just at this time, has induced 'the author to extend this work so as to give a brief account of the contest in the legislature to secure its enactment, provisions of the law, and its relations to the business interest of the valley.

The law simply authorizes the city of Eau Claire in its corporate capacity, to erect a dam sixteen feet high across the Chippewa river, to place piers, booming and sorting works in the river, at suitable points, and to lease the water power and works to responsible parties, and binds the city to make and operate free of charge a lock for the passage of steamboats, a safe and suitable raft slide for two strings in width of rafts over the dam, and unobstructed raft channel past the booming works at all times, and to pay all damages incurred by any and all parties from the erection of these works.

As the city of Eau Claire is a responsible party, and abundantly able to indemnify all parties for such loss if any were sustained, it seems as though no objection could be urged against the measure on that account; and so it must have appeared to the members of the legislature, and the executive of the State as the bill passed both houses, and became a law within two weeks after its introduction.

The personal popularity of our Senator and Assemblyman, Messrs. Graham and Callahan, undoubtedly did much to insure the passage of the bill, an efficient lobby was also on the ground, and the audacity of the Eagle Rapids bill which provided, had it become a law for that institution to collect ten cents per thousand feet for all logs passing that point, may have roused some interested parties in other parts of the State, who in a spirit of retaliation favored the claims of Eau Claire in this contest; but more potent and above all was the conviction throughout the State, that the interest and welfare of the people demanded the law. This conviction has been gaining ground ever since the first agitation of the subject, and it has now found public expression in this enactment. The people of Eau Claire seem very much in earnest in this matter, and will probably vote any amount of bonds necessary to carry out the objects authorized by the law, and it is hoped that all opposition to so beneficent a work will cease.

Whatever cause for alarm or uneasiness, any party may entertain in regard to losses likely to be inflicted upon their interests by these operations, one very favorable aspect of the case is observed in the fact that all the mills between the Dalles and Chippewa Falls, manifest no opposition, but are rather favorable to the projected improvement.

The aggregate amount of lumber annually manufactured at these mills, is greater than the quantity made at the Falls, and if any real danger were apprehended to their interests by the construction of these works, it would seem as though all would make common cause against it. These mills have been erected at great expense, and their success, and even their existence is just as much imperiled as the mills at the Falls, and yet their owners appear very well pleased at the prospect of these improvements.

As some of these establishments have received no attention in these pages a brief reference to each may not be out of place here.

In the summer of 1867, Ed. Coleman and James Mitchell, two enterprising young men at the Falls, erected a steam saw mill, and the necessary booming works at French Town, which after several assignments is now run in the interest of A. K. Shaw & Co.; it is a good little mill. Then comes the Gravel Island Mill, commenced in 1857, by Martin Daniels and Ephraim E. Shaw, and completed the year following by Bussy & Taylor, who established booming works above the Island; it was burnt in the fall of 1863, and rebuilt the year following by James A. Taylor. It is favorably situated three miles below the Falls, and is a very good mill, now run by a company of enterprising Frenchmen, under the firm name of the French Lumber Company. It lacks some of the latest improvements in mill machinery. The mill frequently referred to as the "Blue Mills," first erected in 1842-3, was after many vicissitudes taken down in 1864, and a large establishment driven partly by steam, (the first was propelled by a spring creek), erected in its place by H. Clay Williams & John Barron. A nice arrangement for elevating the logs by water power from the river into the mill pond, where they are safe from freshets and danger, has since been added.

The capacity of this mill is from twelve to fifteen millions for the season, has most of the late improvements in machinery, and is now owned by a corporation with the title of "Badger State Lumber Company." A lath, shingle mill and pail factory are connected with this mill.

Three miles below is the LaFayette mill, erected in 1863-4, by Charles Coleman, of Chippewa Falls, its capacity is about the same as the Badger State Mill, has ample storage booms, and convenient sorting works, and is now owned and operated by John and George Robson, of Winona. A terrible boiler explosion occurred at this mill in the summer of 1869, by which one man was fatally and others badly injured. Two miles lower down is the Wheaton Mill, built in 1869-70, by Ira Mead, Frank McGuire, Saul & Lally, capable of cutting six million feet per season. It is now run by the two latter gentlemen. These are all in Chippewa county.

Two miles below are the mills of Prescott, Burditt & Co., first erected in 1867-8, rebuilt and greatly enlarged in 1873-4, by the same company. The company of Graham, White & Co., own a controlling interest in this mill, and it is complete in all its appointments. Its annual cut is from ten to fifteen millions. The Wilkins Island Booming Works accomodate this mill; it is erected on the East Side, and nearly opposite is the mill built by Mr. Farwell, and now owned by W. T. Weber. And one mile below on the same side is the famous, but now idle mill, erected in 1863-4, by Horton & Van Buren, Barron, and H. Clay Williams, subsequently sold to Nelson, Hunter & Co. It is near this mill that the raft channel cut-off is to be excavated, which will shorten the running distance for rafts more than two miles, and leave the river for more than that distance as a safe reservoir for logs. The mill and peninsular tract of land belonging to it are now owned by various parties amongst whom is the Union Lumber Company of Chippewa Falls.

Then right at the head or upper entrance of the Dalles, is the Eddy Mill, of Ingram & Kennedy, commenced in 1860, by A. M. & S. Sherman, the former of whom entered the army, and the work lingered, and after a sickly existence was sold in 1869, to the present enterprising firm who moved and rebuilt the mill on its present site the year following, and made it one of the best mills on the river. All the last named mills are within the limits of the city of Eau Claire, but with the exception of the last will continue to use and depend upon the Eagle Rapids Boom to store a considerable share of their logs, even after the works are completed at the Dalles.

The report of Colonel Farquhar, of the United States Engineers, lately submitted to the War Department, of a survey made last summer by his assistant, Captain Turner, recommends the erection of dams and locks at the foot of both the lower and upper Dalles, as the only way to improve the navigation of the river at those points, and if the provisions of the law are effectually carried out by the city in the erection of these works, navigation of the river will be greatly improved. as now, in low water, it is with much difficulty that a single string of lumber can be navigated over the tortuous, shallow channel, and too frequently, for the owner's profit or the pleasure of the crew, sticks fast on the rocks and must be taken off in separate cribs, with handspikes. Raftsmen will have occasion to rejoice when relieved from this hardship.

Substantial manufacturing establishments will undoubtedly follow the completion of these works, and a reservoir for logs absolutely safe from the highest flood, will mark the improvement as the best investment and the grandest enterprise of the kind in the valley—because Nature has planned the situation for just such an undertaking, and during all these years has invited man's handiwork to make it available.

The mills below the Dalles to be benefitted by this work are two owned by Ingram & Kennedy, one by the Valley Lumber Company, a corporation, one run by Tarrant Brothers & Bletcher, one by J. P. Pinkum & Co., one by the Daniel Shaw Lumber Company, a corporation, one by W. B. Esterbrooks, one by Boyd & Randall, one by Gorton Brothers, one by the Northwestern Lumber Company, and several others lower down on the river. One of the two first named was built by Adin Randall, in 1858, came into the possession of Stephen Marston some time afterward, who finally sold it to the present owners. It was the third mill started by Mr. Randall, all near the connecting chute to Half Moon Lake. The other was erected by the present owners and Mr. Dole, in 1857-8, was the second steam mill erected in this valley, was destroyed by fire in 1861, was rebuilt and enlarged immediately, and has been one of the most successful establishments on the river. It was the first to introduce the improved patent sawdust carrier and distributor; an invention that substitutes the sawdust made by a steam mill almost exclusively for other fuel.

The third one named was commenced by Adin Randall in 1857, sold to and completed by Ball & Smith, the former of whom sold his interest to G. A. Buffington, since which time it has been operated by the firm of Smith & Buffington until this winter, 1874, when the new company, composed of the last named firm and Carson & Rand, of Eau Galla, an organized corporation, removed the old mill and are erecting on its site one of the largest steam mills in this valley. Their millwright is the well known George Barton, who has superintended the laying the foundations and every part of it, and intends to make it one of the most complete mills in all its appointments in the northwest. The company has a paid up capital of four hundred and fifty thousand dollars already invested in the undertaking. Mr Pond's improved setting and dogging apparatus, and a newly invented log turner, are amongst the improved machinery of this mill. Martin Daniels, Bangs & Fish, and R. F. Wilson built the mill now operated by the Tarrant Brothers, in 1866-7, which, by some means, has been involved in more legal difficulties than any other on the river, but is a good mill and the present proprietors will probably extricate it from all its troubles.

At the outlet of Half Moon Lake stands the mill of the Daniel Shaw Lumber Company, the site for which was selected in 1856, before the introduction of steam mills on the Chippewa. Unable to overcome the difficulties involved in building at the Dalles, Mr. Shaw located here as the next best point, resolved to await future developments.

Half Moon Lake is a safe reservoir for logs, but the uncertainty of getting them in there makes it an important matter to secure other means of storing their logs. The mill was burnt in 1867 and rebuilt the year following by the present able company, composed of Daniel Shaw, Mr. Bullen, Mr. Newell, and Mr. Furgerson, who became incorporated in 1874. Their mill is one of the most extensive and substantial in the valley, with all the new improvements in machinery, and its capacity is over twenty million feet per season. A steam flouring mill has lately been erected by the company. The two next named mills have scarcely any booming privileges, and will find their property very much enhanced in value by the completion of the new works at the Dalles.

The Northwestern Lumber Company's mill occupies the site of the mill commenced by Charles Warner and completed by Porter & Brown in 1864, consumed by fire in the fall of 1867, rebuilt and enlarged by Mr. Porter, who subsequently associated D. R. Moon with him in the business. The establishment is hardly excelled by any in the country, combining farming, merchandizing, and various smaller manufactories with that of lumber. The company's business office is in this city, and connected with the mill six miles below by a telegraph wire. All these mills have suffered for want of storage for logs, and have sometimes seen almost the season's supply float past them to the Mississippi, because no safe reservoir could be provided.

In April, 1866, occurred one of those destructive freshets, bringing down jams of ice, logs, and drift-wood in such force as to carry away booms, piers, and all other obstructions that interfered with the swollen, uncontrollable flood. The entire Chippewa bottom was overflowed and covered with logs and drift-wood. There was no Beef Slough boom, then, and the delta of the river, and even many islands in the Mississippi, were piled with logs, and such quantities deposited on the intervening Chippewa bottoms, that several of our mill men established portable steam mills to manufacture them into lumber. I need hardly add that conflicting claims to those logs involved several of their owners in legal difficulties so complicated and tedious that they seemed like permanent fixtures on the Circuit Court calendar. From the effects of this, and almost every other, destructive freshet, Knapp, Stout & Co., of Menomonie, and Chapman & Thorp, of Eau Claire, escaped, simply because safe, secure reservoirs for logs had been created near their mills, by overflowing low, flat basins, and taking the logs entirely out of the current, but no such place of safety had been provided on the Chippewa, and to-day we should find it little better, for I venture the prediction that the works at Eagle Rapids would not stand one hour against such a flood. My reasons are that the river directly above the "jam boom" is hemmed in between perpendicular walls of rock, and the Chippewa is one of the maddest, most ungovernable streams in the world.

Reposing in such continual security, it is not surprising that the last named companies have gone on in the even tenor of their way and accumulated great wealth, while others are involved in heavy liabilities. It is true the latter came with considerable capital, but it is because they availed themselves of the natural advantages of their position that they achieved success. Their first steam mill, erected during the hard trying times of 1857-8, was consumed by fire in 1867, but replaced the next year by one of the most complete mills in the State; their water power mill on the same site occupied by McCann & Randall's mill, and carried away by the flood of 1847, was rebuilt in 1871, its capacity quadrupled by the introduction of the Leffel turbine wheel, and all the modern improvements, among the most valuable of which are several inventions of L. W. Pond, an improved method of hanging and fastening gang saws, a machine for setting and dogging on circular saw carriage, and many other improvements in mill machinery by this inventor have been adopted.

A steam shingle mill and merchant flouring mill of large capacity, also a new and costly store to replace the one destroyed by fire in 1874, have been added to this company's city property, while title to a large amount of pine land has been secured.

The business operations of the Menomonie and Eau Galla companies have been heretofore set forth in these pages. Mr. Carson, of the latter, has already invested considerable capital at the Falls and in this city, and Knapp, Stout & Co., it is confidently expected, will invest largely in the new works at the Dalles. In addition to the manufacturing establishments already mentioned, there are several in the country around about. Hazen & Son have an excellent flouring mill on Otter creek; Peter Daniels and John Kelly are running each a good grist mill on Lowe's creek; Bump Brothers run the mill at Rock Falls, erected by Weston & Chamberlain; Mud creek, Elk creek, and Sand creek have each a grist mill, and many small steam saw mills are scattered about up the Eau Claire and Chippewa rivers.

Three good bridges for travel, one in Eau Claire and two at Chippewa Falls, also a railroad bridge at the former place, span the Chippewa;

public highways have been opened in every direction; elegant churches and school buildings are seen in every neighborhood, and all the elements of progress, comfort, convenience, and the refinements of Christian civilization have been developed in this country. Our interests are really one and inseparable; here is room for all and free scope for all our energies, and no occasion for envy or sectional bitterness; the few cannot expect to monopolize the advantages that belong of right to the many. The conflict between different localities is more imaginary than real, and the sooner kind and fraternal relations are established, the better it will be for our varied interests.

On the eleventh day of May, 1875, the qualified voters of the city of Eau Claire, in accordance with the provisions of an ordinance passed by the City Council, submitting the question of bonding the city to carry the amendment into effect, voted almost unanimously to issue bonds to the amount of one hundred thousand dollars for that purpose But parties at Chippewa Falls having obtained a writ of injunction, in the name of the Attorney General, from the Supreme Court, restraining the government of said city from issuing such bonds and from constructing any of the works contemplated by said amendment, the case came up for argument before said Court on the 18th and 19th days of May, 1875, and the injunction was sustained on the grounds that the Chippewa river is a navigable stream and a public highway, secured by treaty of cession and constitutional provisions; and that the city of Eau Claire, as a municipality, could not legally and constitutionally become a booming and manufacturing organization, such as the law contemplated.

It may be that the legal impediments that stand in the way of this great improvement will effectually prevent its construction, but its necessity was never more apparent than at this moment, as the breaking up of the ice in the Chippewa this spring completely demolished the booming and assorting works at Eagle Rapids, and more or less injured all the establishments of the kind on the river, and such will probably be the fate of those and all others until some place is adopted where logs can be taken out of the current and made secure in some overflowed marsh or bayou, and no locality on the river can ever vie with the great basin just above the lower Dalles, in natural facilities for such a work.

CHAPTER XLIII.

In the settlement of all new countries frequent changes become necessary in the organization of Senatorial and Assembly districts, and questions often arise in conversation as to the number or description of the district in which a certain locality was included at a given period.

Such changes have occurred in the districts in which this valley is situated at every decade and semi-decade since the organization of the Territory, and a concise statement of the districts in which our valley has been included, time of their formation, and the various Senators and Assemblymen whom the people have delighted to honor with seats in our Legislature, may be of interest to my readers.

But in the first place, a short account of the organization of the Territorial and State governments will claim our attention.

The name, Wisconsin, first of our Territory and since of the State, was derived from its principal river, Wees-kon-san, signifying in Indian, "The gathering of the waters." It contains 53,924 square miles, or nearly 35,000,000 acres of land, beside rivers, lakes, etc.

The act establishing the Territorial government was passed and approved April 20th, 1836, and its organization followed on the 4th of July following, with Henry Dodge, one of the heroes of the Sac and Fox war, for Governor. What is now the State of Iowa constituted part of this Territory, but in accordance with the proclamation of the Governor, the first Legislature convened at Belmont, now in La Fayette county. The second session was at Burlington, Iowa, after which the seat of government was permanently located at Madison, where the first session of the second Legislative Assembly met Nov. 26th, 1838, the Territory having been divided, by act of Congress, in June previous.

As usual in such cases, the general government made an appropriation of forty thousand dollars for the capitol building and other sums were given by Dane county and the Territory equal to twenty thousand dollars more, and a very sumptuous house was erected. As indicating the times of that early day, a quotation from the Legislative Manual of 1874, as given by Col. Childs, one of the early pioneers of the Territory, will amuse the reader.

He says: "The Legislature met for the first time at Madison on the 26th of November, 1838. The new capitol edifice was not yet in a suitable condition to receive the Legislature, so we had to assemble in the basement of the American House, where Governor Dodge delivered his first message at the new seat of government.

"After some time, we took possession of the new Assembly hall, the floors of which were laid with green oak boards full of ice; the walls of the room were iced over; green oak seats and desks, made of rough boards; one fire-place and one small stove. In a few days the flooring near the stove and fire-place shrank so that one could run his hands between the boards. The basement story was all open and James Morrison's large drove of hogs had taken possession; they were awfully poor, and it would have taken two of them standing side by side to make a decent shadow on a bright day. We had a great many smart members in the House, and sometimes they spoke for buncombe. When members of this ilk would become too tedious, I would take a long pole and go at the hogs and stir them up, when they would raise a young pandemonium for noise and confusion. The speaker's voice would be completely drowned, and he would be compelled to stop; not, however, without giving his squealing disturbers a sample of his swearing ability.

* * * *

"The American House was the only hotel in Madison, but Mr. Peck kept a few boarders in his log house, and we used to have tall times in those days—times to be remembered. Stealing was carried on in a small way, and the Territory would occasionally get gouged a little, now and then."

The Territorial government continued from the time before stated, July 4th, 1836, until the 29th day of May, 1848, nearly twelve years.

Until the year 1840, the entire northwestern portion of the Territory was included in Crawford county, and of course the settlements on this river; represented the first year, 1836, in the House by James H. Lockwood and James B. Dallam, no member of the Council being allowed; and the second year by Ira B. Brunson and Jean Brunett.

The first session of the second Legislative Assembly convened and adjourned in 1838; in the Council, Crawford was represented for the first time by George Wilson, and in the House by Alexander McGregor, who established a ferry across the Mississippi and founded the city of McGregor, in Iowa. The next year, second session of the second Legislature, Ira B. Brunson was added to the House from Crawford.

At the third session of the second Assembly, 1839-40, Joseph Brisbois was elected to the Council, Wilson having resigned. St. Croix county was established at the extra session of this Legislature, Charles J. Learned having taken the place of Brisbois in the Council.

At the first session of the third Assembly, Crawford and St. Croix being still one district, Mr. Learned was in the Council, and Alfred Brunson (the Rev. Dr.) and Joseph R. Brown were members of the House, but at the next session 1841-2, the seat of the former was successfully contested by and awarded to Theophilus La Chappelle.

The first and second sessions of the fourth Legislative Assembly, 1842-3-4, found this district the same, with Mr. La Chappelle in the Council, and John H. Manahan in the House, and at the third session of the fourth Assembly, 1845, Wiram Knowlton was Councilman, and Jas. Fisher in the House, for Crawford and St. Croix. At this session acts were passed to organize the counties of Chippewa and La Pointe, but the four counties still constituted one district, and in the fourth session of the fourth Assembly, 1846, were represented by the same parties, Knowlton in the Council and Fisher in the House.

Benjamin F. Manahan, afterward a prominent lumberman on O'Neil's creek, in Chippewa county, was member of the Council and Joseph W. Furber of the House, during the first session of the fifth Assembly, 1847, from this district, the same four counties, but for the special session Henry Jackson was in the House. The same members were in the Council and House for the second and last session, 1848.

On the 5th day of October, 1846, the first Constitutional Convention assembled and submitted the result of its deliberations to the people, who rejected it on the first Tuesday of April, 1847. Peter A. R. Brace, of Crawford county, and James P. Hays, of La Pointe county, were members from this district; and Chippewa and Crawford counties were represented in the second Convention by Daniel G. Fenton. Its wisdom was embodied in our present State Constitution and submitted to the people for their adoption on the second Monday of March, 1848, a large majority voting for it.

Under the Constitutional apportionment, the four counties of Crawford, Chippewa, St. Croix, and La Pointe, composed the Third Senatorial District, and the counties of Crawford and Chippewa made an Assembly district. The State was also divided into two Congressional districts, the second embracing all the western portion and of course this valley. Five Judicial districts were also created by the same instrument, and the fifth comprised about one-half of the territory of the State, including Crawford county, to which Chippewa was attached for judicial purposes.

This arrangement of the various Senatorial, Assembly, and Congressional districts continued until 1853, nearly four years. Where then were the great populous counties of La Crosse, Monroe, and Vernon, now so potent in directing the political destinies of the State, the territory of which, with half a dozen other counties, lay between Crawford and Chippewa?

D. G. Fenton was our first Senator, and Wm. T. Stirling the first to represent us in the Assembly of the State, which assembled, as before stated, on the fifth day of June, 1848

But in 1849 we find James Fisher in the Senate and James O'Neil, of Black River Falls, in the Assembly, the former for two years, and in 1850 Mr. Stirling was elected to the Assembly.

Hiram A. Wright, of Prairie du Chien, was on the floor of the Senate for this wide-spread district for the next term, 1851-2, and Wm. T. Price (our Billy) the first year, and Andrew Briggs, of Bad Ax, the second year, in the Assembly. At the last session, 1852, the districts were reorganized, and we find ourselves in the nineteenth Senatorial district, comprising the counties of Crawford, La Crosse, Bad Ax, Chippewa, St. Croix, and La Point. Chippewa and La Crosse constituted an Assembly district.

This arrangement continued four years, during which time Hon. Benjamin Allen, of Pepin, was in the Senate the first term, 1853-4, and W. J. Gibson, of Black River Falls, for the next, 1855-6, and in the Assembly for 1853 we find Albert D. La Due, of La Crosse; 1854, Wm. J. Gibson; 1855, Chase A. Stevens, of La Crosse; 1856, Dugald D. Cameron, of La Crosse.

At the session of the last named year, the State was re-districted under the State census of 1855, and this valley is included in the twenty-eighth Senatorial district, composed of La Pointe, Douglass, Polk, (now Barron), St. Croix, Chippewa, Pierce, Dunn, Clark, and Burnett, while Clark, Chippewa, Eau Claire, Dunn, and Pierce made an Assembly district.

Hon. Wm. Wilson, of Menomonie, was chosen the first Senator, for one year, 1857, Daniel Mears, of St. Croix, the second term, 1858-9, Charles B. Cox, River Falls, the third, 1860-61.

And our Assemblymen for those years were, 1857, Orrin T. Maxon, Prescott; 1858, Lucius Cannon, Pepin; 1859, Richard Dewhurst, Neilsville; 1860, W. P. Bartlett, Eau Claire; 1861, Rodman Palmer, Chippew Falls. This was the fourteenth session of the State Legislature, and being the year following the national census, a new organization of the districts was necessary, and the counties of Jackson, Clark, Trempealeau, Buffalo, Pepin, Eau Claire, Dunn, and Chippewa were included in the thirty-second Senatorial district, while Chippewa, Dunn, and Eau Claire made one, and Buffalo, Trempealeau, and Pepin another, Assembly district.

Hon. M. D. Bartlett, of Durand, was chosen the first Senator in the thirty-second district, 1862-3; Carl C. Pope, Black River Falls, for the next term, 1864-5; and for 1866-7, Hon. Joseph G. Thorp was elected. There was no change in this Senatorial district until 1871. A. W. Newman, Trempealeau, was our next Senator, 1868-9, and for the next term, 1870-71, Wm. T. Price, Black River Falls.

Our Assembly districts were represented as follows, during this period: Chippewa, Dunn, and Eau Claire: 1862, Horace W. Barnes, Eau Claire; 1863, Wm. H. Smith, Eau Galla; 1864, Hon. Thadeus C. Pound, Chippewa Falls; 1865, Francis R. Church, Menomonie; 1866, T. C. Pound, Chippewa Falls. Buffalo, Pepin, and Trempealeau: 1862, Orlando Brown, Gilmantown; 1863, Alfred W. Newman, Trempealeau; 1864, Fayette Allen, Durand; 1865, John Burgess, Maxville; 1866, Wm. H. Thomas, Sumner.

At this session the Assembly districts were so remodeled that Pepin and Eau Claire constituted one district, and Chippewa and Dunn another. The latter was represented in 1867 by Thad. C. Pound, Chippewa Falls; 1868, Samuel W. Hunt, Menomonie; 1869, T. C. Pound; 1870, Jedediah Granger, Menomonie; 1871, James A. Bate. The former, in 1867, by Fayette Allen, Durand; 1868, Horace W. Barnes, Eau Claire; 1869, Fayette Allen, Durand; 1870, Charles R. Gleason, Eau Claire; and 1871, Henry Cousins, Eau Claire. The apportionment of 1871 made the counties embraced in this valley one Senatorial district, the thirtieth; Chippewa, Dunn, Eau Claire, and Pepin; while Chippewa and Eau Claire each constitute one Assembly district, and Pepin and Dunn another. Hon. Joseph G. Thorp, of Eau Claire, represented the thirtieth district in 1872-3, and Hon. Hiram P. Graham, of Eau Claire, in 1874-5.

Chippewa county was represented in the Assembly in 1872 by John J. Jenkins; 1873, Albert E. Pound; 1874, James M. Bingham; 1875, Thomas L. Halbert: all of Chippewa Falls. Eau Claire county was represented in 1872 by Rev. Bradley Phillips; 1873, Hon. Wm. Pitt Bartlett; 1874, Thos. Carmichael; 1875, Jonathan G. Calahan. Dunn and Pepin was represented in 1872 by Elias P. Bailey, of Menomonie; 1873, Horace E. Houghton; 1874, Samuel L. Plummer, of Waterville, Pepin county; and in 1875 by R. G. Flint, editor of the Dunn County News.

The Blue Book, or Legislative Manual, abounds in valuable statistical and other information, and persons in possession of the consecutive numbers as annually issued, could easily collate the facts contained in this chapter, but very few are so fortunate, and I therefore give a complete list of the members of Congress from the several districts since the organization of the State government.

Until 1863 this valley was included in the second district, then for the next decade in the sixth, and since 1871 the counties of Chippewa, Dunn, and Barron have composed part of the eighth, and the remainder is in the seventh.

REPRESENTATIVES IN CONGRESS SINCE THE ORGANIZATION OF THE STATE GOVERNMENT.

District	Representative	Congress
1st District.	Wm. Pitt Lynde.*	30th Congress, 1847-49.
2d "	Mason C. Darling.*	" "
1st "	Chas. Durkee.	31st Congress, 1849-51.
2d "	Orsamus Cole.	" "
3d "	Jas. D. Doty.	" "
1st "	Chas. Durkee.	32d Congress, 1851-53.
2d "	Ben. C. Eastman.	" "
3d "	John B. Macy.	" "
1st "	Daniel Wells, Jr.	33d Congress, 1853-55
2d "	Ben. C. Eastman.	" "
3d "	John B. Macy.	" "
1st "	Daniel Wells, Jr.	34th Congress, 1855-57.
2d "	C. C. Washburn.	" "
3d "	Chas. Billinghurst.	" "
1st "	John F. Potter	35th Congress, 1857-59.
2d "	C. C. Washburn.	" "
3d "	Chas. Billinghurst.	" "
1st "	John F. Potter.	36th Congress, 1859-61
2d "	C. C. Washburn.	" "
3d "	Chas. H. Larrabee.	" "
1st "	John F. Potter.	37th Congress, 1861-63.
2d "	Luther Hanchett.†	" "
2d "	Walter D. McIndoe.	" "
3d "	A. Scott Sloan.	" "
1st "	James S. Brown.	38th Congress, 1863-65.
2d "	Ithamar C. Sloan.	" "
3d "	Amasa Cobb.	" "
4th "	Chas. A. Eldredge.	" "
5th "	Ezra Wheeler.	" "
6th "	Walter D. McIndoe.	" "
1st "	Halbert E. Paine.	39th Congress, 1865-67.

2d	"	Ithamar C. Sloan.	"	"
3d	"	Amasa Cobb.	"	"
4th	"	Charles A. Eldredge.	"	"
5th	"	Philetus Sawyer.	"	"
6th	"	Walter D. McIndoe.	"	"
1st	"	Halbert E. Paine.	40th Congress, 1867-69.	
2d	"	Benj. F. Hopkins.	"	"
3d	"	Amasa Cobb.	"	"
4th	"	Chas. A. Eldredge.	"	"
5th	"	Philetus Sawyer.	"	"
6th	"	C. C. Washburn.	"	"
1st	"	Halbert E. Paine.	41st Congress, 1869-71.	
2d	"	Benj. F. Hopkins.‡	"	"
2d	"	David Atwood.	"	"
3d	"	Amasa Cobb.	"	"
4th	"	Chas. A. Eldredge.	"	"
5th	"	Philetus Sawyer.	"	"
6th	"	C. C. Washburn.	"	"
1st	"	Alex. Mitchell.	42d Congress, 1871-73.	
2d	"	Gerry W. Hazelton.	"	"
3d	"	J. Allen Barber.	"	"
4th	"	Chas. A. Eldredge.	"	"
5th	"	Philetus Sawyer.	"	"
6th	"	Jere. M. Rusk.	"	"

*Elected May 8th, and took their seats June 5th and 9th, 1848.

†Died Nov. 24th, 1862, and W. D. McIndoe elected to fill the vacancy Dec. 30th, 1862.

‡Died Jan. 1st, 1870, and David Atwood elected for balance of term, Feb. 15th, 1870.

Hon. J. M. Rusk was re-elected in 1872 for the 7th District, and Hon. Alex. S. McDill to represent the 8th District in the 43d Congress.

The 8th Judicial District has embraced all the counties of our valley since its organization in 1853, except one year, 1861, when, by a strange freak of legislation, we were placed in the 12th District. It, the 8th, has been presided over by Hon. S. S. N. Fuller from 1854 to 1861, by Hon. L. P. Wetherby from 1861 to 1866, by Hon. H. L. Humphrey from 1866 to 1872, and re-elected for six years.

CHAPTER XLIV.

OUR PROMINENT MEN.

In the preceding pages reference has been made to most, perhaps all, of the subjects of these sketches, nearly all of whom are still living and prominent actors in some department of life in this valley, and further notice of some of them may seem unnecessary or as involving repetition, but as the object in view is to exhibit the qualities that command success, as well as to pay a just tribute to the deserving, the reader will pardon the iteration.

HIRAM S ALLEN

Is undoubtedly the oldest settler and perhaps the only man now living in this valley who came here at the early period in which the subject of this notice came. He was born in Chelsea, Orange county, Vermont, in the year 1806, received such education as the common schools of that State afforded, and was reared in the business of lumbering, but soon conceived the idea that the one-horse establishments of that ancient State were inadequate to the realization of his hopes and aspirations, and in 1833 resolved to try his fortunes in the far West; came first to Illinois, and the year following up the Chippewa, and on the Red Cedar the year following bought the first mill ever erected in this valley of Street & Lockwood, and laid the foundation of a flourishing business and an active business life. He was identified with every public enterprise undertaken in this valley during the early days of hardship and trial—building steamboats to navigate the shallow, ever-changing current of the Chippewa, opening roads to the Mississippi and establishing a stage line over the same, and as early as the year 1856 was mainly instrumental in fitting out a surveying party to locate a road to connect Chippewa Falls with Stevens' Point. It was run by Wm. J. Young, now of California, and ten miles of the route immediately opened for travel. He has always had boundless faith in the future of Chippewa Falls, and to him more than any other one man is due the credit of building the railway last summer that now connects that place with the West Wisconsin railway.

In politics, he was a Whig until the organization of the Republican party, since when he has uniformly acted with that party; has repeatedly been urged to accept positions of trust and honor to which he could easily have been elected, but has constantly refused all political preferment.

In religion, though educated a Presbyterian, he is and always has been very liberal.

LUKE INMAN.

Cnotemporary with the earliest settlers was the humble individual whose name is here given. He represents a class, only a few of whom remain. Luke is an American by birth, and was for many years a soldier in the regular army of the United States; was in Florida during all the long years of the Seminole war; was with General Atkinson and Colonel Zachary Taylor in the Black Hawk war, and repeats with much gusto the orders of the corpulent Colonel, at the battle of the Bad Ax, as he found himself unhorsed in a soft marsh and sinking to his waist in the mud: "Bear me up, boys, bear me up; there, that'll do; now give 'em hell; don't let 'em cross the river; kill 'em, damn 'em, kill 'em!" Luke tells some curious stories about himself and other soldiers while stationed at Prairie du Chien. Whiskey being strictly forbidden by the officers, he and others had very frequent occasion to get permission to wash their blankets at the river bank, near which was a saloon, and a Mackinaw blanket, when thoroughly saturated, would absorb at least two gallons of the regular "red eye," and the whole mess would be unfit for duty the whole day; and for a long time the utmost vigilance of the officers was unable to detect the manner in which the liquor was obtained. Amongst others, Luke was sent up the Red Cedar for lumber, and having served his time out has made his home at some one of the mills here ever since, now more than forty years; has always worked by the month, a faithful, trustworthy, unassuming man, always contented, and through all the many hard sieges to which he has been subjected as a soldier, boatman, raftman, or millman, he was never known to complain. Many laughable anecdotes are told by Luke and by others at his expense. In his younger days he had been awakened at and participated in a religious revival, and amongst other exercises had learned to sing many tunes appropriate to such occasions. During the first religious services held in this valley, Luke made himself useful by joining the choir, but on one occasion, at a funeral service, he found himself almost alone but volunteered to raise the tune, which not being appropriate to the words. he broke down; again and again he made the attempt, but finally gave it up with "h—l, I used to sing that tune, but d—d if I can get it now." Luke is a living monument of human endurance, having been lost in the Eau Galla woods in 1837 for seven days at one time without food.

DANELIE DUCH, M. D.,

Was the first regular bred physician that settled on the Chippewa, and represents a class, though not numerous, to be found amongst the pioneers of a new country. An Italian by birth but educated at Cambridge, England, and receiving a diploma from the Royal College of Physicians and Surgeons, London, and the best medical schools on the continent of Europe, he soon obtained a position in the British army in India, congenial and lucrative, rose high in his profession, accumulated a handsome fortune, and allied himself by marriage with an excellent family. What, the reader will ask, could have driven such a man to this out-of-the-way corner? Alas, what are birth and fortune, talent, education, and advancement, when the wine-cup has obtained the mastery! An insatiable thirst for strong drink soon unfitted him for the duties of his profession, for society and the enjoyments of home, and on the death of his wife, which occurred soon after the birth of a daughter, he became a wanderer—his property and child cared for by legal provision— and died amongst strangers; as a fool dieth, died this courteous, genial, refined, and talented man, remembered only for his follies and lost opportunities.

Considering its natural advantages, Eau Claire has afforded better opportunities for enterprising men of limited means to establish themselves in business, than almost any other locality. At other points the most eligible situations became early absorbed by individuals or organizations who supposed their interests would best be subserved by excluding others; while the first settlers of Eau Claire held out all the inducements in their power to all who had the boldness to invest their means and energies in any undertaking that would enhance the interests of the place; which, more, perhaps, than natural position, has induced a large number of active, intelligent business men to locate there, and hence, quite a number of these sketches will recount the early strggles of what may appear a larger proportion of its prominent citizens.

DANIEL SHAW.

To no single individual, perhaps, is the city of Eau Claire indebted for the development of its resources and the establishment of its most important industries than to him who is the subject of this sketch. He was born in 1813, in the town of Industry, Franklin county, Maine. He chose the business of lumbering for a vocation, and located first in Alleghany county, New York, where he was quite successful, but wishing to enlarge his sphere of operations, came to this State and reconnoitered the Chippewa pine district in 1855, and the year following, having, in company with Mr. Clark, father of Dewitt C., purchased a large amount of pine land on the Chippewa river and its tributaries, came with his family.

His location at the outlet of Half Moon lake was induced by the assurance that logs, when once in there, would be perfectly secure; the booming and assorting works he was less confident of, and the disasters attending the operations of the first and second years were not altogether unexpected, but the terrible collapse in business affairs throughout the West and the almost total prostration of the lumber trade immediately after he commenced operations, was an unlooked for calamity, and although he worked with untiring energy, and took upon himself hardships that few business men could endure—always superintending the drive in person, and on one occasion carrying one hundred pounds of flour forty miles in a day on his back to feed his men, success seemed for a long time beyond his reach and the struggle against adversity unequal: but having associated Mr. C. A. Bullen in the business with him, the firm finally succeeded in establishing their business on a firm basis, when in 1867 the mill was consumed by fire, which once more brought discouragement and almost despondency; but capital was now more abundant, and by taking Messrs. Newell and Ferguson into the firm, a much larger and more perfect establishment was erected, and in 1874 the concern was incorporated with the title of Daniel Shaw Lumber Company.

Few men have been happier in their domestic relations than Mr. Shaw, though bereaved of a very promising son in 1863. The two surviving sons are model young men in filial regard for their parents and their attention to business, the result of sound moral and religious training at home.

Mr. Shaw worships at the Congregational church, though more liberal and advanced in his religious views than the tenets of that organization. And in politics, he is a steadfast Republican, but has always refused political preferment and the seductive influence of office.

SIMON RANDALL.

A lumbering country, especially in its incipient settlement, offers very few situations for any one to get a living without work; there are few, if any, easy positions; whatever one gets he must work for, and those who come without means, only their hands to help themselves with, must of course work for some one who has got a start. Simon was of this class, who, with his brother George, came up the Chippewa in June, 1840.

Simon was born in the town of Baldwin, (now Sebago), Cumberland county, Maine, in 1817. The strongest, healthiest, and most robust of a hardy family, he prided himself more on his physical ability than upon his intellectual acquirements. Other members of the family were proud to be at the head of the class at the Centre school house, he cared not who was at the head or foot, nor whether his lesson was learned or neglected. His stay in Muscatine county, Iowa, to which place he and George emigrated in 1838, was too short to deplete his energies with fever and ague, and on their passage up the Mississippi, the boat having landed at Wabasha to put off a large amount of pork, and being short for help on deck, the two brothers offered their services, and instead of rolling the barrels over deck and gang-plank, they seized them by the chimes and carried them ashore and up the bank with as much ease as the deckhands carried kegs of nails. These displays of strength sometimes excited the envy of his fellows, but his good nature and free and easy way made him a great favorite amongst the boys, and few could tell a story with a better zest or more telling effect on the crowd.

It was natural that a young man of such a temperament should fall readily into the ways of his associates, and the lessons the boys first learned on this river were not calculated to improve their morals or raise their aspirations for something better; the example and influence of some of the business men then on the river being very pernicious.

In any industrial pursuit or department of business, to rise from the condition of a common laborer to the management and successful prosecution of business for one's self, requires pluck, energy, economy, and persistent endeavor; but the lumber business of that early day, when stumpage and titles to land were unknown, though replete with hardships, required less capital than at present, and the two brothers, after more than a year's struggle. took out their first raft, which was sold in Muscatine—lumber and pine logs being almost the only commodity that would sell for cash in that market at that time.

Availing themselves of credit, which was freely offered, they extended their operations, and in 1846 formed the partnership with Allen & Branham elsewhere referred to in this work, and after its dissolution became the principal factor in building the first mill in Eau Claire, only to see it carried away by the flood the next day after it started, together with piers, booms, and ten thousand logs. Credit had been used to the utmost to accomplish this, and heavy liabilities remained—a clog and burden upon all succeding operations. But over all these difficulties pluck and perseverance finally triumphed, and a fair competence, if nothing occurs to prevent, seems likely to relieve the anxieties of the downhill of life.

NELSON C. CHAPMAN. JOSEPH G. THORP.

It very frequently happens, especially in new countries, that enterprises are commenced by parties who find themselves inefficient or wanting in business capacity to conduct them when more fully developed. Of all the varied business pursuits in which men engage in this country, perhaps none require more ability and active energy to conduct it successfully than the manufacture of lumber; and the original settlers and operators on the Eau Claire began to realize very soon their inability to fully develop the resources of the situation, and to invite men of capital to visit their premises, with a view to sell.

Unable to command the means to purchase the interest of Gage & Reed, Adin Randall, who came to Eau Claire in the summer of 1855, obtained a bond for the transfer of the property at a fixed price and applied himself to find a purchaser, and, by chance or fate, came in contact with and made the acquaintance of the gentlemen above named, then operating in real estate at Clinton, Iowa, which led to their investment here and identified them at once with the growth and development of Eau Claire and its surroundings, and made their names conspicuous throughout the Northwest.

Nelson C. Chapman was born in Durham, Green county, New York, in 1811. The death of his father occurring when he was quite young, his education was limited to such as the common school of that period could bestow, and at the age of sixteen he went into the store of Benjamin Chapman, in Norwich, Chenango county, where industry and fidelity won him the confidence of his uncle, and he was taken into the business as partner at the age of twenty.

Here he remained, the house doing a successful business until 1846, when he removed to Oxford and became a partner with J. G. Thorp, under the firm name of Chapman & Thorp, continuing in business with the latter until the time of his death in 1873, which occurred in St. Louis, to which place he removed in 1857, conducting the business of the firm with signal ability in that city, where he was regarded as a prominent citizen and thorough business man, being chosen president of a leading railroad corporation, and elected to many important positions under the city and State governments.

Joseph G. Thorp was born in Butternuts, Otsego county, New York, in 1812, was bereaved of both parents at the age of fourteen, and for three succeeding years continued to work on a farm, receiving such common school education as he could acquire in the winter season.

In 1829, he obtained a situation, on trial, in the store of Ira Wilcox, a thorough merchant of Oxford, Chenango county, New York, where he remained until his majority and three years after as clerk at a good salary, when, in 1836, he was given a partnership under the name of I. Wilcox & Co., which continued ten years, when Mr. Wilcox sold his interest to N. C. Chapman, and thus was formed the firm of Chapman & Thorp, their business being carried on in the same place, Oxford, until 1857, when it was removed to Eau Claire, Wis. Thus we see that Mr. Thorp was twenty-seven years in the same store and place, having risen from a boy on trial to a partnership in a prosperous business, and the credit of the firm was now fully established. Mr. Thorp married Miss Chapman, sister of his late partner, who was allied by marriage to the Messrs. Gilbert, since so well known in this State.

Sufficient capital had been accumulated in 1855 to make investments in real estate at Clinton, Iowa, without affecting the business of the house in Oxford, but their transactions here soon called for all their means, having closed an engagement with Gage & Reed for their property, at forty-two thousand dollars in May, 1856, and soon after bought the entire property of Carson, Eaton & Downs, on the Eau Claire.

Quite an amusing incident grew out of the contract with Gage & Reed, the payments being in installments—gold being plenty and commanding no premium when the bargain was made, no stipulation had been made to satisfy the claims in anything else—but before the last fell due, money in any shape, but especially gold, had disappeared utterly throughout the West, and few people hereabouts, Gage & Reed among them, believed it possible for so much gold, nine thousand dollars, to be obtained in the United States, and the payees having signified their determination to receive nothing else, looked confidently forward to a foreclosure, but when the day came were astonished to find the whole sum ready, principal and interest, in American gold. But those were days that tried men's souls, and however successful as merchants this firm had been, they could not but realize that as lumbermen they lacked the experience necessary to command success; however, they were fairly in for it and must go on, as heavy liabilities had been incurred, and now the value of credit and a good name was to be fully tested, which, with pluck and untiring perseverance, carried them successfully through the crisis while thousands became bankrupt. In ten years all these difficulties had disappeared and large accessions been made to their real estate, when, by act of incorporation, the Eau Claire Lumber Company was organized with a paid-up capital of one hundred and sixty thousand dollars, now worth ten times that amount, the head of which is Joseph G. Thorp.

Mr. Thorp has filled many positions of trust with honor to himself and advantage to the public; was several years a member of the county board, and shares the credit of ferreting out delinquencies in the management of its funds, and of raising the credit of the county which for a long time was fifty per cent. below par; has been twice elected State Senator, and was a delegate to the convention in Philadelphia that nominated Grant and Wilson in 1872. Having traveled extensively in Europe, he has now returned to business and the enjoyments of private life.

In answer to my inquiries, he says; "My experience from my boyhood up leads to this opinion as regards my success. When a boy I was lazy, and if I had had anything in expectancy to rely upon might have made a worthless fellow. Necessity showed me only one way to be anybody, and that was to establish a good character. Trusting in God, I have succeeded. My motto has been, and my advice to all young men is, always honest, ever plucky, and your word better than your bond."

In politics, Mr. Thorp was formerly a Clay Whig and since a steadfast Republican, and in religion a sound Presbyterian.

HON. HIRAM PEASE GRAHAM.

Modest and unassuming, without parade or ostentation, this individual has raised himself to positions of trust and honor, and acquired distinction among men by positive merit. He was born in Windham, Green county, New York, March 29th, 1820; received a common school education; learned the trade and for several years followed the occupation of millwright. The first steam mill erected by Chapman & Thorp was built under his supervision. Mr. Graham has held various local offices, was for five years general inspector of lumber for the Chippewa district, was elected the first Mayor of Eau Claire in 1872, and State Senator for the Thirtieth district in 1873, but he is one of the men that office has sought, and being a Democrat has on more than one occasion been the only hope of his party in the district or city—his own popularity electing him against overwhelming Republican majorities. Though by no means opposed to the war measures of the Government during the rebellion, it was a matter of surprise and regret to many of his best friends that a man of such influence and high moral worth should adhere so tenaciously to a party whose prestige and success could only in the very nature of things afford comfort and inspire hope in the enemy's camp, and thereby serve to protract the war. Conservative in all things, it must have been a great sacrifice of party fealty to find that he could no longer be true to the Government and yet follow the dictum of his party leaders, but throughout the entire war there was not the remotest suspicion of his want of loyalty to the country, and as an individual he performed with alacrity his duty to the Government. A life-long Democrat, accustomed to regard the policy and principles of the party as next to infallible, it was a far severer test of his patriotism than if his sympathies had always been with the party now wielding the Government. Mr. Graham was emphatically a War Democrat, and as such exerted a powerful influence against the re-actionary measures of those who favored the Ryan Address. In this respect he represents a class, and I have chosen him as one of its most prominent representatives.

CHAPTER XLV.

MR. AND MRS. LORENZO BULLARD.

Few persons in private life are better known than this veteran couple; the former from Wayne, the latter from Genessee, county, New York, where they were married in 1833. Came to Menomonie in 1847, with Captain and Mrs. Wilson, where for fifteen years they shared all the hardships of that early period. Mrs. Bullard was one of the patriotic women who called the first war meeting in this valley, and walked over the battlefield of Gettysburg in quest of her boy Eugene, who was wounded in that fearful conflict, while the battle was still raging in the distance.

As an operator in the lumber business, in which Mr. Bullard engaged in 1848-9, he does not seem to have been very successful, but as host and hostess in a hotel, first in Menomonie and for twelve years at Reed's Landing, in Minnesota, they won a reputation second to none and acquired a handsome competence for old age; have purchased an elegant residence in the city of Eau Claire, where their son Eugene located after his return from the war, and where peace and plenty bid fair to crown the days of their long and useful lives.

GILBERT E. PORTER.

A soldier in a regiment of hussars recounted the many battles he had taken part in and produced testimonials of his valor on many a hard-fought field, and added, "For this, Colonel ——— was promoted to brigade commander, and for this, General ——— was made commander of division." But how happens it, I remarked, that you performed so much for your country, served so long and so faithfully, and are nothing but a private soldier still, while so many others are advanced to high positions by your valor? "Well," he answered, "all those had fathers or uncles in Parliament, or other powerful friends at headquarters to give them a boost, and so they got in ahead of me." And such is the secret of advancement and good fortune to a great many, perhaps most, men who attain high position in the world.

Not so, however, with the subject of this notice, for he had nothing but his own unaided efforts and indomitable energy by which to climb the hill of distinction. He was born in the town of Freedom, Cataraugus county, New York, July 6th, 1829, but his boyhood and youth was spent in a heavily-timbered, unhealthy district of Michigan, whither his father removed in 1836, and being too poor, as he says, to return, Gilbert, being the eldest of the children, soon became inured to the toil and hardship of clearing up a farm in the woods. At the age of eighteen he obtained a clerkship in a store, and by assiduous attention to business was permitted to attend one term at Albion Seminary, where he made good progress.

In 1856, Mr. Porter came to Eau Claire in the service of Chapman & Thorp, having entire charge of their business the first year after their purchase here—a very laborious and trying position for one so young.

In the year 1858, Mr. Porter furnished a small amount of means to assist Mr. Charles G. Patterson in starting the Eau Claire Free Press, a Republican newspaper, in Eau Claire, an enterprise of very doubtful success, and Mr Patterson soon became discouraged and induced Mr. Porter to take the unpromising thing off his hands, which, as the politics of the county and valley were largely Democratic, induced him to feel that he had a pretty large elephant to manage, especially as he knew nothing of type-setting or the business of printing, but he had pluck, energy, perseverance, literary taste, and a nice discrimination; and, notwithstanding all those difficulties, soon made the Free Press a power in the land—one of the best country papers in the State.

Its success and zeal gave Mr. Porter the appointment of Register in the United States Land Office at Eau Claire, which position he held for almost nine years. Being threatened at one time with dismissal if he would not "Johnsonize," he replied that he would not hold the office a moment on such terms, and if his minions wanted it they could take it. The columns of the Free Press while edited by Mr. Porter, exhibit but few lengthy, labored articles from his pen, but as a paragraphist he was pointed, terse, and sometimes witty. Mr. Porter gave convincing proof of his business capacity before he engaged in the manufacture of lumber, as the following anecdote, related by himself, will show. "For several years the Free Press was the official organ for Eau Claire, Dunn, Pepin, and Chippewa counties, the legal advertising for which, and especially the enormous tax-list of the latter, created a good deal of envy on the part of neighboring journals, and repeated efforts were made to start a paper at Chippewa Falls, but I always found means to discourage such attempts or to buy out the concern before the public patronage was bestowed upon it." The destruction of the mill owned by Porter, Brown & Meredith utterly discouraged the last named partners; not so with Mr. Porter; he knew the mill-site was a good one, and the means to rebuild in his name alone was soon proffered, and as president of a great lumbering corporation or as Mayor of the city of Eau Claire has displayed marked executive ability.

H. C. PUTNAM.

Few men have been more fortunate in their business relations than this gentleman. He was born in Madison, Madison county, New York, March 6th, 1832, was a graduate of an engineering school at Cornwall, Conn., and adopted the profession of Civil Engineer. Came to Wisconsin in 1855, and worked in that capacity one year on the Milwaukee & Prairie du Chien railroad; thence to Eau Claire in May, 1857, with a capital of only two thousand dollars, which, by judicious investment, and the salary and perquisites of several local offices to which he was soon elected, he was soon able to establish himself permanently in the real estate business.

But the most fortunate position, perhaps, that he ever secured was that of principal assistant in the United States Land Office while Messrs. Porter and Bartlett successively held the office of Register. It was here that he laid the foundation of an immense fortune. As agent for Eastern capitalists, many of whom remitted him large sums for investment; he has the reputation of never having made a bad location, seeming to know by instinct just where lands were likely to rise in value, and frequently to secure an interest without investing his own means. His name is introduced here not because he represents a class, but because he and his operations are an exception to all other operators in the same line in this part of the State.

STEPHEN MARSTON.

In the person of this individual, the old Pine State furnished another prominent operator in the settlement of this valley. He was born in Kennebec county, Maine, in 1821; came to Eau Claire in 1856, making the journey in a one-horse buggy, with his wife and little daughter, and averaging sixty miles per day. The year following he visited Cincinnati and returned to Eau Claire with seventy-five tons of merchandise—the heaviest invoice of manufactured goods ever ordered for this locality at that time. As a merchant he was honorable and obliging, and so well adapted to the wants of this community was his assortment of goods, that he was proverbial for keeping everything that other dealers failed to supply, which in a new country was a very great convenience.

Succeeding in 1860 to the ownership of the Randall saw and planing mill, door and sash factory,—the latter for several years being the only one in operation in the valley—he availed himself of the facilities these offered and invested largely in building on both sides of the river, his hall over the post-office being for some years the only one in the place, and his own sumptuous residence denotes taste, refinement, and culture. Mrs. Marston claims the honor of bringing the first piano to Eau Claire.

He held the office of Postmaster from 1863 to 1871, and although his business precluded him from personal attendance, he saw that his assistants were courteous and obliging. During the war he was active in procuring enlistments, and did much toward filling up the various companies recruited here. In 1872 he was the candidate on the Greeley ticket for Representative to Congress in the seventh district, leading his ticket in eight out of eleven counties in the district, including his own.

GEORGE A. BUFFINGTON.

Cataraugus county, New York, furnished another active business citizen for Eau Claire in the person whose name heads this notice. He came in 1856, run a livery, kept a hotel, and in 1859 bought Mr. Ball's interest in the mill owned by the firm of Smith & Ball, West Side, formerly one of the Randall mills, and for fifteen years was the resident managing partner in the firm of Smith & Buffington; is now at the head of a corporation known as the Valley Lumber Company, and Mayor of the city of Eau Claire.

ISAAC W. SHELDON.

Came from McHenry county, Illinois, in 1855, and settled on a farm in the town of La Fayette, Chippewa county.

With a somewhat limited common school education, he possesses business qualifications that have raised him to a fair competence and distinction among men.

For the past twelve years he has resided at Chippewa Falls, has twice been elected Mayor of the city, and shares the esteem of his fellow citizens. He is now successfully engaged in merchandising.

JOHN F. STONE

Was one of the first settlers of Augusta, in Eau Claire county. He erected a saw and grist mill at that point on Bridge creek in 1856. As one of the proprietors of the village, he pursued a very liberal policy and afforded assistance to a great number of farmers of feeble means, as one after another located in the fertile valleys around him, and upon these, and all others who have made homes in the village and surrounding country, to a certain extent stamped the impress of his own unsullied character, so that Augusta has ever been noted for its moral, religious, and social advancement.

Mr. Stone's religious convictions accord with [those of the Baptist church, of which he is an exemplary member.

O. H. INGRAM

Is a born lumberman, and what he don't know about the business is not worth knowing. He came to Eau Claire in 1856, in company with Messrs. Dole and Kennedy, the former of whom soon retired, and the firm have since done business under the title of Ingram & Kennedy. They were previously operating in Canada, whence they migrated to this river, and the hard times which followed the crisis of 1857 taxed their resources to the utmost, and before fully recovering from the difficulties of that trying period, their mill was consumed by fire.

Mr. Ingram is the financial and general manager, and has always maintained an unblemished reputation as an able financier and straightforward business man. Socially, he likes a good joke, and is not always very particular at whose expense, but his feelings are always kindly and his employes are always treated with consideration and respect; which secures their confidence and esteem, as the following pithy incident will attest. Some two years ago a little girl about seven years old came one forenoon to the residence of the writer, crying bitterly, and saying she had lost her way to Mr. Ingram's Eddy mill, having left Shawtown on foot early in the morning. Having quieted and refreshed the little thing with a lunch, I proceeded to place her on the right road, and to cheer her up made many inquiries about herself, and amongst other things told her I had seen Mr. Ingram an hour before on his way to the Eddy mill.

Her face instantly brightened, and full of animation she exclaimed: "Oh, I wish I could have seen him, for Mr Ingram is a good man; my papa works for him, and he is a good man."

Mr. Ingram owns mills, stores, and bank stock, and enjoys all the distinction that wealth and position can bestow, but dearer by far must be the tribute paid to his goodness by this little Scandinavian girl; and the brightest jewel in his diadem when he shall have finished his course will be the testimony of his workmen that he "is a good man—for she but echoed the voice of the hundreds of men in his employment.

R. F. WILSON.

Having so often referred to this gentleman in the body of this work, little can be added here, especially as he has failed to give me the necessary data.

As one of the proprietors of the village of Eau Claire as first platted, he succeeded beyond his expectations. His temperament is hopeful—almost too sanguine—and his faith in Eau Claire and its future is boundless.

It is not given to all men to be successful in their undertakings, and Mr. Wilson has seen his purposes frequently fail, but he still works on, and is confident still that there is a good time coming.

WILLIAM CARSON.

Ever since the year 1839 the little crooked river which takes its rise in the big woods that divide the Chippewa and St. Croix valleys, known as the Eau Galla, has been the theater of action for an emigrant from Upper Canada of the above name who at that early period settled upon its banks, and is undoubtedly to-day the only person in the Chippewa valley occupying the same premises as a home that he then occupied.

Accommodating himself socially and domestically to the peculiar circumstances with which he has at various periods been surrounded, he has witnessed change after change in the development of the country, and transfer after transfer of the premises of other operators in the same business, even his own partners selling out and seeking more favored localities as they imagined, but he has kept right on in the even tenor of his way, cautious and conservative, carefully husbanding all his resources and prudently investing his accumulations, he has succeded beyond all who came to the valley with him in building up a fortune and a name. As a common laborer he was faithful and diligent, and is now literally realizing the promise that "he who is faithful over few things shall be made ruler over many things."

Surrounded by a numerous and amiable family and all that wealth, taste, and refinement can confer, the retired spot that has so long been his home must be dearer to him than any of the great marts of trade or the most attractive centers of fashion.

Lawyers, it is said, are a necessary evil, but on the principle that opposing evils correct each other, society is compelled to tolerate a good many of them—there being so many other evils in the world that many of these not only exist but attain distinction and honor among men; and quite a number are found in this valley, some of whom came so long ago as to make their lives historic, and like all other men in a new country had a pretty hard struggle to get started, and are proper subjects for these sketches as prominent actors in all our stirring events.

The profession was poorly represented at first in this section, but a bad beginning sometimes makes a good ending, they say.

The first was a wild Irishman, Patrick M. McNally, who came to Chippewa Falls in the summer of 1854—was advised to locate there by Judge Fuller, and for want of something better was immediately retained by H. S. Allen & Co. as their regular counsel, which enabled him to make the two ends meet.

How baleful is the evil example of a man placed in high position! It is an undeniable fact that a large majority of the practicing attorneys in Judge Fuller's circuit contracted the bad habit of drinking to fearful excess during his term—even carrying a demijohn of "Old Bourbon" with them as they followed the Court from one shire town to another. I could name more than one who in the prime of life has gone down to a drunkard's grave, the incipient cause of whose fall could be traced to the bad example and pernicious influence of that erring judicial functionary. P. M. McNally, George Mulks, and H. Clay Williams died as a fool dieth, and these are far from comprising the list, to say nothing of those who barely escaped.

The Greggs, father and son, came next, the former a man well versed in law, and on one occasion he aspired to the judicial ermine, but the people thought otherwise; his habits and character were too well formed to be led astray by the prevailing vice referred to above, but the son succumbed and has removed elsewhere.

HON. W. P. BARTLETT

Is a native of Maine, was born September 13th, 1829, graduated at Waterville College in that State in 1853, taught school and studied law until the fall of 1855, when he came to Wisconsin, arriving in the State October 1st, was admitted to practice in Jefferson county in 1856, and came to Eau Claire the next spring, 1857—the first lawyer that settled in Eau Claire county.

Perhaps it was because the youthful attorney refused to resort to the same measures to get on the right side of Judge Fuller that some others did, that he failed to secure favorable recognition; indeed, it was apparent to every one who attended his court when Mr. Bartlett was managing a case that the rulings were invariably against him, which made it up-hill work for the young barrister. But he worked on in spite of these and many other discouraging circumstances with a zeal, energy, and industry that showed conclusively that neither Judge Fuller nor any other Judge could always keep him down.

If as a pleader he has not always satisfied the expectations of his friends, he seldom fails to impress a jury favorably, and in examining a witness he has no superior for skill and tact on this circuit—perhaps, I may say, in the State.

Mr. Bartlett has held several positions of trust and honor; twice elected to the Assembly, in 1860 and 1872; was six years district attorney for Eau Claire county, and one term County Judge, and now holds the position of Register of the United States Land Office at Eau Claire.

Mr. Bartlett has alway taken a deep interest in the cause of education, especially the common schools of Eau Claire; having been elected a member of the School Board within three weeks after he became a resident of the district; and it is to his energy and efficiency in some degree that the Second and Third ward school, now and for twelve years past conducted by Mr. Howland, owes its high standard of excellence and usefulness.

CHAPTER XLVI.

Pioneer life exhibits peculiar habits and phases of character and amongst others the disposition to rove; to move from place to place becomes a ruling passion with a certain class, and a retrospect of the coming and going shows that many of the early settlers in every locality in this valley have found homes, or are still roaming, elsewhere.

From Chippewa Falls, Wm. J. Young, afterwards a member of the Nebraska Legislature and now editor of a prominent paper in California;

John Judge, for two years one of the most prominent men at that place and secretary of the Chippewa Falls Lumbering Company, now in the South; Judge Whipple and Andrew Gregg, lawyers and bankers; D. Skinner, at one time County Treasurer and a successful merchant; the Masons, father and sons, and the Gilbert brothers, from Yellow river: from Eau Galla, Henry Eaton, of the old firm of Carson & Eaton: from North Pepin, Hon. Benjamin Allen, State Senator and Colonel of the Sixteenth Regiment: and from Eau Claire, Drs. Ketchum and Day and Col. Chas. Whipple are now on the Pacific coast; Hon. N. B. Boyden, counsellor at law and first Receiver in the United States Land Office, and now Municipal Judge in Chicago; John Wilson, in Montana; Rev. W. W. McNair, in New Jersey; C. Howard, a worthy citizen, the first and for a long time Register of Deeds in Eau Claire, and now Postmaster at Osage Mission, Neosho county, Kansas; Peter Wyckoff, a very successful merchant, now of New York; and Hon. Horace W. Barnes, for many years a prominent member of the bar in this judicial district, and many others who made their homes here at an early day, are now scattered over the country from Maine to Oregon.

Death, also, has claimed two of our prominent and esteemed pioneers. Hon. A. K. Gregg, an eminent member of the bar at Chippewa Falls, died in 1867, and Hon. Rodman Palmer, formerly of the same place, land agent and dealer in real estate, an upright man and much honored citizen, died in 1871, having previously removed to Eau Claire.

Of those above mentioned, one claims more than a passing notice, as a self-made man who, in spite of early privations and discouraging circumstances, made for himself an honorable name and acquired a competence and distinction.

HORACE W. BARNES

Was born in the town of Colesville, Broome county, New York, in 1818. His boyhood was spent in the family of an uncle who settled in a dense beech and maple forest, in Medina county, Ohio, where he lived a life of constant toil, without one day's schooling until his majority, and Shakespeare's lines would then forcibly apply to the youthful Buckeye.

> "This boy is forest-born, and hath been tutored in
> The rudiments of many desperate studies."

How many men famous in American history, have laid the superstructure of their education and built up an honorable name from such rough materials as poverty and the adverse circumstances of pioneer life always impose! There seems to have been something inspiring in the grand old woods where the early days of many of our most distinguished men first saw the light; and in overcoming the many natural obstacles always encountered in new districts, high aspirations and a determination to achieve grander results take possession of the hardy backwoodsman and frequently leads to victory, honor. and fortune.

These feelings inspired Mr. Barnes, and with indomitable energy he set himself to earn the means to educate himself. By the most rigid economy and assiduous attention to his studies, he acquired a good English and mathematical education and considerable proficiency in the classics at Oberlin Institute, Ohio. Acquisitions that he utilized in teaching and surveying until 1852, when he commenced the study and practice of law, in which he soon won distinction as a sound legal adviser and laborious faithful advocate.

As a pleader, Mr. Barnes displayed qualities which, if not always insuring his own success, were well calculated to quench the ardor and paralyze the force of his adversary.

Carefully noting, as the cause proceeded, the points which his antagonist intended to make, he would anticipate him and tell the court and jury precisely what his opponent would say, frequently using the exact language in which it would be clothed, and emasculating the argument of all point or power before it was uttered. He felt defeat intensely and seemed to suffer even more than his client the loss incurred by any want of skill or foresight in managing a suit, and hence in all civil suits was wary and cautious, always exacting a full, impartial statement of the case from his client before taking it, and not then unless the evidence, justice, and a reasonable prospect of success justified it.

In serving the public, no matter in what capacity. his industry and perseverance were untiring, and he shares with Mr. Thorp the honor of exposing frauds in the accounts of the Eau Claire County Treasurer and of restoring the credit of the county.

Mr. Barnes came to Eau Claire in 1858, and was elected District Attorney the next year, 1859, and County Judge in 1865; was a member of the Legislature in 1861 and 1867. In politics, was a steadfast Republican, and during the war zealous and active in carrying forward any and every measure for its prosecution.

In his friendship, he utterly ignored position or caste, and wherever he found what he considered a true man, he was his friend; but scorned obsequious or patronizing airs, and was sometimes so impolitic as to prefer blunt honesty to assumed gentility. In 1872 he removed to Oswego, Kansas, with his family, where he now resides in the practice of his profession.

ALEXANDER MEGGETT

Is probably so well and so widely known that only for posterity can I say aught that will interest my readers. But all may not know that he is a son of toil; that in his boyhood and youth he worked in a cotton factory in Uxbridge, Massachusetts, to which place his father emigrated in 1827, from Glasgow, Scotland, where he was born in 1824. By his own exertions he acquired the means to defray his expenses for a year at Wilbraham Academy, and by close application to study, fitted himself to enter Middleton University, Connecticut, where he managed to support himself one year; was a teacher in the public schools for ten years, and then studied law in the office of Hon. C. B. Farnsworth, of Pawtuxet, Massachusetts, and Hon. Thos. A. Jencks, Rhode Island; was admitted to practice in the State courts in 1853 and in the United States Circuit Court in 1856. His first settlement in Wisconsin was in Milwaukee county, where his half-brother, Hon. Arthur McArthur, presided, but Eau Claire, then just growing into importance, attracted his attention and he made his home here in 1857.

Says John Neal;

> Language is the power,
> The only omnipresent present,
> "hereby man holds communion with his God;
> Whereby he does imperishable things.
> * * * The outlet to a mine of wealth
> And of power ten thousand times more precious than the earth
> Glittering with diamonds and charged with ore
> That man, short-sighted man, would perish for.

This power Mr. Meggett certainly wields and uses as few men in this part of the State can. Not alone as a lawyer in the line of his profession where as a pleader he perhaps has no rival in the circuit, but in the arena of politics, religion, social and moral improvement, reform, science, and the arts. With attainments so diversified and a felicitous adaptability of speech to every department of thought and knowledge, he is perfectly at home in any assemblage and almost invariably the chosen exponent of its views and behests.

A large practice and strict attention to the duties of his profession has enabled Mr. Meggett to accumulate a handsome competence and to devote considerable time to social and intellectual enjoyment. Brief extracts have been made from the remarks of Mr. Meggett on two occasions—at a war meeting and a religious festival—to which, as indicating the versatility of his genius, I will add a few passages selected from his addresses on other occasions. Smith Whittier, now of Chicago, Illinois, built the second hotel which was erected in Eau Claire, which he called the "Metropolitan," and which was opened with a dance, superb supper, speeches, and congratulations, one evening in September, 1857.   Mr. Meggett was one of the latest accessions to the place but was selected as spokesman of the occasion.

After a few preliminaries, he said : "Ladies and gentlemen, Your experiences in Western life have already taught you how quickly our sympathies spring into vigorous life in a new country and unite man with man and heart with heart that under other circumstances would each have known only self.

"It is these common sympathies that have brought us together to-night, and in the absence of some things incidental to a more mature development grown aristocratic with age and boasting of its refinement, where envy, pride, selfishness, all luxuriate, no fair one here to-night will have her peace of mind destroyed by the bitter reflection that her crinoline is less beautiful than that of some fancied rival. (Uproarious applause). No, ladies, everything here is too fresh from Nature—from the hand of God—to permit the growth of these pernicious weeds, so thrifty in the soil of a more mature civilization.   *   *   *   I rejoice as a citizen of Eau Claire in the freedom and equality which characterize the festivities of this occasion, with no aristocracy of wealth, position, or dress, to mar its joys."

Elsewhere in this work it is stated that Mr. Meggett was chosen to welcome the visitors to Eau Claire when the advent of the West Wisconsin railway was celebrated in August, 1870, a brief outline of his address being given. It was an able and comprehensive statement of the growth, prosperity, and resources of Eau Claire and the Chippewa valley; a few paragraphs from which without the risk of repetition may find a place here.

"While so much may be justly said of ourselves as the metropolis of the Chippewa valley, we must not forget the claims and virtues of the sister counties and cities within its limits. They are most excellent neighbors of which equally good, but, perhaps, not quite as many great, things can be said. In some respects much our superiors, and having citizens equally enterprising and public-spirited, were it not for our advantageous geographical position we might have to compete with some of them for the palm of being the commercial center of this valley. As it is, however, we altogether form a great people in a great valley, with power and resources sufficient to make our influence felt in all matters of public concern."

In his intercourse with men, Mr. Meggett is more than genial, he is jovial; and one would not suspect that bereavement had repeatedly invaded his household; twice has he been called to follow the wife of his bosom to the grave, and on the 22d of August, 1864, a promising son, then his only one, the child of his early love, met with a fatal accident, being accidentally shot while taking a loaded rifle from a wagon at Bridge creek. He had recently come from Rhode Island at the age of later boyhood, very intelligent, and justly his father's pride. It was a grievous affliction, but borne with Christian patience and fortitude.

And now, no longer a disconsolate widower, but a happy husband and father, Mr. Meggett's declining years bid fair to be peaceful and full of honor.

The foregoing brief sketches, though undoubtedly very imperfect, embrace the principal points in the lives of such of our distinguished citizens as have not been set forth in the preceding chapters of this work, quite a number of whom, including the members of the firm of Knapp, Stout & Co., of Menomonie, and T. C. Pound, of Chippewa Falls, it was thought required no further personal illustration.

And it will be seen that almost every one of our most active successful business or professional men have been reared in comparative obscurity and trained in the school of toil and hardship, and by their own exertions raising themselves to positions of trust, honor, and affluence.

In the medical profession, three only of the early comers remain, all of the allopathic school.

The first was Doctor McBean, formerly from the island of Jamaica, West Indies; came to Chippewa Falls in 1856, entered the Union army as physician and surgeon in 1862, and served till the close of the war. The other two, Drs. W. T. Galloway and F. R. Skinner, hail from the same Alma Mater, though as different in every trait and characteristic as two men can be, came to Eau Claire in 1857; the former a demonstrative politician, a Democrat, appointed by Buchanan Register in the newly-created Land Office; speculated in village lots, mill property, and lumber, and then returned to his profession, where an extensive practice awaited him, and wherein he has been very successful. Judiciously investing its avails in manufacturing and other village property, he has accumulated an estate that yields handsome dividends. He is still distinguished for his skill as a physician and surgeon, and as a leader in the Democratic party, though now less demonstrative than before the war. The latter is the son of the late Reverend Doctor Dolphus Skinner, a highly distinguished Universalist clergyman of Utica, New York; a quiet, unobtrusive man; came to Eau Claire the same year, 1857, and started the first drug store in this valley. He, too, has acquired a reasonable share of this world's goods, and is a much respected citizen.

Continual changing in the local whereabouts of the clergymen who have labored here, has taken most of the early incumbents beyond the writer's observation.

Reverends McNair and Phillips, frequently referred to, were co-laborers and students from the same theological school, and their churches here were established, and for some years partly sustained, as Presbyterian missions of the Home Missionary Society. The diversified religious views of the first settlers, and the feeble, struggling condition of many or most, precluded the possibility of any denomination being able to organize a self-sustaining church at the early period when the subject of the following sketch came to Eau Claire and organized the first church in the Chippewa valley.

Rev. Alberoni Kidder was born in Wardsboro, Vermont, February 14th, 1814, the youngest but one of a family of eight sons and six daughters.

Having been educated for and chosen the profession of the ministry, he received license to preach in 1847, and commenced his ministerial labors at Alexander, Genesee county, New York, the year following, and was ordained as pastor of the Congregational church at that place in 1849.

A revival that added seventy to the membership encouraged his labors here. At other points where he subsequently preached his zeal was rewarded by greater activity in, and large accessions to, the church.

In September, 1856, he was invited to visit Eau Claire by a former member of his church, who had previously migrated thither. The barroom of the Eau Claire House, then just enclosed, was the only room in the place large enough to accommodate the audience, in which, by invitation, he held religious services, and was requested by many devout people to remain and organize a Congregational church and society. During the ensuing winter, these services were continued in bar-rooms and private dwellings, Chippewa and Dunn counties visited, and religious instruction given where the Gospel had never before been heard. His church in Eau Claire consisted at first of seven members, the nucleus of what is now one of the most flourishing religious organizations in the West. Much credit is due Mr. Kidder for the zeal with which he urged forward the completion of the church edifice, which was dedicated in 1859.

Having resigned his pastorate, he was elected in 1863 County Superintendent of Schools, a position which he ably and satisfactorily filled for seven years and three months—one term to fill a vacancy occasioned by the resignation of Prof. S. A. Hall. An account of his subsequent and contemporary pastoral labors in Augusta, Bloomer, Mondovi, and Durand is given elsewhere.

It is hoped that no one will be offended at the freedom with which the character and conduct of the parties are discussed, whose personal history is herein placed before the public.

And now, though unconscious of intentional error in any statements herein made, should the reader discover discrepancies, let the mantle of charity cover any mistakes as due to the head, not the heart.

THE END.

www.ingramcontent.com/pod-product-compliance
Lightning Source LLC
Chambersburg PA
CBHW020909230426
43666CB00008B/1371